Knowing Human
Movement

Knowing Human Movement

Steven G. Estes
East Carolina University

Robert A. Mechikoff
San Diego State University

Allyn and Bacon
Boston • London • Toronto • Sydney • Tokyo • Singapore

Senior Editor: Joseph Burns
Senior Editorial-Production Administrator: Joe Sweeney
Editorial-Production Service: Walsh & Associates, Inc.
Composition Buyer: Linda Cox
Manufacturing Buyer: Megan Cochran
Cover Administrator: Jenny Burns

Copyright © 1999 by Allyn & Bacon
A Pearson Education Company
160 Gould Street
Needham Heights, MA 02494

Internet: www.abacon.com

Library of Congress Cataloging-in-Publication Data

Estes, Steven.
    Knowing human movement / Steven G. Estes, Robert A. Mechikoff.
      p.   cm.
    Includes bibliographical references and index.
    ISBN 0-205-15841-2
    1. Kinesiology.   I. Mechikoff, Robert A., 1949–   . II. Title.
QP303.E86   1999
612.7′6—dc21   98-55944
                                            CIP

Printed in the United States of America

10 9 8 7 6 5 4 3 2 1   03 02 01 00 99

Contents

Preface

This textbook is the product of years of teaching introductory courses in kinesiology, where our goal was, and continues to be, to use the humanities to introduce students to our field. We have used the materials in these chapters to "brief" our new students on what one should know if one is to be described as knowledgeable in our field, and the approach that we use here has been very effective compared to the more traditional, survey-style approaches that were used when we were undergraduates. Our approach—to use types of knowledge to organize studies in kinesiology—works well for us, and we hope it works well for the reader as well. We note, though, that this approach is a living test of how we go about helping our students acquire an understanding of the nature of our field. This effort to help our students learn will evolve as we do. We hope you will work with us to help us do our jobs better.

With every rewrite the materials in this textbook changed, sometimes subtly, sometimes not. Change proceeds at an uneven pace. While our courses are still titled, for instance, "History and Philosophy of Physical Education and Sport," we speak of the field as if there is consensus that it is now called "kinesiology." No matter the name of our courses, the changing names of our departments, or the new name of our field, it is still "understood" that the humanities are the best way of introducing our students to the field. Consequently, we use a significant amount of the textbook to discuss the humanities, especially philosophy, so that our students can grasp both the detail and the richness of our field.

The two of us have seen thousands of students pass through our classrooms, and we have used a variety of perspectives to achieve our end of introducing our students to the field of kinesiology. These approaches included simply surveying the field, using disciplinary perspectives in history and philosophy to interpret changes over time, and using argument to explain different perspectives toward the field. More recently, we have begun using computer-aided instructional technology to interact with our students in a variety of ways. Some of these approaches and teaching techniques worked better than others, and this textbook reflects those approaches that worked best for us. And, of course, we used a variety of textbooks. To those authors and scholars who helped us achieve the end of explaining the field to newcomers, we say "Thank you!"

This textbook is the latest in a series that seek to accomplish the goal we outlined above: introducing our students to the field of kinesiology. Most of the original textbooks that described the field of physical education used a *survey* approach. Jesse Feiring Williams' *The Principles of Physical Education*, which went through at least eight editions beginning in 1927, is one of the earlier efforts, and it provided a standard against which all foundations textbooks are compared. There were a half-dozen or so textbooks, written between 1934 and 1960, that used this survey approach, and there are another half-dozen introductory textbooks currently in print that use this survey approach as well. Any discriminating reader in the field *must* ask one question: What makes this textbook different from these many surveys written in the last sixty years?

This textbook does not *survey* the field of kinesiology; instead, it *interprets* the field. *Knowing Human Movement* provides a very definite perspective from which to view the field. Specifically, this textbook asks a question: What do we call knowledge in the field? We can question the name of the field, its subject matter, or if there is enough activity in the field, and all of these questions could be used to provide some unique perspective to organize the content of a course.

This textbook argues that kinesiologists use a variety of *types of knowledge*, and a good kinesiologist uses them frequently and well. Put differently, to "know" kinesiology one will "learn" using different types of knowledge. A quality educational experience in our field would provide students with the opportunity to:

- Be told what is true (authority)
- Use their powers of reasoning to understand the principles of the field (rationalism)
- Use their powers of observation to understand the principles of the field (empiricism)
- Use science to investigate movement in the material world (pragmatism)
- Expand their awareness of the moving, lived experience (somatics)
- Experience the meanings behind the stories that define the field to its members (narrativism)

The above outline explains the part of the textbook, Chapters 7 through 13, that makes it unique in the field, and that provides our students with insights as to what makes our field unique. Yet to emphasize only this part of the textbook would be to place in a vacuum our approach to understanding the field. Students, and faculty, must move to new approaches from some common base.

Without some basic terms and definitions, no discussion can take place. Chapter 2 provides such a common language, and this chapter will be very familiar to all who have ever taught a foundations class. Chapter 3 outlines our approach to understanding the field of kinesiology, organizing the professions and subdisciplines by the types of knowledge that are emphasized in each.

Chapters 4 and 5 are traditional descriptions of the professions and how our field evolved into an academic area of study composed of the subdisciplines. We simply *tell* the students where we have been, what we are, and how we have changed over time. Using the epistemological method of *authority*, as surveys do, we rely on those who came before us to describe the field and what students must know if they choose to be a part of it.

Chapter 6 provides a description of how our field has evolved over time and of the themes that continue to define our field in spite of all of the changes. No course can be described as *introductory* without such a history. Chapters 7 through 13 then describe the types of knowledge that we use most frequently in our field and provide an explanation of what these types of knowledge are. Such an understanding is in the best traditions of *liberal* education, expanding the perspectives of our students, and places this course, and our field, directly within the mission of our modern universities. Kinesiology so described helps create liberally educated citizens in the modern world.

Chapter 14 discusses the nature of movement itself, using the perspectives of contemporary theorists like Rudolf Laban and Sy Kleinman. Following a discussion of the traditional types of knowledge that have been used in the academy since its inception, movement theory is a new area of study and is best understood with a firm grounding in the liberal arts. Chapter 15 provides a discussion of the political aspect of our field, of how we have gone about trying to change our field in the context of the educational reform movements that continue in the modern world. Such information is rarely included in survey classes; indeed, it is rarely part of the undergraduate curriculum. Students usually find themselves in professional situations upon graduation having never discussed how education reform occurs, and we hope to rectify this situation somewhat by at least introducing our students to the idea that it is *they* who will carry on the battles after they have left the higher education environment.

As the field continues to evolve, and how we go about introducing our students to the field similarly evolves, we will make many changes in the presentation of our course materials. One of the most exciting changes coming our way is the use of computer-aided instructional technology. This textbook and all support materials are now available on the internet. Our lecture notes, tests and quizzes, popular readings, and other course materials are available either on disk or on the internet and e-mail. Used as a course management system, the internet is a wonderful tool that faculty can use to contact the authors for help in using this textbook. We look forward to working with you in helping our students become members of our field.

Acknowledgments

This textbook is dedicated to the students who helped in its creation. Years of teaching "History and Philosophy of Sport and Physical Education," "Philosophy of Sport," "Principles of Physical Education," and other "intro" courses led to the development of this book. Those students—and after ten years there are many—attended The Ohio State University; California State University, Fullerton; State University of New York, Cortland; and East Carolina University. Many of these students worked with some very rough drafts of this textbook, and their persistence, interest, and contributions show up in many ways in the following text. Thank you for your help!

In addition, my own experience at San Diego State University, as both an undergraduate student and as a graduate student studying under my co-author, Bob Mechikoff, helped form the basis for this textbook. I still remember what it is like to be a student, although the images are not as vivid as they once were. Lyle Olsen at San Diego State University taught this course when I took it in 1977, and his enthusiasm for this material had a wonderful impact on me as both a student and as an instructor. The late Reet Howell, another wonderful professor and friend, also deserves mention. And, of course my co-author Bob Mechikoff, whose encouragement led me toward graduate work in the area of "foundations," deserves mention. Bob's work is evident throughout the textbook as both lead author of many of these chapters and as editor of the rest. My thanks to you all.

The idea for this textbook was first delivered at the 1992 Conference of the Western College Physical Education Society (WCPES), for which I received the Arthur G. Broten Young Scholar Award. To that organization, and to Art, for your support, I say "Way to be!" The theme of that paper and for this textbook, how epistemology can be used to organize our field, is actually one of the few ideas I've come up with on my own! Yet even here I must acknowledge Sy Kleinman, under whom both Bob Mechikoff and I studied at The Ohio State University. Sy's scholarship, and especially his course "Concepts of the Body," had a tremendous impact on the two of us. It was a small step to follow Sy's original work, and we hope that this textbook helps students in the way that Sy helped us. Thank you, Sy!

Kevin Stone of Allyn and Bacon was the first of several editors, and he was followed by Joe Burns. Thanks to you both for your patience and your support. Also deserving of mention at Allyn and Bacon is Sue Jones, who kept me on task as the project came to an end. Kathy Whittier of Walsh & Associates did a wonderful job as copy editor—well done! It is always pleasantly surprising to read the final drafts and note how much better they get! Also, my thanks to the reviewers for their insights and edits: Stanley Brown, University of Mississippi; John Charles, College of William and Mary; John Massengale, University of Nevada at Las Vegas; Dirk Nelson, Missouri Southern State; Donald H. Sussman, Bemidji State University. Those of you who have written books know how important these comments are, and I very much appreciate the suggestions that made their way into this textbook.

Last, and not least, this textbook is dedicated to Erin, Katie, and Cheryl, who are with me always. And to Bubba, who sat on my lap and purred through the writing of many of these chapters.

Introduction to Human Movement

Chapter Objectives

Upon completing this chapter, the reader will be able to:

1. Understand the significance of human movement as the essence of existence.
2. Understand the significance of the philosophical position of the body.
3. Understand the impact of metaphysics and dualism on the development of physical education.
4. Understand the nature of kinesiology and physical education and how these two areas articulate to help establish the scope and significance of the field.
5. Understand the nature of the debate relative to a proper name that identifies the content and methods of the field.

When you proudly announced to your parents or significant other that you intended to major in physical education, do you remember the look on their faces? Was it one of confusion, a look of "Where did we go wrong?" Or perhaps they went into shock. After all, they were probably hoping that you would choose a major that they thought of as prestigious, highly intellectual, or leading to a career path that held the promise of a "better life" than they had. Sensing their concern, you may have assured them that you are not really planning to major in physical education, but in (pick one) kinesiology, sports medicine, or exercise science, which no doubt caused their faces to light up and thus assure you that the "Mom and Dad Scholarship Office" would be open for the next four to five years.

It should come as no surprise to you as a student of physical education that your chosen field of study is, at the very least, misunderstood. Perhaps you have even found that your major is looked upon with a great deal of suspicion or even contempt by educators as well as parents. Why does this perception exist? More to the point, Is the public's perception of Physical Education as a nonintellectual or frivolous area of study an accurate one?

The general public, as well as many people who consider themselves to be well educated, often look upon physical education as merely a formalized recess. Professional physical educators, on the other hand, argue that physical education is not frivolous, that it is the area of study that is concerned with one of the most important aspects of human existence: the joy and meaning that people derive from engaging in human movement. Who is right?

One might think that both descriptions of physical education are extreme, and that the answer is somewhere in the middle. A few observations, however, reveal that the area of study with which physical education is concerned is central to our existence in the contemporary world. Recent studies conducted jointly by the Centers for Disease Control, the American Alliance for Health, Physical Education, Recreation, and Dance (AAHPERD) and the American Medical Association reveal that physical activity is perhaps the most important aspect of one's health. Monuments to sport, such as the huge sports arenas and stadiums that are located in any modern city, rival those associated with religions, fallen soldiers, and North American heroes. Institutionalized competitive sport occupies major sections of the evening news, entire cable channels, and the most widely read section of the daily newspaper. Our interests in physical challenges like mountain climbing, surfing, or hang gliding seem to be more evident every passing year. Dance—both artistic, such as ballet and modern dance, and popular as seen on "Soul Train," MTV, and VH-1—is an integral part of contemporary culture. Indeed, all of these activities have one thing in common: the human body in motion. Physical education as an area of study is concerned with all of these aspects of culture.

Few would argue that human movement is central to our existence. Movement, along with our ability to engage in intellectual activities such as logic and critical thinking, defines our existence. Without movement as an aspect of our being, humans would be entirely different. Indeed, the idea that we are not creatures of movement is so foreign to us that it is seems silly to even consider! To name just a few of an infinite number of examples, human movement manifests itself in dance, athletics, education, and recreation. Ignoring or downplaying the physical parts of our existence, which really *does* happen at peculiar moments in the contemporary world, is to deny the obvious. Without human movement there would be little, if any, meaning to life. There would be no health, sports, Super Bowls or World Series, dance, exercise, or joy. Indeed, there would be no existence at all!

The above question—How did physical education acquire its peculiar status in culture—is the type of question that is asked by scholars and professionals in the field. It is our nature as humans to ask such questions, to study, investigate, and analyze those things that have a significant impact upon our lives. For instance, scholars study medicine in the hope of curing diseases, or the natural world because of the obvious impact nature has upon our existence and survival. Along these same lines, physical educators study, investigate, and analyze human movement because of its significance and impact upon the quality of life.

This study of human movement, in its broadest form, is called *kinesiology*: the art and science of human movement. We shall use the term kinesiology to refer to all studies that focus on human movement: physical education, human movement studies, exercise science, and so on. One might wonder how kinesiology came to be regarded as an "unworthy" area of scholarly inquiry. One answer can be found in the philosophical arguments regarding the most basic ideas of what humans are. These arguments began with the ancient Greeks, continued through the development of Western civilization, and still define western civilization today. In short, we find that, at the most fundamental level, the Western world believes that "mind" is more important than "body." And if we begin with this position, kinesiology, no matter how we define it or name it, will always be viewed with some suspicion.

One example of how the Western world has valued the mind more than the body might be helpful in understanding how kinesiology came to be viewed with some suspicion. Rene Descartes, a sixteenth-century French philosopher, believed that matters of the mind are much more important than those of body. Descartes began his famous inquiry into the nature of knowledge and existence by dismissing all knowledge that he could not prove with absolute certainty. One of the types of knowledge he dismissed was anything that he could know with his five senses: seeing, hearing, touching, tasting, and smelling. Descartes eventually came to the conclusion that, at the most basic level, his existence was that of a "thinking being," and from this point worked forward to *logically prove* that we have a physical body. On a side note, Descartes is considered one of the greatest intellectuals of all time, and to this day his philosophical methods inspire and define just how one "does" philosophy.[1]

Our point is that in the Western world philosophers like Descartes have argued that the mind is much more important than the body. The problem with Descartes' philosophical position, however, is that it has profound consequences for anyone who deals primarily with the physical, material world, and this includes professionals in kinesiology. Specifically, kinesiologists argue that one *can* come to know something through the five senses. But if one follows Descartes' logic, everything we do in kinesiology must be thrown right out the window! Who is right? It depends on one's starting point, on the philosophy one accepts as the beginning point of all discussions regarding what is "real" and what is "knowledge." And once one understands the philosophical basis of Western civilization—that mind is more important than body and that we come to "know" and understand primarily through intellectual means—one more easily understands why kinesiology came to be regarded as an "unworthy" area of scholarly inquiry.[2]

Our point here is not to dismiss or refute Descartes' philosophy—known as "rationalism"—or to prove that Western civilization got off on the wrong foot 2500 years ago accepting philosophies like Descartes'. Rather, it is important to us in this discussion that students of kinesiology understand that Descartes' philosophy is shared by many Americans, and once one begins with Descartes' philosophical position, it makes sense to value kinesiology less than that of other, more "intellectual" pursuits. The consequence, then, of Descartes' logic is that many Americans believe that there is little to be gained education- ally by participating in human movement activities. Perhaps now we can understand why your parents hoped you would choose a more prestigious, "intellectual" course of study that would lead to a different career.

The purpose of this textbook is to place Descartes' argument, and others like his, in a context that makes more sense to us in kinesiology. Specifically, we hope to describe the many ways of generating knowledge that are used in kinesiology, and in so doing both jus- tify the study of kinesiology and help students progress through their studies with some sense of where they are going and why. While doing so we will argue and disagree with Descartes' assumption that his philosophy is the *only* one that can explain reality and knowl- edge. It is our position, and that of your instructors in kinesiology, that human movement is a fundamental part of our existence, and as such is worthy of our scholarly efforts. It is no less important a part of our existence than thought.

It is our position that kinesiology deserves the attention that other scholarly areas deserve. In our discussions we will elaborate on what is central to the field of kinesiology: human movement. Movement is the "soul" of kinesiology and sport, and it is the focus of the specific areas of research that constitute the "body of knowledge," the essence of your studies. Kinesiology, then, can be understood as the area of study that examines human movement from every possible perspective: intellectual, historical, social, and physical. It is concerned with the nature of the *experience* of moving, as well as studying everything that can be known *about* moving. The study of kinesiology includes the language of express- ing movement: by moving, by writing about movement, by speaking about movement. Kinesiology includes the study of the history of movement, as well all of the reasons that we use to justify movement. In sum, kinesiology is an area of study that is both liberating and historical, meaningful and expressive.

To ignore the place of human movement in the development of the human race and its impact on our personal, social, and cultural institutions is to commit a grave philosophical and historical error. Kinesiology is a field that is both on the cutting edge of scholarship and central to the understanding of what it means to be human: "cutting edge" in that it uses a variety of philosophical perspectives to understand the centrality of the body and human movement in our everyday lives, and "central" in that movement is critical to our existence as humans.

Naming the Field and the Field Defined

You may ask, Why worry about a name? Upon reflection you will see that there is a lot at stake. The title or name that is associated with an academic or professional course of study communicates the nature of the field. The title will often proclaim whether the field is a profession, as in the case of a School of Architecture or School of Law, or an academic dis- cipline, such as philosophy or biology.

The problem regarding the nature of our field manifests itself in our name for it. Sim- ply put, there has been quite a bit of debate regarding a proper name for our field. There are several terms and phrases that have been used, some common and some not so common. The word kinesiology, the one we have chosen to use in this textbook, is a term that is used more and more frequently in higher education (colleges and universities). Kinesiology can be compared to the more traditional phrase physical education, an area of study that focuses on the professional preparation of teachers of human movement such as physical educators and coaches. Another option for a name for the field is "Human Movement Studies." This phrase has been used twenty years or so and is still recognized by some professionals, but it has not generated a significant following.[3]

Although physical education has been the label used historically by most programs that study human movement in colleges and universities, many are changing the name in an attempt to more accurately portray our changing field. For instance, in 1989 the American Academy of Physical Education (AAPE), whose membership is composed of the leading scholars and researchers in the field, changed its name to the American Academy of Kinesiology and Physical Education (AAKPE). Furthermore, AAKPE recommended that "kinesiology" be the name for the field formerly titled physical education:

> Therefore, be it resolved that the American Academy of Physical Education recommends that the subject matter core content for undergraduate baccalaureate degrees related to the study of movement be called Kinesiology, and that baccalaureate degrees in the academic discipline be titled Kinesiology. (Charles, 1994)

Without some consensus on what we call ourselves, it is difficult for people in the field, much less those outside of the field, to have a discussion regarding what we do, how well it should be done, who is good at it, and so on. Again, to facilitate our own discussion, and accepting what seems to be the prevailing argument within the field, we will use the term kinesiology as the most inclusive descriptor of the field. We will use the phrase physical education to describe the profession charged with preparing teachers to work in education, whether it be in public or private school settings, or any other area where knowledge is passed from one to another that deals with human movement.

Kinesiology is the more inclusive term: All physical educators are in the field of kinesiology, but not all kinesiologists are professional physical educators. While a physical educator has been trained to teach certain aspects of human movement, he or she may not be expert in other areas of kinesiology such as exercise physiology or sport history. Similarly, while an exercise physiologist may be an expert researcher, he or she may know very little about how to teach human movement. Both the exercise physiologist and the physical educator are included in the field of kinesiology, but only one is a "Physical Education" expert, the oldest profession in kinesiology.

Defining the Body of Knowledge

It is relatively easy to state that kinesiology will be the term used to describe the scholarly study of human movement in activities such as work, exercise, play, dance, instruction, or competition. However, it is a little harder to describe the body of knowledge of our field (Corbin, 1989; Newell, 1990). For example, if one were to study engineering or accounting, the body of knowledge of these two fields—whether they be theoretical or applied—has been determined over time by both academics and practitioners. Unlike engineering or accounting, however, the body of knowledge in kinesiology continues to be the subject of some debate. Kinesiology includes a great many areas of study that continue to be discussed, and these areas of study can be approached from intellectual, social, and physical perspectives. This complexity presents the field with a problem that does not lend itself to an easy solution: What constitutes the body of knowledge of kinesiology?

Again, the one thing that kinesiologists claim as our own is human movement. Most professionals agree that our field must be defined by this one distinctive aspect of our existence. And if human movement is the one thing that kinesiologists will study, then any aspect of human movement that one can imagine becomes appropriate for our studies. The "body of knowledge" in the field of kinesiology will be that information created through research that deals with human movement. It would seem that if the body of knowledge of human movement can be added to with academic, scholarly methods, then so be it.

So far the logic of our argument has been fairly simple: We study human movement, and any knowledge created that helps us understand movement is part of the body of knowledge of the field. In real life, however, it is not this simple. There have been many attempts to define the body of knowledge in kinesiology, and none of these attempts has produced an argument that is acceptable to everyone in the field. The reasons are philosophical, political, and historical, and all of these arguments seem to divide the field rather than unite it.

One argument that seemed to generate much debate occurred when the field was labeled an academic discipline. Franklin Henry called for this change in his address at the National College Physical Education Association for Men in 1964 (Henry, 1964). Henry's call met resistance from those who believed that kinesiology is primarily concerned with *teaching* human movement (physical educators), and only secondly with creating the body of knowledge. Those concerned with teaching saw little evidence that scholarly academic research yielded anything of use to those who were "in the trenches" working with children and young adults in school settings. These two positions have generally defined the debate within the field as to what constitutes the body of knowledge.

As we near the year 2000, the debate over what constitutes the name for the field, the body of knowledge, and other important issues in the field of kinesiology has yet to be resolved in a manner that is acceptable to all professionals. That these issues remain unresolved is not necessarily bad, though. Debate and discussion within any field, whether academic or professional, can be an indication of a healthy field if that debate is conducted in a respectful and collegial manner. Hopefully, at some point there will emerge a consensus over the important issues that confront the field. We will now begin defining many of the terms that are used in kinesiology so as to build a common understanding of what kinesiologists study.

Summary

This chapter introduced the topics that this textbook will examine—specifically the nature of the field of kinesiology, the name of the field, the approach that this textbook will take in examining the field—and provided an overview of the significance of movement to the meaning of being human. An understanding of the way that the Western world has viewed the human body is of critical importance to the student of kinesiology, and this understanding is implicit in what we call knowledge in our field.

If students of kinesiology are to truly understand the many different aspects of our field, then their understanding must have both breadth and depth. The different types of knowledge that are used must be, at the very least, acknowledged by scholars and professionals, and in the best of all cases are to be used in ways deemed appropriate by practicing professionals. What these types of knowledge are, and how these types of knowledge ought to be used, will be the subjects of study for many years to come. This study begins with the overview of the terms most commonly used in the field of kinesiology.

Discussion Questions

1. What do you think is the best name for the field of kinesiology?
2. Why are you studying this field? To get a job? Because you enjoy sport?
3. What is the attitude of your parents and friends toward the field of "kinesiology"? Toward "physical education?" Toward "human movement studies"?
4. What is more valuable, the human "mind" or the human "body"? For the purpose of this question you have to choose and justify your answer!

References

Charles, J. (1994). *Contemporary kinesiology*. Englewood, CO: Morton Publishing Company.

Corbin, C. (1989). The evolving undergraduate major. *The Academy Papers, 23*, 1–4.

Henry, F. (1964). Physical education as an academic discipline. *Journal of Health, Physical Education, and Recreation, 35*(7), 32–33, 69.

Newell, K. (1990). Kinesiology: The label for the study of physical activity in higher education. *Quest, 42*(3), 269–278.

Endnotes

1. It is interesting to note that most Americans "dismiss" philosophy because of assumptions like this one. The idea that thinking is the best way of coming to know what is important bumps up against "good ol' American know-how," or common sense and experience.

2. Descartes' position does make sense from the perspective of how one can come to know things. To play devil's advocate, do you believe everything you hear or everything you see? Many of us believe that "truth" is determined by rational thought that takes place in the mind, and not in the body. Using similar reasoning, Descartes concluded that there is nothing that we can know for certain from the five senses, that there is nothing "intellectual" about the body or of human movement. Following this line of reasoning, many believe that only "intellectual" methods are capable of creating new knowledge, or even of understanding old knowledge. And continuing this line of reasoning, education is concerned with

acquiring knowledge. So on what types of knowledge should the institutions of education focus? Why, intellectual types of knowledge, of course! Again, this is one of the philosophical ideas that is the foundation of Western civilization, and we in modern times often accept these Western ideas uncritically—sometimes to the detriment of kinesiology.

Descartes' philosophical position that the mind is separate from and superior to the body is similar to that of many other philosophers in Western civilization, and this position is known as "metaphysical dualism." Most of us in North America uncritically accept Descartes' logic and his belief in dualism, which separates human existence into two parts, mind and body. Dualism most frequently places the mind in a superior position to that of the body. As a result, the intellectual ability of each person is valued more highly than one's corporeal (bodily) existence or one's physical attributes. Indeed, as you have experienced yourself, dualism is alive and well in the nation's schools today. The majority of the curriculum (the courses one takes to achieve a degree) is focused on cognitive skill development. Important, "scholarly" courses are those in science, mathematics, social sciences, and the humanities. Ironically, the body, the primary mode of our existence, is relegated to a single daily Physical Education class, if that.

3. One of the more thorough studies regarding the name of the field can be found in Newell, K. (1990). Kinesiology: The label for the study of physical activity in higher education. *Quest, 42*(3), 269–178.

Chapter 2

Terms and Definitions

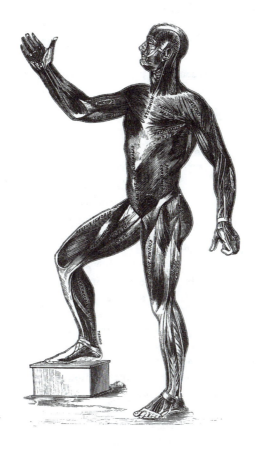

Chapter Objectives

Upon completing this chapter, the reader will be able to:

1. Develop a common language to describe human movement.
2. Provide a history of the words that define the field.
3. Explain the use of contemporary terminology in a way that defines where the field is headed.
4. Help students understand the relationship between the most important concepts and terms in the field of kinesiology.

We use many words in kinesiology to describe the areas of study of human movement. Sport, physical education, exercise, athletics, play, games, leisure, and a host of other words have in common humans in motion, and they all describe different attitudes and qualities of people as they move. It is the differences between these activities and concepts that make them important and worth studying, and you will find that the experiences you bring with you to your studies will help you understand the subtleties that distinguish them. It is important to students of kinesiology that we discuss its many parts with a common understanding of these activities and concepts so that we discuss common experiences. For instance, many students enter the profession of physical education thinking that it is the same area as athletics, when in fact the two areas are very different. An understanding of the differences between these types of movement experiences will facilitate the quality of both of them.

Kinesiology and Biomechanics

The first term we have defined is *kinesiology*, which is the study of the art and science of human movement. "Kin" refers to movement, as in "kinetic"; "-ology" refers to the study of an area of knowledge. Kinesiology literally translated, then, means "the study of movement."

In practice, however, kinesiology has not always had the same definition, and the definition we use is relatively new. During the early 1900s, scholars who used science to study movement from the perspective of how bones and muscles articulate created the word kinesiology to describe what they did. Scholars in this area of study, which has come to be known more recently as *biomechanics*, were the first to use the word kinesiology and probably created the word from the Greek roots because of its literal translation, "the study of movement." Slowikowski and Newell (1990) noted that one of the earliest documented uses of kinesiology was found in Baron Nils Posse's textbook, *The Special Kinesiology of Educational Gymnastics* (1890). Posse used the term to describe "either a system of gymnastics; animals or humans in motion; the study of animal or humans in motion; or a combination of the three" (Slowikowski & Newell, 1990, p. 283).

During the 1960s scholars of physical education began to use kinesiology as the term that encompasses all aspects of human movement. Anne Atwater noted that in the 1960s, scholars began to view the field of *kinesiology* "more as a broader discipline, and less as a specific course of study" (Slowikoski & Newell, 1990, p. 293). Barham (1963) proposed a framework for the discipline of kinesiology that included anatomical kinesiology, mechanical kinesiology, physiological kinesiology, psychological kinesiology, and sociological kinesiology. Each of these areas of study developed its own body of knowledge as a subdiscipline, and yet each was also a part of the larger field of kinesiology. The movement toward a broader definition of kinesiology had begun.

In the 1970s scholars interested in "anatomical kinesiology" agreed that kinesiology and biomechanics were not the same thing, but there was little incentive to change the name of the more narrow discipline that focused on skeletal and muscular articulation. When the Academy of Physical Education changed its name in 1989 to the Academy of Kinesiology and Physical Education, many college and university departments of physical education began the process of changing the name of their academic department to kinesiology because of its broader and more general definition. The older area of anatomical kinesiology has come to be known by the more specific term biomechanics, and in 1990 the name Biomechanics Academy was adopted by the old Kinesiology Academy to promote the study of muscular and skeletal articulation.

Physical Education

The oldest and most well known profession associated with kinesiology is *physical education*. Kinesiology as a field grew out of physical education, and the scholars who coined the term kinesiology were, for the most part, physical education professionals. There is a fair amount of agreement about the goals of the profession of physical education, a process through which an individual obtains fitness and physical, mental, and social skills through physical activity (Gerber, 1972). More importantly, physical education is *education*, which literally means to make a person more knowledgeable.[1] Gerber (1972) noted that three positions were described early in the 1930s in the great debates between Charles McCloy, who argued for fitness and health through movement; Jesse Feiring Williams, who argued for the development of citizenship and social skills through movement and sports; and Jay B. Nash, who argued for lifetime skills to be used in one's leisure time.

Physical educators seek to understand the best methods by which education through movement occurs, so physical education is, most importantly, *education*. This emphasis on education through movement is what makes the profession of physical education a part of kinesiology. Physical educators are interested in using movement to change people, to help them realize their full potential as human beings.

The relationship of physical education to kinesiology is still subject to debate, however. Many professionals in the field argue that the distinction between kinesiology and physical education is an artificial one, and that the term physical education should be the only one to describe the field. However, many scholars of human movement argue that they are not particularly interested in the methods of *teaching* human movement. Rather, they are interested in researching various aspects of human movement, in promoting sport as a business, or in other aspects of kinesiology. Consequently, professionals in kinesiology not interested in teaching needed a word that describes what they do.

It has also been argued by many that the term "physical" in physical education is limiting and does not include the whole person. For instance, if one is developing social skills through movement, many have argued that the word *physical* is not appropriate. Similarly, recent studies indicate that early physical activity may promote intellectual development.[2]

As a result of these debates and others, kinesiology has come to be the umbrella term that encompasses all aspects of human movement, and physical education has come to be the term to describe the profession of those who specifically teach movement skills.[3] Over time the distinction between kinesiology and physical education may come to be more clear as these words and their corresponding functions are used more frequently in the general culture.[4]

Sport

Another term important to students of kinesiology is *sport*. Sport is closely associated with our field because for most of the twentieth century it was both the "subject matter" as well as the preferred method of teaching physical education from kindergarten through high school (K–12). Since the early 1900s children and college students in the United States were taught movement skills almost exclusively by participating in sporting activities. These activities— primarily team games such as baseball, basketball, and football—have become almost synonymous with physical education.

The problem with using sport in physical education is that people participate in sport for many reasons, and only a few of these reasons have anything to do with education. Because so many people participate in sport as an end unto itself, it becomes difficult to separate playing a sport and using sport to teach a person a skill by *using* sport. Consequently, sport and physical education are, in many schools, moving away from one another. This split is occurring because sport is not the best method available for the types of learning that physical educators wish their students to experience.

A definition of sport is helpful in explaining just why this split is occurring: Sport is defined as a competitive physical activity governed by formal rules and played by individuals and teams seeking to win (Calhoun, 1987). More carefully, sport is an *institution*, a socially accepted set of attitudes and behaviors that guide our lives (Calhoun, 1987). Note the difference between *physical education* and *sport*: Physical education has as its goal changing a person, while sport is an end unto itself.

Modern sport has a variety of characteristics that make it recognizable: It is has formal organizations such as the National Football League and the National Basketball Association, rules are formal and written, competition is national and international in scope, competitors are highly specialized, public information is disseminated through a variety of media, and statistics and records are kept (Adelman, 1986). It should be noted that by learning a particular sport it is arguable that an individual acquires certain health, fitness, social, and movement skills. Indeed, this has been the justification for the "sport model" in physical education for almost a century.

The problem with the sport model, however, is that while learning does occur in the sport environment, this learning is *incidental* to the sport experience. Indeed, it appears that all too often the very act of participating in sport undermines the educational goals one seeks to achieve through participation. This understanding of sport is not accepted by all professionals in the field and is clearly subject to debate. Yet the movement away from sport *as* education by many physical education professionals supports the idea that there may be better ways of achieving physical, social, and mental growth through movement.

Athletics

Closely associated with sport is *athletics*. Where sport is an institution in which there is a place for everyone (including spectators), athletics is associated with an individual's skilled performance in a sport. The following truism illustrates the relationship between sport and athletics: Athletes play a sport, but not all people who participate in sport are athletes.

This distinction between athletics and sport is often lost on those who spectate. It has been noted that many people who attend a major sporting event believe that, given a bit of time to train, they could perform as well as the athletes they are watching on TV! Yet the years of preparation on the part of the athletes is entirely different from the experience of the spectator, and this distinction is apparent when spectators cross the line from spectator to participant. For instance, the simple physical skills required to run in Olympic level competition are well beyond the abilities of spectators. And the physical requirements of this level of competition are only one part of what elite-level athletes have to do to be able to perform at that level. The intellectual understanding of the performance, the psychological preparation necessary to compete well, and the dedication necessary to train hard enough to perform at an elite level are well beyond the understanding of most spectators.

Even more basic levels of athletic competition, such as interscholastic sport at the high school level, are beyond the ability levels of most spectators! The preparation of even the lowest level of athletic competitors, compared to the activity levels of most spectators, elevates athletics into a different category of human movement. Our point here is not to show disrespect to spectators. Rather, we wish to emphasize just what an athlete is and what a spectator is *not*.

Play

One characteristic that is common to both sport and athletics is *play*. Play can be described as those amusements engaged in voluntarily, for fun, with no limitations imposed on it from without. Perhaps the most famous definition of play was put forth by the early twentieth century philosopher Johan Huizinga (1955), who argued that play is the defining element of human nature. As such, play is a more basic category than either sport or athletics, and the relationship between sport and play can be described in much the same way as the relationship between athletics and sport. While it can be argued that all sport is play, it does not follow that all play is sport. So play, which is both more fundamental and more varied, includes sport as well as many other types of human activities.

It is important to note just how central to our lives play is. Huizinga argued that play is "pre-cultural," that is, it existed before there was anything like human culture. As such, humans were playing long before there was anything like civilization. Furthermore, Huizinga (1955) argued that play is an aspect of all parts of life. It is a "significant function" in that people make sense out of the games they play, and that the playful aspect of human existence defines the nature of being. Put differently, the defining characteristic of the human being is that humans are playful, and in a word, seek activities that are simply *fun*. Huizinga's (1955) definition of play is that it is

> a free activity standing quite consciously outside "ordinary" life as being "not serious," but at the same time absorbing the player intensely and utterly. It is an activity connected with no material interest, and no profit can be gained by it. It proceeds within its own proper boundaries of time and space according to fixed rules and in an orderly manner. It promotes the formation of social groupings

which tend to surround themselves with secrecy and to stress their difference from the common world by disguise or other means. (p. 13)

Huizinga's work is generally considered to be one of the best points to begin the study of play, and it has been added to by Roger Callois (1961), Brian Sutton-Smith (1972), and others. If one can understand Huizinga, then one is in a good position to understand the relationship of all playful activities to each other, and to culture.

Games

One type of play that physical educators use to teach movement skills is that of *games*. Games are activities that create winners and losers, and range from simple diversions to competitions with significant outcomes governed by rules. A game is a somewhat more organized effort at play, where the organized and playful elements of the activity become more evident. All of us have played games at some point in our lives, so we have a good idea as to what to expect when we play a game. Good physical educators choose games that are appropriate to the educational goal. This act of choosing explains why many physical educators are moving away from *traditional* games like football and basketball: Our *expectations* in that game inhibit our ability to learn something new in those games. Games with which we are not familiar, though, allow for new learning opportunities. Our understanding of just what a game is helps the learning process. Ager defines a game as

a play activity which has explicit rules, specified or understood goals. . . the element of opposition or contest, recognizable boundaries in time and sometimes in space, and a se quence of actions which is essentially "repeatable" every time the game is played. (1976, p. 47)

From this definition one can see how games fit nicely within the definition of sport. Games, like volleyball or softball, can either be highly organized and institutionalized into a sport, or they can be more playful.

The relationship between play, games, sport, and athletics has been subject to much debate. One of the best ways to understand all of these activities is to put them into a continuum where the most playful is compared to the most competitive:

Play—Games—Sport—Athletics

Another way to look at these movement activities is to put them in hierarchical order, where the most restrictive activity is supported by the ideas of the least restrictive:

Athletics
|
Sport
|
Games
|
Play

These diagrams describe the relationship of these activities to each other. It is most important for us to emphasize, however, that no one diagram can describe completely the complex set of relationships of play, games, sport, and athletics. Each activity is too complex to be limited by a single chart. Even more important to understand is that no one type of activity is best for teaching human movement. All of these activities have their virtues, and it is up to the qualified physical educator to understand when a particular activity, with its particular characteristics, is best for achieving a specific educational outcome.

Exercise

There are several other terms associated with kinesiology. *Exercise* has become one of the central areas of study in kinesiology. Most simply, to "exercise" is to practice, strengthen, or condition the human body through physical activity. Kinesiology has become increasingly concerned with understanding the consequences of exercise, and the most progress has been made in understanding its physiological consequences. A stronger heart and other muscles, decreased fat, and improved circulation are just a very few of the benefits that have been associated with exercise. Indeed, it is now argued that the single most important aspect of health is one's activity level, and exercise is the most direct method of raising one's activity level.

Leisure

Leisure is another term often associated with human movement and play. Leisure is often defined as freedom from work and other responsibilities, yet it may be more accurately described as an *attitude* rather than an *activity*. The English word leisure is derived from the Latin word *licere*, meaning "license or freedom." As such, leisure implies that one is "free" to choose one's activities. A richer definition of leisure, and one that dates back to the ancient Athenian Greeks who developed Western traditions of democracy, is that the freedom of choice associated with leisure is the way of life necessary to create a truly democratic community. As such, leisure is the condition needed to create a rich sense of self and a truly democratic community where people are truly free to pursue their wishes, whatever those wishes may be. Perhaps leisure, like play, is best understood as one end of a continuum, with work on the other:

leisure--------------------------------work

It should be noted that leisure may or may not involve physical activity. For instance, playing cards is a form of leisure and a form of play, but it is not considered physical because of the relatively low level of activity. This characteristic of playing cards in no way diminishes its value as play, however. In fact, there are many who play cards *because of* its low activity level, and this characteristic may be the one that makes it either possible or desirable to its participants. Regardless of one's motivation, however, card playing is a time-honored leisure pursuit. So are badminton, football, and mountain climbing, and one can pursue these activities and other leisure. In sum, leisure is an *attitude* of the participant more than it is a type of activity.

Recreation

Closely associated with leisure is *recreation*, which in the twentieth century has become an area of study in its own right.[5] One definition of recreation is the use of time to refresh or renew one's strength and spirit. Again, recreation may or may not include physical activity. Recreation has come to be associated with how one goes about using one's leisure *time*. The modern concept of recreation dates back to New England Puritans in the 1600s and 1700s, who argued at length over how one should use time, which was considered to be a gift from God. Prayer and hard work were, of course, considered the best use of time by the Puritans, whose main goal was to serve God in earth and to demonstrate that they were the chosen few who were destined for heaven.

As much as the Puritans valued work and prayer, they also understood that no person could *only* pray and work. In fact, it was argued that it was one's religious duty to spend an appropriate amount of time at recreation so that one could recover from one's labors, and that doing so would allow one to work and pray harder after the recreation occurred. In short, proper use of one's time literally "re-created" an individual, and from this term came the concept of "re-creation," or recreation (Calhoun, 1987).

You will hear these terms many times throughout your studies in kinesiology, and understanding their origins and meanings will aid in the creation of a mental image of all that kinesiology encompasses. There are other terms as well, and when we come across these terms we will highlight them for you so that you can fit them into the "big picture" in kinesiology. But the above terms are the most general, and any discussion of the field begins with these words and concepts.

Summary

The terms that we use in the field of kinesiology must be understood so that we can communicate effectively with our students, peers, and the public. Without a common vocabulary quality discussion and a common understanding are not possible. Indeed, without discussion and understanding we do not even have a field!

Also, what we find from an overview of the terms and definitions in kinesiology are two benefits, first that many of us have used these terms inappropriately in the past. Physical education and athletics are not the same thing, and to assume that they are undervalues both of these unique areas. Next, by defining the many terms that we use in kinesiology one finds that our field is a rich one composed of many interesting options. Students of kinesiology may never have known that athletic training is a professional opportunity available only to the highly trained *professional* practitioner. Similarly, many students entering the field believe that the only options available were coaching and teaching, and that new areas such as sport management are an option in our field. A discussion of the various terms we use in kinesiology opens many doors that those new to the field did not know existed.

So an examination of the words we use serves many helpful purposes. We will use these terms frequently throughout the textbook, so refer back to this chapter as you proceed through other readings in order to make sure you understand fully the topic you are covering.

Discussion Questions

1. What is the definition of *kinesiology*? Of *physical education*? What is the difference between the two?
2. What is the definition of *athletics*? How is athletics different from *kinesiology*? From *physical education*?
3. What is *play*? How is play different from *work*?
4. Can you think of examples of how our field uses *play* to be *education*? Hint: You have to define education before you can answer this question. Use a dictionary to help you do so.

References

Andelman, M. (1986). *A sporting time: New York City and the rise of modern sport*, 1820–70. Champaign, IL: University of Illinois Press.

Ager, L.P. (1976). The reflection of cultural values in Eskimo children's games. In D. Calhoun (1987), *Sport, culture, and personality* (p. 47). Champaign, IL: Human Kinetics.

Barham, J. (1963). Organizational structure of kinesiology. *Physical Education, 20*, 21.

Calhoun, D. (1987). *Sport, culture, and personality*. Champaign, IL: Human Kinetics.

Caillois, R. (1961). *Man, play, and games*. New York: Free Press.

Gerber, E. (1972). The ideas and influence of McCloy, Nash, and Williams. *Proceedings of the Big Ten Symposium on the history of physical education and sport* (pp. 85–100). Chicago, Illinois: The Athletic Institute.

Huizinga, J. (1955). *Homo ludens: A study of the play element in culture*. Boston: Beacon.

Slowikowski, S., & Newell, K. (1990). The philosophy of kinesiology. *Quest, 42*(3), 279–296.

Sutton-Smith, B. (1972). *The folkgames of children*. Austin: University of Texas Press for the American Folklore Society.

Endnotes

1. "Education" is derived from the Latin word *educare*, which means "to bring up." Romans understood the process of education to be one that makes a person "larger," a process that allows an individual to be in possession of the type of knowledge that was necessary to the Roman citizen.

2. A recent study argued that boys develop cognitive skills and mathematical reasoning abilities because of their active lifestyles when they are young. Apparently there is some association between movement and an understanding of spatial relationships that facilitates the development of mathematical

reasoning. To the extent that an understanding of spatial relationships is an "intellectual" activity, movement builds intellectual "ability."

3. We should note that even physical education is being used less. Professionals in Europe and many in the United States prefer the phrase *sport pedagogy*.

4. A recent article in *Sports Illustrated* is typical of the change that is taking place. Jon Peters, who in 1989 became the only high school baseball player to make the cover of *Sports Illustrated*, went on to study kinesiology and then pedagogy in graduate school. "Peters returned to A&M in the fall of '92, serving as the baseball team's undergrad assistant and graduating two years later with a degree in kinesiology. He earned his M.A., also in kinesiology, from Sam Houston State. . . Next week Peters, now 26, leaves Brenham. . . for Louisiana State to pursue a doctorate in pedagogy." Gutierrez, P. (1997). Catching up with. . . . *Sports Illustrated, 87*(6), p. 13.

5. One reason for the development of the field of recreation was the emphasis in physical education on competitive sport. If physical education was devoted to highly competitive, physical activities, then an area of study was needed that would study the social and psychological attitudes associated with play and leisure. Recreation as a discipline has served this purpose. As physical education and kinesiology move away from competitive sport, it will be interesting to follow the relationship of that field to that of recreation.

Chapter 3

Knowing Kinesiology

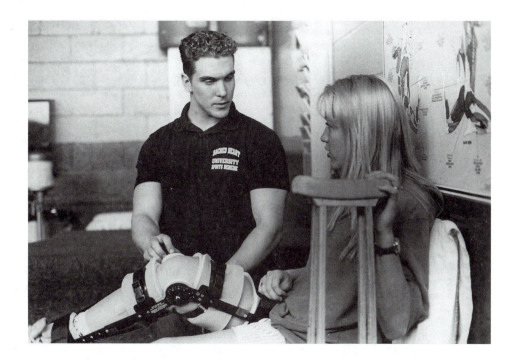

Chapter Objectives

Upon completing this chapter, the reader will be able to:

1. Define academic disciplines and their counterparts in kinesiology, the subdisciplines.
2. Define *profession*, a *professional*, and identify the *professions* that are based in kinesiology.
3. Understand the difference between academic subdisciplines and professional positions.
4. Understand the importance of a *body of knowledge* in one's academic and professional work.
5. List the types of knowledge used in kinesiology and the relationship of knowledge to the courses that students take.

Many students enter the field of kinesiology with the idea that they will be trained *specifically* to get a job that deals with human movement. Teachers and coaches are the best examples of these types of jobs, but other jobs such as athletic training, sport management, and physical therapy are recent additions to the professional options available to kinesiology students. All of these jobs have human movement in common, and consequently are served by the area of study we have described as kinesiology.

What makes a job "professional" is that the person who holds that job "owns" the knowledge that is special to it. For instance, doctors "own" medical knowledge, priests "own" knowledge of their religion, and lawyers "own" the knowledge of the law. This concept of the "ownership" of knowledge is an old one, an idea that had its beginnings in the training that was necessary to do the first simple tasks associated with civilization. The first people to grind grain, to make wine, to explain the "meaning of the universe" to their communities passed their knowledge on to a select few, and in so doing protected their "trade secrets." The "professions" listed above are, from this perspective, merely a modern version of this practice. Fortunately in the modern world, to gain admission to these "guilds" one needs only the virtue of a good work ethic, desire, opportunity, and native ability to become of a member of these and other professions. One then can acquire the knowledge to gain admission to the profession of his or her choice.

So the questions in kinesiology become: What is the knowledge that is special to the profession of my choice? And how do I get it? Corbin (1991) answered these questions in part when he described the definition of a field: A field has "a *discipline* (unique subject matter) using *intellectual techniques* that are delivered by *professionals* through *formal agencies* created by those in the field" (p. 225).

Each one of these words and phrases requires its own explanation. A *discipline* is an area of study, like biology or math. For the most part, your education has consisted of the learning of a number of traditional disciplines: math, biology, language, history, art, and so on. Each of these disciplines, in turn, is divided into a number of smaller components. Math, for instance, is divided into algebra, geometry, calculus, and others. History is divided into ancient history, western civilization, medieval history, and on. Each discipline organizes itself differently, choosing the best methods developed over time to make all the information known in that area of study most available to those who are interested in it. Specifically, an academic discipline has been defined as:

> an organized body of knowledge collectively embraced in a formal course of learning. The acquisition of such knowledge is assumed to be an adequate and worthy objective as such, without any demonstration or requirement of practical application. The content is theoretical and scholarly, as distinguished from technical and professional. (Henry, 1964, p. 32)

You are already familiar with the disciplines, courses that you have studied throughout elementary and high school: physics, biology, chemistry, philosophy, history, sociology, psychology, mathematics, and so on.

The sum total of all of the research or scholarship in a discipline comprises its *body of knowledge*. The body of knowledge in each discipline is created with *intellectual techniques*, which often include logic, scientific experiments, observation, or a number of other methods. The intellectual techniques that are the best are often subject to debate by members of a discipline, and over time consensus develops as to the best way for a discipline to create knowledge.

Once a body of knowledge is created, this body of knowledge is used by *professionals* who are "learned" or knowledgeable in that discipline. We gave examples above: Doctors use the knowledge of the medical profession to heal the sick. The clergy use the knowledge of their faith to spiritually fulfill the lives of their congregations. And teachers use the knowledge of their special discipline to educate their students. Professionals must continually be updated on the latest developments of their discipline, and one way that professionals do this is to join *formal agencies*, such as the American Medical Association (AMA) or the American Bar Association. Formal agencies are charged with making sure that the information or knowledge of a discipline is, in fact, the best or latest knowledge of the discipline.

Applying these terms and phrases to kinesiology reveals the following: The discipline of kinesiology houses the body of knowledge of human movement. It provides for the learning of this knowledge through formal courses of study, which is usually done at the university level. One can earn a degree in kinesiology, just as one can earn a degree in any other discipline.[1] There are kinesiology professionals who are "learned" in the subject matter of their specific kinesiology profession: teaching, athletic training, sport management, sport medicine, and a number of other professional fields (see Chapter 5). In other cases kinesiology students go on to more traditional professions such as law or medicine. In many of these professions, such as teaching, athletic training, law, and medicine, one must be certified to practice. This process involves study, testing, internships, and other professional certification processes. Only after having completed this certification process is one allowed to work in a profession.

The subject matter of kinesiology is organized into a number of *subdisciplines* in order to distinguish between different types of knowledge that are used by professionals. Each subdiscipline (see the Table 3-1) is based on the disciplines described above. The formal agencies of kinesiology are those professional organizations that create and house human movement knowledge, the most prestigious of which is the American Academy of Kinesiology and Physical Education (AAKPE), composed of 150 scholars who represent the best

TABLE 3-1   Relationship of the Academic Disciplines to the Subdisciplines

Discipline	Subdiscipline
Pedagogy	Sport Pedagogy
Biology, Physiology	Exercise Physiology
Physics, Mechanics	Biomechanics
Philosophy	Sport Philosophy
History	Sport History
Literature	Sport Literature
Sociology	Sport Sociology
Psychology	Sport Psychology
Mathematics, Statistics	Measurement and Evaluation
Psychology	Motor Behavior, Motor Learning

research done in kinesiology. The oldest organization is the American Alliance of Health, Physical Education, Recreation, and Dance (AAHPERD), which was founded in 1885. Another well known organization in kinesiology is the American College of Sports Medicine (ACSM). All of these organizations have in common the creation and maintenance of the body of knowledge of their specific discipline.

The Subdisciplines

As we stated above, the subdisciplines constitute organized bodies of knowledge that are created and studied in kinesiology. The relationship of the subdisciplines to the traditional disciplines is described in the Table 3-1. As soon as one discusses the subdisciplines, though, one finds there is some discussion as to which subdisciplines are the *real* subdisciplines, or perhaps the "more important" subdisciplines. It is our contention, though, that this debate is an indication of the youth of these various areas, and that all of the subdisciplines add to the body of knowledge if they meet certain criteria. Our selection of the set of subdisciplines in Table 3-1 was based on the courses that most students take to graduate from college and does not reflect negatively on any subdiscipline not specifically addressed.

There is much agreement among kinesiologists that exercise physiology, biomechanics, motor behavior (which includes motor learning, motor control, and motor development), sport psychology, sport sociology, and sport history are subdisciplines. Sport pedagogy, while it is relatively "young" in a subdisciplinary sense, is firmly established because of its link with the very well established profession of physical education. Some of the sport humanities, though, such as sport philosophy and sport literature, are not as well recognized because of their small size and relative youth. In addition, new subdisciplines such as adapted physical education have recently evolved and have very active participants, large numbers of members in their professional organizations, strong academic journals, and annual conferences that are well attended.

What we do know for sure is that subdisciplines do exist, and that they become viable when large numbers of academics and professionals engage in these specific areas. In fact, that is the process of creating a subdiscipline: Professionals with common interests study an area, gather among themselves to share ideas, organize themselves into a professional body, publish scholarly work, and are eventually accepted by the parent discipline (in this case kinesiology). Once a group goes through this process, it is an "accepted" subdiscipline.

Each of the subdisciplines uses distinct methods of research to create a particular type of knowledge, and these methods are recognized by other scholars in that subdiscipline if the research is up to its standards.[2] If a scholar in one of the subdisciplines claims to have made a discovery, then that person's published claim can be verified by other scholars who are familiar with the type of work he or she has done. It does not matter who does the study or where the discovery is published, only that the methods used are tried and true, that the information builds upon previous research, and, in a professional setting, that this information can be used to benefit the clientele. We will talk more about the specific subdisciplines in the next chapter.

The Profession/Subdiscipline Debate

The decision to use academic, disciplinary methods to create knowledge in kinesiology has been the subject of much debate for the past thirty years in the field among professionals and academics. The cause of this discussion is that there are competing views on what professionals ought to be doing, and what should be considered the most important tasks of professionals—teaching or research. For instance, it is easy to understand the disciplinary content of history, of biology, and so on. Historians study history, biologists study biology, and chemists study chemistry. But what is the content of kinesiology if we are using the methods of history or biology? The answer would appear to be "sport history," "exercise biology," and on through the subdisciplines.

This answer is unacceptable to many professionals, especially teachers, who believe that our field should be composed of people who actually "do" human movement and who serve a clientele: coaches, physical education instructors, and so on. These professionals argue that to know human movement one must be a mover. Clearly this is a powerful argument, one that argues that to know something one must actually experience it.

Some professionals also charge that kinesiologists who try to be too "scholarly" are actually trying to be historians or biologists in disguise. This argument states that scholars using the methods of the disciplines are *embarrassed* to be teaching physical education and are therefore, at best, second-rate historians and biologists who happen to study human movement.

Finally, another argument states that scholars in the field of kinesiology should be creating their own methods to understand the "essence" of human movement. To use the methods of other disciplines is an admission that there is no academic, scholarly nature to kinesiology. This argument, like the preceding one, implies that kinesiology scholars are really trying to be academics in the parent disciplines.

Kinesiology scholars have answered these charges, stating that the methods of the disciplines are as appropriate to kinesiology as they are to any other area of study. Furthermore, to invent "new" methods would be wasted effort. The reason that older methods are used to study human movement is that these methods *work*, and that the reason kinesiologists use these methods is that scholars in the parent disciplines have failed to study human movement with any consistency or rigor.[3] Kinesiology scholars argue that it is the task of kinesiologists to study human movement, and members of traditional disciplines are free to use the methods of their discipline to study it. The only criterion that is important is that the scholarship that is done should be done well.

While this debate has gone on for over thirty years, it appears that the use of disciplinary knowledge is here to stay in kinesiology research. This condition is evident in that most undergraduate programs of kinesiology and physical education are supported by an academic "theory core." This theory core is a list of courses that emphasize the type of knowledge created and housed in the subdisciplines of pedagogy, biomechanics, exercise physiology, motor behavior, sport history, sport philosophy, sport psychology, and sport sociology (see Table 3-2). From a very practical standpoint, then, it is important for undergraduates in kinesiology to understand how we create knowledge in the subdisciplines, what the subdisciplines are, and to understand how this information is passed along to the next generation of scholars and professionals in the field of kinesiology. It is just as important for professionals to understand how knowledge is created in the various subdisciplines so that they can best use the information created.

So far we have discussed the subdisciplines and the professions as if all professionals agree with the idea of studying these academic subjects, but there are some very practical questions that are often asked about the relationship of these two. One question asked by many undergraduates is, "Why do I have to study the disciplines at all? I want to be a professional, and I need to know only the information that I will use in my job." The answer is that the type of information in the subdisciplines *is* essential to professional positions. It is not obvious that this is so, however, so this relationship needs to be justified.

Corbin (1991) argued that the essential subject matter of the field is what kinesiologists and physical educators "sell." That is, without the unique subject matter created in the subdisciplines we would have nothing to talk about! The relationship of the field of kinesiology to the subject matter of human movement is described in the characteristics of the field itself (Corbin, 1991):

1. **A field must have a *discipline* that uses intellectual techniques.**
   The discipline of kinesiology is the study of human movement.
2. **A field must have *disciplinarians* who have a long period of training in the unique subject matter and its intellectual techniques. Disciplinarians must have a dedication to *scholarly* endeavors that will contribute (a) to the *preparation of professionals* in the field and (b) to providing the field's *social service*.**
   The disciplinarians are the scholars in the field of kinesiology. Usually they are college professors, but they are sometimes located in research institutions such as the Cooper Institute in Dallas, Texas, and the Centers for Disease Control in Atlanta, Georgia. These disciplinarians generate the research that is used by professionals, such as the recent Surgeon General's report that argued for increased levels of physical activity among children in the schools to improve their health.
3. **A field must have a *subject matter* related to the delivery of the *social service*.**
   The subject matter of kinesiology is "human movement."
4. **It must have professionals who have a long period of training in the *disciplinary* and *professional subject matter*. Professionals must also have expertise in the intellectual techniques of their particular profession as well as autonomy in providing their social service.**
   Professionals in kinesiology, such as athletic trainers and teachers, are required to study in the subdisciplines, study their specific professional techniques in certified programs, and serve internships before receiving professional certification. Usually this certification process includes testing of the understanding of the subject matter of the profession.
5. **A field must have a clarified *code of ethics* and *organizations* that govern the field and enforce the code.**
   The code of ethics of teaching, athletic training, and other professions are created and published by various organizing bodies including the American Alliance for Health, Physical Education, Recreation, and Dance (AAHPERD), the National Athletic Training Association (NATA), and the American College of Sport Medicine (ACSM).

6. **It must have agencies that are dedicated to preparing** *disciplinarians* **and** *professionals* **who have studied all types of knowledge and who have a dedication to the field and the social service it provides.**

> The agencies that prepare disciplinarians and professionals are our nation's colleges and universities.

7. **A field must have a** *clientele*, **or a group of people, that needs and demands the field's services.**

> The clientele in our example are the students of kinesiology, health professionals, and the public.[4]

Using the above guidelines, one can see that a field of kinesiology is concerned with some unique subject matter that distinguishes that field from others (law, medicine, or religion). This subject matter is created and passed along by disciplinarians to professionals who are providing some social service. Organizations facilitate the cooperation of professionals and scholars in the field, and students are the beneficiaries of this collaboration.

Knowing the Field of Kinesiology

The first task of students beginning their studies of the field of kinesiology is to take some sort of an introductory course, one where students will become familiar with the general nature of the field. We have been doing just this, describing the nature of a field, applying this understanding to kinesiology, and explaining the relationship of knowledge to the professions. Usually this study of the field of kinesiology is started by memorizing the many subdisciplines, and then memorizing the various professions. As the subdisciplines and the professions have become increasingly specialized, this task has become increasingly difficult. This memorization, in practice, can be tedious. Another problem is that, when kinesiology students begin their studies, it can be hard to distinguish between the subdisciplines. This is so because all of the information you have acquired is, at least for right now, more similar than different. This is so because all of the subdisciplines share one characteristic: You have *memorized* them all! This act of memorization is not really bad. In fact, it is convenient and is a tried and true method of starting the learning process. Yet exercise physiology and sport psychology, for example, are very different, and students should know how and why these subdisciplines are so different.

Our plan is to approach kinesiology in a manner that will help students make sense of the information that the field now includes. The central theme of this textbook is that there is a way of organizing all of the subdisciplines and professions to make it easier to understand their differences. This organizational scheme involves an area of philosophy known as *epistemology*, which is literally defined as "the study of the nature of knowledge."[5]

An approach to the study of the field of kinesiology using epistemology has several points in its favor. Such an approach constitutes an "organizer," the principal function of which "is to bridge the gap between what the learner already knows and what he needs to know before he can successfully learn the task at hand" (Ausubel, 1968, p. 148).

An organizer is a plan of learning, one that a student becomes familiar with so as to make the body of knowledge the student is trying to understand a little easier to know. An organizer is introduced in advance of the material to be learned, and is presented at a high level of abstraction, generality, and inclusiveness. (Ausubel, 1968, p. 148)

We organize the field of kinesiology by using epistemology to understand the types of knowledge that are used in the subdisciplines and the professions. We have found that kinesiology can be organized by using six different types of knowledge: authority, rationalism, empiricism, pragmatism (the scientific method), subjectivism, and narrativism. By becoming familiar with these epistemologies one can more easily understand, and with greater perspective and appreciation, the different types of knowledge generated in the subdisciplines. This makes sense if one stops to think about it: The subdisciplines are composed of *knowledge*. It stands to reason that if one understands the *type* of knowledge that is used in a subdiscipline, then that subdiscipline is better understood.

Subdisciplines can be categorized by the type of epistemology that they emphasize, and this commonality can be used to distinguish the parts of the field of kinesiology by providing a common approach to these subdisciplines. This is easier than it sounds, and you have been doing it your whole life: The sciences (chemistry, biology, physics, etc.) are different than the humanities (literature, philosophy, languages, history, etc.), and the humanities are different than the social sciences (psychology, sociology, and anthropology). Activity courses (basketball, softball, swimming, etc.) are different than science, and so on. What we are going to do is make clear the differences between the types of knowledges of these disciplines.

This approach to organizing the subdisciplines can be viewed in Table 3-2. How knowledge is gained and the subdisciplines that emphasize specific ways of knowing are related to one another by tracing the specific way of knowing (epistemology) to the specific subdiscipline. The matrix is useful in that it graphically represents that all ways of knowing are evident at one time or another in all of the subdisciplines. The subdisciplines chosen to illustrate this approach are exercise physiology; biomechanics; motor learning, control, and development; sport sociology; sport psychology; sport pedagogy; and the sport humanities (sport history, sport philosophy, and sport literature). Again, we chose these subdisciplines because they are evident in most university kinesiology programs.[6]

This textbook uses six epistemologies: authority, rationalism, empiricism, science, somatics, and narrativism. These six epistemologies are valuable primarily for two reasons. First, these six are chosen because their extreme positions on knowledge make them easy to contrast with one another. *Rationalism*, for instance, argues that knowledge is intellectual and deductive. *Empiricism*, on the other hand, argues that knowledge can be had by using the five senses, or what philosophers call "experience." These two epistemologies are often contrasted with one another, and it is this contrast that helps makes each comprehensible.

Science limits knowledge to the observable, measurable world and emphasizes objectivity. The consciousness of an individual being studied, or the state of being aware, is irrelevant to good science. In contrast, *somatics* limits knowledge to the internalized, conscious experiences of the individual. Awareness is crucial to somatic ways of knowing. Because

TABLE 3-2   Epistemologies—"Ways of Knowing"

Subdiscipline	Authority	Rationalism	Empiricism	Science	Subjective	Narratives
Sport Pedagogy	*	*	*	*	*	*
Exercise Physiology	*	*	*	*	*	*
Biomechanics	*	*	*	*	*	*
Sport Philosophy	*	*	*	*	*	*
Sport History	*	*	*	*	*	*
Sport Psychology	*	*	*	*	*	*
Sport Sociology	*	*	*	*	*	*
Measurement and Evaluation	*	*	*	*	*	*
Motor Behavior	*	*	*	*	*	*
Sport Literature	*	*	*	*	*	*

of their differences, these two ways of knowing are easily contrasted with one another, and both are important to understanding human movement.

Authority and narrativism are more difficult to distinguish philosophically, but at the same time students are quite familiar with these ways of knowing. *Authority* is the method of knowing that you have been most exposed to in education. Indeed, while we have been making this argument, we have been using the epistemology of authority. We are the "experts," the authority, because of our role as authors and professors. You, in contrast, are the student, and are distinct from the professor because you do not have the knowledge of the professor.

Narratives, in contrast, are the stories that you have heard your whole life. Cultures throughout history have relied on telling stories to pass along important information to their young, and to maintain the essence of their culture. Hearing a story is fun, and so is telling a good one. In fact, hearing a really good story puts one in a unique state of mind— young children appear almost hypnotized when they are read a good story before going to bed. In a sense, the listener to the story and the story itself become one. This distinct aspect of a story—that the listener and the story become one and the same—puts it in an absolutely different category of knowledge from authority.

Using epistemology to organize disciplinary content is not a new idea.[7] After Henry's (1964) argument that physical education has a disciplinary content, several scholars did just this (Brown, 1967; Phenix, 1967; Schwab, 1967). Epistemology is a particularly effective mechanism for understanding disciplinary content because different subdisciplines can use radically different epistemologies in the process of creating knowledge. By emphasizing how one creates knowledge, one can see an obvious connection between how one gains knowledge and the knowledge gained.

Failure to use epistemology makes it difficult to appreciate the differences between the subdisciplines. In philosophical terms, knowledge claims become "relativized." Relativized means that one cannot tell the difference between two different categories, that one category seems just as good (or bad) as another. Relativized is the opposite of the "absolute," where the differences between two categories are clear and complete.

An example is helpful. Modern scholars of ethics are concerned that young people do not know the difference between right and wrong. Often these scholars argue that the social fabric of the 1960s is the origin of this problem, and that the "do your own thing" philosophy of the 1960s led to the idea that one idea of right and wrong is as good as another. This means that the values of right and wrong are relative to the person. In contrast, the Ten Commandments of the Bible are absolute. "Thou shalt not kill" is an absolute. It is the same for all people, regardless of where the person lives, how old one is, and so on. The idea of "thou shalt not kill" is *absolutely* the same for you and me.

The differences in the types of knowledge used in the subdisciplines are absolute, and your own experience bears this out. Scientific knowledge is absolutely different than knowledge you get from reading fiction. Similarly, statements based on the methods of science are of a different quality than statements based on your teacher's authority. Knowledge you gain by watching Tiger Woods play golf is absolutely different than knowledge you get from jumping off a diving board.

Another, and perhaps more practical, reason for using epistemology to organize your introduction to the field is that it helps explain the differences between the professionals in the field and the scholars who study it. If you recall, we described earlier the differences between physical education teachers and college professors. College professors generally work in the world of theory, while physical education teachers work in the world of practice. Using epistemology to organize the study of the field reveals that professional teachers and professors rely on different epistemologies, and consequently the two groups often view the field from two very different perspectives. The argument over the heart of the field may really be as simple as fundamental differences over how these two groups of people create knowledge.

Looking at the types of knowledge in the field allows one to ask, and answer, certain questions that help distinguish between the subdisciplines and the professions:

1. **How reliable is the particular type of knowledge that one is using to understand various aspects of human movement?**

   Is science the best way to "know" playing basketball? Or should one use observation to learn how to play? Is the feeling one gets when tumbling in gymnastics really knowledge at all? Is the lesson of persistence learned by watching the movie *Rudy*, a story of a young man's desire to play football for Notre Dame in spite of many obstacles, valid knowledge? These questions, when answered, reveal that human movement uses several types of knowledge, and that these types of knowledge are very different.

2. **How should research be done in a particular subdiscipline or profession?**

   Research is systematic investigation, and each subdiscipline lends itself to certain systems of investigation. What is the best method of research for a subdiscipline? For instance, is science the best method to understand biological processes in exercise physiology? Or should one use logic? The answer is that science best answers questions about biological processes.

3. **How should one best teach the subdisciplines?**

While science may be the best way to do research in exercise physiology, is it the best way to teach it? Teaching and research are very different acts, and sometimes it is better to simply lecture than it is to do a scientific experiment. When should students learn by doing research, and when should they learn by listening to a teacher? Scholars who study teaching have answered these questions.

The six epistemologies we have chosen are valuable because they help answer the above three questions. Perhaps more importantly, these six ways of knowing are *absolutely* distinct, and are therefore easily contrasted with one another. Kinesiology students can easily grasp each epistemology and then follow its application in various subdisciplines. In so doing, the student is provided with some perspective into each discipline. Put more simply, students can more easily see the differences between the subdisciplines and the professions and can therefore *know* better the subdisciplines and the professions.

An example might be helpful at this point to demonstrate how different subdisciplines use different types of knowledge. Our example represents the difference between pragmatism, which is philosophy behind science, and experience, which is the philosophy behind applied sport psychology.

Pragmatism, which is the philosophy of the scientific method, is the epistemological method of choice in doing research in the subdiscipline of exercise physiology. Science operates on very specific assumptions (see Tables 3-3 and 3-4): that space, time, and matter are "real"; that the material world is observable and measurable, that all events are "determined" or caused; and that scientists can be objective in their observations (Martens, 1987).

Because the operating conceptions and fundamental axioms of science are so clear and so much agreed upon by scientists, science is perhaps the most respected method of creating knowledge in the modern world. As a result of this agreement and consistency in the

TABLE 3-3   Fundamental Axioms of Science

Axiom	Scientists' Belief
Reality of space	Belief that space is real.
Reality of time	Belief that time is real.
Reality of matter	Belief that matter is real.
Quantifiability of matter	What exists, exists in some amount; what exists and even relationships between existing phenomena are amenable to observation and measurement.
Consistency in the universe	The universe is organized in an orderly manner; there is regularity, constancy, consistency, and uniformity in the operation of the universe.
Intelligibility of the universe	Science holds that we can observe, know, and understand the universe in which we live.
Determinism	All events are determined or caused.
Empiricism	Knowing is the result of first-hand, direct original observation.

TABLE 3-4   Operating Conceptions of Science

Concept	Scientists' Belief
Conception of objectivity	Scientists must remain impersonal, impartial, and detached in making observations and in interpreting data; the scientists must maintain a disinterested attitude.
Conception of amorality	Science is not moral or immoral, it is amoral.
Conception of caution	Scientists must maintain meticulous caution and painstaking vigilance in their methods.
Conception of skepticism	Scientists reject the notion of absolutism; scientists refuse to acknowledge authoritarianism or dogmatism as a source of knowledge; even the data of science are viewed as tentative.
Conception of theory	Science tries to build and test theory construction and utilization.
Conception of parsimony	Science should be conservative in stating the implications of its data; the data should be interpreted in the simplest, most succinct form possible.
Conception of reductionism	Science strives to reduce specific data to succinct statements of consistency; ultimately, reductionism demands that generalizations be specified in terms of precise mathematical formulae.

methods of creating knowledge, scientists are probably the most prestigious of all of the scholars in the modern world.

However, while science is clear and consistent, it also has some *absolute* limitations. While science is an excellent way of coming to know the material world, it is of less use for research in the social sciences. For instance, it has been argued that science is of only marginal use in the subdiscipline of sport psychology because the mind—the *object* of research—is not observable or measurable (Martens, 1987). Indeed, in some psychologies, such as behavioral psychology, the existence of mind at all is questionable. The method of science is simply unusable in another subdiscipline, sport philosophy. This subdiscipline creates knowledge by methods that emphasize logic, critical thinking, and argument.

Our argument here has been to distinguish between the different types of knowledge that we use in the subdisciplines and the professions. Another way of describing these differences in types of knowledge is by graphing their relationship. In Table 3-5 the different types of epistemologies that are discussed in this textbook are displayed, and their relationship to the subdisciplines is described. It is worth noting again that all of the epistemologies listed in Table 3-2 are used, at one time or another, in all of the subdisciplines. *How* they are used, however, and *how well*, makes all the difference between one epistemology and another, and this relationship is described in Table 3-5.

Table 3-5 asks specific questions and allows students to answer these questions to show differences between the subdisciplines and the professions: What epistemology offers the most reliable knowledge in that subdiscipline? How does the epistemology in question develop knowledge in that subdiscipline? Does a particular epistemology have anything to

TABLE 3-5 Ways of Knowing in the Subdisciplines

Subdisciplines	What knowledge is most reliable or important in	How does knowledge arise in	How ought the search for knowledge be conducted in	How is this knowledge best taught in
Sport Pedagogy	Rationalism			Empiricism
Exercise Physiology				
Sport Biomechanics				
Sport Humanities				
Sport Psychology		Authority	Narrativism	
Sport Sociology				
Measurement and Evaluation				
Motor Behavior	Pragmatism-Science			Somatics

Each question can be asked in the subdisciplines while using the four epistemologies. Each epistemology provides answers to the questions of a different kind.

say regarding the methods of searching for knowledge in a subdiscipline? Does a given epistemology have any particular teaching advantages?

Summary

In this chapter we attempted to justify the use of studying different types of knowledge to come to know the field. The differences between the subdisciplines becomes more clear when they are examined in light of the different types of knowledge that each subdiscipline uses. Similarly, different professions use different types of knowledge, and knowing the differences enables professionals to do their jobs better.

It is our argument that knowing these differences will help the student of kinesiology move better through the field and to study areas that are of more interest to the student. In fact, by studying the different types of knowledge in the field, a student may choose a different profession than one that was originally selected.

Discussion Questions

1. What is an academic discipline? What does this aspect of education look like in kinesiology?
2. What is a profession? Name three professions in the field of kinesiology.
3. What is a professional? How can this concept be applied to our field?
4. What is the *body of knowledge* of kinesiology?
5. What is meant by the term *epistemology*? How can this concept be used to organize one's studies in kinesiology?

References

Ausubel, D. (1968). *Educational psychology: A cognitive view*. New York: Holt, Rinehart and Winston.

Barham, J. (1966). Kinesiology: Toward a science and discipline of human movement. *Journal of Health, Physical Education, and Recreation*, October, 65–68.

Brown, C. (1967). The structure of knowledge of physical education. *Quest, 9*(Winter), 53–67.

Brownell, C., & Hagman, E.P. (1951). *Physical education—foundations and principles*. New York: McGraw-Hill.

Corbin, C. (1991). Further reactions to Newell: Becoming a field is more than saying we are one. *Quest, 43*(2), 224–29.

Gaesser, G. (1996). *Big fat lies: The truth about your weight and your health*. New York: Fawcett Columbine.

Henry, F.M. (1964). Physical education: An academic discipline. *Journal of Health, Physical Education and Recreation, 35*, 32–33.

Lee, M. (1937). *The conduct of physical education*. New York: A.S. Barnes.

Martens, R. (1987). Science, knowledge, and sport psychology. *The Sport Psychologist, 1*, 29–55.

Nixon, E.W., & Cozens, W.C. (1941). *An introduction to physical education*. Philadelphia: W.B. Saunders.

Oriard, M. (1983). On the current status of sport fiction. *Arete: The Journal of Sport Literature*, 1(1), 7–20.

Phenix, P. (1967). The architectonics of knowledge. *Quest, 9*(Winter), 28–41.

Schwab, J. (1967). Problems, topics, and issues. *Quest, 9*(Winter), 2–27.

Sharman, J.R. (1934). *Introduction to physical education*. New York: A.S. Barnes.

Sharman, J.R. (1937). *Modern principles of physical education*. New York: A.S. Barnes.

Shepard, N. (1960). *Foundations and principles of physical education*. New York: Ronald Press.

Siedentop, D. (1990). *Introduction to physical eduction, fitness, and sport*. Mountain View, CA: Mayfield.

Singer, R., Lamb, D., Loy, J., Malina, R., & Kleinman, S. (1972). *Physical education: An interdisciplinary approach*. New York: Macmillan.

Staley, S. (1939). *Sports education: The new curriculum in physical education*. New York: A.S. Barnes.

Thomas, J., & Nelson, J. (1990). *Research methods in physical activity* (2nd ed.). Champaign, IL: Human Kinetics.

Williams, J.F. (1959). *The principles of physical education*. Philadelphia: W.B. Saunders.

Endnotes

1. In 1993 all of the California State University physical education degree programs changed the name of their human movement studies degree to *kinesiology*. The purpose of this change was to reflect the change in the nature of their degree, which was no longer professional but instead was disciplinary. Many of these programs also offer professional certifications, ranging from teacher certification to physical therapy.

2. This relationship was made very clear recently when Glen Gaesser, an exercise physiologist at the University of Virginia, along with the Cooper Institute in Dallas, Texas, asserted that *obesity* is not a health risk. *Lack of exercise that leads to obesity* is a health risk. Many physicians disputed this finding, claiming that obesity is, in fact, a cause of heart disease and numerous other health problems. But Gaesser's and the Cooper Institute's claims are hard to dispute. His research is based on the same method of research as that of the medical profession: the scientific method. Either Gaesser's science is well done, or it is not—his research will be examined and discussed in numerous professional bodies throughout the country. If his research withstands this examination, then it will become part of the medical profession's, as well as kinesiology's, body of knowledge. See Gaesser, G. (1996). *Big fat lies: The truth about your weight and your health.* New York: Fawcett Columbine.

3. Michael Oriard argued that literary critics have failed to study sport literature seriously for a variety of reasons, among them embarassment, that sport is not "serious," and that there is a resultant lack of quality research in this discipline. See Oriard (1983), On the current status of sport fiction. *Aethlon: The Journal of Sport Literature, 1*(1), 7–20.

4. There is quite a bit of debate in the profession about whether students constitute a "clientele," which implies that students "buy" a good or a service. As professionals, teachers are much more concerned with having students learn, a difference that makes teaching very different from selling.

5. We owe Sy Kleinman much for this idea. We began with Kleinman's use of metaphysics and ontology to organize one's understanding of the body. Using the same philosophers, but looking at epistemology, we found that the subdisciplines took on a new look. See Singer et al. (1972).

6. We should also note that we are not alone in our choice of these particular subdisciplines. We have chosen to use the those described by Siedentop (1990) because his treatment of is one of the most comprehensive, and the manner in which he groups the subdisciplines is already somewhat organized by knowledge types.

7. Researchers in kinesiology have long been aware of how different epistemological approaches yield qualitatively different types of answers. Thomas and Nelson (1990), writing to provide a context for scientific research, describe the methods of tenacity, intuition, authority, rationalism, and empiricism in order to give the reader some background regarding the reliability of scientific inquiry. Thomas and Nelson provided this information to contrast science and other ways of knowing. This contrast legitimizes the difference between science and other ways of knowing and helps students see how science is a superior way of knowing the material world. Similarly, the epistemologies of authority, rationalism, empiricism, science, subjectivism, and narrativism can be contrasted to one another.

C h a p t e r   *4*

The Subdisciplines

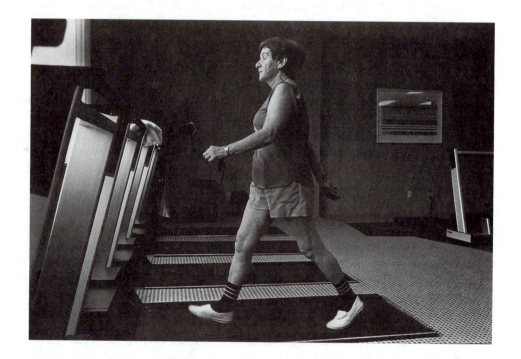

Chapter Objectives

Upon completing this chapter, the reader will be able to:

1. Describe and define the most frequently encountered subdisciplines.
2. Explain the development of the subdisciplines.
3. Understand the methods of scholarship used in particular subdisciplines.

In the previous chapters we argued for several ideas: that the study of human movement was a worthy pursuit, that this study results in the creation of "bodies of knowledge" that are housed in areas called "subdisciplines," and that professions use this knowledge to help their clients. We also argued that there is more than one way to create knowledge, and that every way of creating knowledge is used in every subdiscipline.

What we do now is to describe, or survey, the most frequently used and studied subdisciplines. While there is a fair amount of agreement among kinesiologists as to what these subdisciplines are, it is worth noting that the development of the subdisciplines is in various stages of maturity. Probably the oldest of the subdisciplines is exercise physiology, and the youngest may be sport pedagogy. While scholars have studied exercise physiology for over 100 years now, it "became" a subdiscipline only in the 1960s when the subdiscipline movement took shape.

Age is not the only factor to consider in the viability of a subdiscipline, though: The number of active participants is probably the best indicator of a subdiscipline's health. For instance, sport philosophy is one of the oldest of the subdisciplines, yet it is also one of the smallest with roughly 100 active members throughout the world. The first issue of *Quest*, a journal that discusses interdisciplinary issues in kinesiology, was devoted entirely to the discussion of philosophical issues. Other subdisciplines, such as athletic training and sport management, are much more active even though they are more recent in origin.

Regardless of the age of a subdiscipline, students are well served to begin their studies in kinesiology by learning the subdisciplines most frequently encountered in their studies. We start with what should be the most familiar of the subdisciplines, *sport pedagogy*, which historically has been known as "physical education." While the profession of physical education is the oldest and best known of all areas of kinesiology, its scholarly body of knowledge, known as sport pedagogy, has only recently organized itself as a subdiscipline. We then describe the rest of the subdisciplines by their locations in the sciences, the social sciences, or the humanities.

Regardless of their location in the professions, the sciences, the social sciences, or the humanities, the subdisciplines have in common the study of human movement. Keep this commonality in mind as you study these bodies of knowledge, for this theme is the heart of our field: *The quest to understand human movement is the reason we are using disciplinary methods.*

Sport Pedagogy

Sport pedagogy is most simply defined as the "science of teaching human movement." The study of sport pedagogy makes possible an understanding of the distinction between a subdiscipline and a profession: Sport pedagogy is a subdiscipline because it is an area of study that can be pursued for its own sake. College professors are usually involved in sport pedagogy. When the body of knowledge generated in sport pedagogy is used by teachers, we have moved into the profession of physical education. With the development in the 1970s and 1980s of graduate programs in sport pedagogy that study teaching and learning and pass new methods on to future teachers, sport pedagogy generated its own body of knowledge and stands on its own as a field of scholarly inquiry. Since this textbook is concerned first and foremost with how we generate knowledge in kinesiology, and then how it is learned by students, it is appropriate that we begin with the subdiscipline that studies just how this is done.

Professional physical educators have long been concerned with just how human movement should be taught. It is this quest to understand and improve upon teaching techniques that led to the development of the subdiscipline of sport pedagogy, which we define as the science of teaching human movement. Teaching human movement is the oldest and most honorable of all of the professions in kinesiology, and even in the 1990s most kinesiology students enter the field with the idea of teaching in mind. This should not be surprising, as for most of this century (certainly since the 1930s), physical education as a field was concerned primarily with teaching.

As we noted in the previous chapter, since the development of the subdiscipline movement in kinesiology in the 1960s physical education began to diversify its mission. New names became necessary to describe the various missions of the different parts of the field. Sport pedagogy is the area of study that examines teaching methods in human movement. Put differently, sport pedagogy studies teaching. It would ask, How can one better teach human movement? The answers to this question become part of the body of knowledge of that subdiscipline.

There is still some confusion over names, however, and we will try to clarify how we are using these names to describe the areas of study and the field in general. Sport pedagogy is obviously similar to the name "physical education." Why change? Or why should we distinguish between the two? The field seems to have created more problems than it solved by making new names. There is confusion between the following names: sport pedagogy as a subdiscipline, the historic name "physical education," and the new name for the field of kinesiology. These names are frequently used inexactly, and interchangeably. This practice of using these names synonymously causes much confusion.[1]

Throughout the late nineteenth century and through the first half of the twentieth century the primary concern of professionals in the field was the quality of the instructional program.

> Until the 1960s, physical education was defined as a teaching field (and) not as an academic discipline. Leaders in the field gave considerable attention to the quality of physical education programs. However, there were no systematic programs of research on curriculum or instruction in physical education and no doctoral programs to train experts in pedagogical research. Most of the professors who taught "methods" classes to undergraduate students were chosen not on the basis of formal training but because they had extensive experience teaching or coaching. And most of the content of the methods courses was based on a view of teaching as a craft learned primarily through apprenticeship. (Bain, 1996, p. 3)

In the 1960s sport pedagogy began to define itself as an area of scholarly inquiry. There were a number of reasons for this change, among them the effects on education in general from the Cold War, which caused many scholars to identify the theories particular to their disciplines; the publication of the *Handbook of Research on Teaching*, which proposed the use of scientific methods to study teaching; and the effort to define physical education as a scholarly discipline that studies human movement (Bain, 1996). Yet while scholars interested in the study of pedagogy began in the 1960s to utilize a variety of perspectives to expand the body of knowledge, there was no attempt to create new academic journals or societies until the early 1980s. Bain argued that the relatively late development of specialized scholarly pedagogy societies may stem from the historical affiliation of teachers with AAHPERD, and that researchers presented and published their research through that organization in the *Journal of Health, Physical Education, Recreation, and Dance*. However, lacking organizations that emphasized the research into teaching methods, pedagogy scholars struggled to gain academic respectability throughout the 1960s and 1970s.

Those on the cutting edge of each area of research need new names to describe what they do. The old words simply do not fit any more. Once something like scholarly research began to be done, a word or phrase needed to be generated that described the *study* of human movement from the practice of teaching human movement. Sport pedagogy is the *area of study*, or the subdiscipline, that uses scholarly techniques to create a body of knowledge. The body of knowledge that sport pedagogy creates is used by professionals, and these professionals are *physical educators*. Physical educators are concerned with *teaching* human movement. Most physical educators are not concerned with research, except of course to the extent that it helps them be better professionals. Professionals are concerned with teaching and hope that the skills they teach are based on good research. We will talk more about the profession of teaching human movement, or physical education, in the next chapter.

We are not alone in the United States in making this change. Sport pedagogy is the term used in Europe to describe the science of teaching in kinesiology, whereas North Americans generally use the term "pedagogy" (Bain, 1996; Siedentop, 1994). Both names are recognized by professionals in the United States, and scholars on both continents share a common definition of the field:

> Disciplined inquiry from different perspectives into teaching and coaching in a variety of contexts in order to inform and improve practice. (Bain, 1996, p. 2)

Similarly, Siedentop defined sport pedagogy as:

> the study of the processes of teaching and coaching, of the outcomes of such endeavors, and of the content of fitness, physical education, and sport-education programs. (Siedentop, 1994, p. 320)

Sport pedagogy is generally understood to be the most sweeping and inclusive phrase that describes research into understanding how to teach human movement. The name "sport pedagogy" includes the science of teaching all areas of human movement, from sport to physical education, and in schools to other institutional settings like health clubs and corporate fitness programs. Siedentop argued that, because this phrase is recognized internationally, it consequently may be the phrase that will define this subdiscipline in the future.

We believe that the problem with the name sport pedagogy will continue for some time, however, and students of kinesiology should recognize the names that others may use to describe both the study of human movement and its corresponding profession. Other names for sport pedagogy include physical education teacher education (PETE), teacher education, and curriculum and instruction (Siedentop, 1994). Programs that have been designed specifically to train physical education teachers often use the acronym PETE. The phrase "teacher education" can be defined as "teaching learners how to be teachers." The "curriculum" of "curriculum and instruction" refers to the courses one takes to achieve the desired ends of an academic program. The study of curriculum involves the philosophy of physical education, the specific goals of courses within a program of study, and of what a program of study should consist. Put more simply, curriculum is the study of what one studies, and why. "Instruction" is how one teaches in the curriculum.

The scholarly study of sport pedagogy often occurs at the graduate level, and this activity can be compared to those states where an undergraduate degree in physical education teacher education *certifies* one to teach physical education. In the former case, one studies good teaching and hopes to expand the body of knowledge as to just what good teaching is. In the latter, one becomes a teacher by becoming familiar with the latest additions to the body of knowledge. Often the two occur in parallel, but the two do not necessarily go together. For instance, one can be certified as a teacher in a university where no research is taking place in sport pedagogy.

New publications were developed in the 1980s to promote research into pedagogy, perhaps the most important being the *Journal of Teaching in Physical Education* (JTPE). This publication, along with the Big Ten Symposium on Research on Teaching in Physical Education in 1982, helped establish pedagogy as a scholarly area of inquiry in the field of kinesiology. Since the early 1980s scholars in sport pedagogy have debated the virtues of quantitative (studying what can be observed and measured) research, qualitative (emphasizing the student's awareness of an activity) research, and critical research, which studies the contextual constraints on behavior.

Perhaps the most important discussions involving sport pedagogy, however, deal with its centrality to the field itself. How much of the efforts of professionals in the field should be devoted to the study of sport pedagogy? Should the field shift away from its traditional emphasis on teaching? These questions have yet to be answered. Still, the quality of the research on teaching has improved significantly in the last twenty years. It remains to be seen just how this research will be used in educational settings.

The Sciences

Exercise Physiology

Exercise physiology may be the most well known of all of the subdisciplines. It is the oldest when one considers the historical nature of scholarly inquiry into human movement. For centuries it has been known that health and exercise are closely related, and the modern subdiscipline of exercise physiology can trace its roots back to this relationship. Ancient physicians like Herodicus (c. 480 BC), his student Hippocrates (460–377 BC), and Claudius Galen (130–201 AD) prepared athletes for competition, treated their injuries, and recommended exercises for health purposes. Philosopher and historian Ellen Gerber noted that essays written by Galen on exercise and injuries were "sufficiently detailed and accurate to rank with those written today" (Gerber, 1971b).

The famous philosopher Aristotle (384–322 BC.) is known as the "father of biology" for his systematic classification of living organisms, both plant and animal. In a sense Aristotle was the first "scientist," both because of his systematic classification of the natural world and his ability to develop theories based on his observations. All of these ancient physicians and scientists had a significant impact on the development of the subdiscipline of exercise physiology in that they related health to human movement in a systematic manner.

In the nineteenth and twentieth centuries the use of physiological principles to study human movement became increasingly important. Leading physical educators like Dioclesian Lewis (1823–1888), Edward Hitchcock (1828–1911), and Dudley Allen Sargent (1849–1924) all had training in medicine, although Lewis' claims to his medical degree were misleading (Lewis held an honorary degree in medicine). All of these physical educators believed in exercise as preventive medicine (Gerber, 1971b). George Fitz (1860–1934) was one of the first scholars to argue that the principles of physiology should be used to support claims of exactly how exercise can improve health, and in so doing helped develop the modern subdiscipline of exercise physiology:

> As physiologists, we should study the conditions under which the exercises are done, and the results of these exercises upon the system. . . . What we want is the clear scientific study of the physiology; the exercise, whether presented in one form or another. (Gerber, 1971b, p. 302)

While Fitz argued for physical educators to base their claims on scientific research, his arguments went largely unheard. During his lifetime most systems of physical training were based on rumor and myth more than on scientific research. However, it can be argued that Fitz's arguments and those of his contemporaries carried the day, for in the 1990s exercise physiology is seen as the subdiscipline that provides the answers to all questions that deal with human movement and metabolic function. What classical scientists and contemporary exercise physiologists have in common, though, is that they are both interested in how the body functions. The exercise physiologist is interested specifically in how the body functions as a consequence of movement.

The origins of the phrase "exercise physiology" help define the subdiscipline. Physiology can be understood as the branch of biological science that has to do with the functions of living tissues and organisms. The word *physiology* is derived from the Greek root *physis*, which means nature. *Physis* is evident in both *physician* (literally translated as a practitioner of *physic*, an old word for the science of medicine) and *physics*, the area of study that deals with the elementary properties of inorganic materials and the forces that affect them.

Combine *physis* with the word *logos* (the Greek word for *discourse*) and we have *physiology*, a word that can be literally translated from Greek to mean the "discourse of nature." In contemporary usage, the modern *logos* is read as *-ology* (as in sociology, biology, psychology, etc.) which means the "scientific study of. . . ." Modern physiological discourse takes place through the scientific method and the publication of research in scholarly journals. Contemporary exercise physiologists use the scientific method to investigate the functioning of the human body with respect to movement.

What makes physiology important to kinesiology is the "exercise" that is associated with it. Muscle contractions move the human body, and the consequences of these contractions can be studied using physiological techniques. Exercise physiologists utilize the principles of both physics and chemistry to understand how the moving body functions. For instance, one must understand how gravity, heat, and light provide the basic causes of metabolic change. A runner must overcome the forces of gravity and inertia to run, and in doing so gets hot and perspires, fatigues, and recovers. Swimmers overcome friction and deal with the specific gravity of water when propelling themselves from one end of the pool to the other. Their heart rate increases, their intake of oxygen increases, and they produce heat, lactic acid, and carbon dioxide as by-products of their work. The movements of these athletes cause various chemical reactions that can be measured: Glycogen is metabolized, heat is created, carbon dioxide is expelled, and oxygen is utilized to create energy. The chains of chemical reactions involved in the functioning of a human body are incredibly complex, and the science of the study of these chemical reactions is known as *physiological chemistry* or *biochemistry*. This area of study is important in the subdiscipline of exercise physiology, and has even become an area of specialization within the subdiscipline itself.

There are three main areas of study within the subdiscipline of exercise physiology: *cardiovascular and metabolic exercise physiology, exercise biochemistry,* and *cardiac rehabilitation or adult fitness* (Siedentop, 1994). These areas of study form the subdisciplinary basis for *professional* opportunities: athletic training, strength training, adult fitness and wellness programs, corporate fitness, and personal fitness training. Graduate programs in exercise physiology are found in most kinesiology departments, and in some instances exist as discrete programs of study.

It has been argued that the specialization of researchers into this subdiscipline has its bad points as well as its merits. In short, some kinesiologists feel that narrowly focused research has little value because it is not applicable to the human condition. Others argue that some exercise physiologists are more interested in pure physiological research than they are in applying the principles of physiology to exercise. In both cases it is argued that very little information that is useful gets to the physical education teacher or coach. While these arguments may be true to some extent, it is clear that much that is positive in kinesiology has come from the subdiscipline of exercise physiology. Exercise programs, equipment such as heart rate monitors, and professional positions such as personal fitness trainers are just a few of the many benefits of this subdiscipline.

Biomechanics

When a coach comments on the movement patterns or technique of an athlete in a sport, the coach is using knowledge from the subdiscipline of *biomechanics*. While the coach tries to teach the most efficient movement patterns with which to perform a particular movement, the athlete tries to move the appropriate muscles in the correct sequence to put his or her skeletal system into the desired positions. Biomechanics is the area of study that examines particular movement patterns, which in sport and physical education are often called "technique" or "form." One can have "good" form or "bad" form in a given movement. Biomechanics studies bodies and uses the scientific method to determine just what is "good" or "bad" about a given movement.

Biomechanics, most broadly defined, is the study of the human body in motion, and uses both geometry and *mechanics* (an area of study in physics) to develop knowledge about proper movement. More narrowly, "human" biomechanics or "sport" biomechanics is defined as "the science (that) investigates the effect of internal and external forces on human and animal bodies in movement and at rest" (Wilkerson, 1996). Movement is central to the subdiscipline. As Wilkerson notes, all of the subdivisions of biomechanics study different types of motion:

> Biomechanics and mechanics have two major subdivisions defined as statics and dynamics. Statics is a state of balance or equilibrium and dynamics is a state of motion. The subdivision of dynamics is further divided into kinematics and kinetics. Kinematics is concerned with the geometry of motion and kinetics with the forces that produce motion. (Wilkerson, 1996, p. 3)

A closely related area of study to biomechanics, *anatomical kinesiology*, studies how muscles move bones.

The word biomechanics is relatively new to the field and was used to define an area of study, perhaps for the first time, in 1935 in Steindler's *Mechanics of Normal and Pathological Locomotion in Man* (Wilkerson, 1996). At one time what is now "biomechanics" was called "kinesiology," probably due to the literal translation of "kinesiology" from its Greek roots. "Kin" refers to movement, as in "kinetic," and "ology," as we noted earlier in this text, refers to the scientific study of an area of knowledge. Kinesiology literally translated means "the scientific study of movement," and during the 1930s those who used science to study movement created this word to describe what they did.

Through the 1960s, however, the word "kinesiology" came to be associated more and more with all the subdisciplines of the field. Barham (1966) argued that the term "kinesiology" did not need to be defined because "it is generally accepted as being the science of movement" (p. 65). Barham proposed a framework for the discipline of kinesiology that included anatomical kinesiology, mechanical kinesiology, physiological kinesiology, psychological kinesiology, and sociological kinesiology. Each of these areas of study developed its own scholarly body, and yet all of them were "kinesiology."

In the 1970s scholars interested in "anatomical kinesiology" agreed that kinesiology and biomechanics were not the same thing, but there was no consensus as to what to call the discipline. However, as Wilkerson noted, once the Academy of Physical Education changed its name to the Academy of Kinesiology and Physical Education, many college and university departments of physical education changed their name to "kinesiology." In 1990, the Kinesiology Academy, formed in the 1960s to promote the study of anatomical kinesiology, changed its name to the Biomechanics Academy.

Looking back at the development of this subdiscipline over the past 100 years, Wilkerson argued that 1900 to 1960 can be considered the "Kinesiological Era," and from 1960 to the present can be considered the "Biomechanical Era" (Wilkerson, 1996). At the beginning of the twenty-first century it appears that biomechanics will be the term of choice of researchers in this area.

Humans have been applying the principles of physics to motion ever since the beginning of civilization. The ancient Greeks were the first to study the human body with respect to movement, mechanics, and anatomy (Wilkerson, 1996). Aristotle made the first attempt to describe movement in some systematic fashion, and discovered that without flexion one could not walk. Archimedes (287–212 BC) understood that much of human motion can be understood by viewing the human body as a system of levers and pulleys. Galen, a Roman, distinguished sensory and motor nerves, as well as agonist and antagonist muscles, information that is used by coaches and teachers today.

Galen's work remained unchallenged until the Renaissance, when the writings of the ancient Greeks and Romans were read and used as a foundation to expand what is known about the material world. This change in attitude toward the material world led to research about the nature of the human body. The founding of modern anatomy is attributed to Andreas Vesilus (1514–1564), whose artistic renderings of the human body in his book *De Humain Corporis Fabrica* (*The Fabric of the Human Body*) revealed the relationship of the skeletal system and muscles. Galileo Galilei (1564–1642) influenced significantly the development of physics by expressing basic physical laws in the language of mathematics. This contribution is evident today in biomechanics in that all human movement can be described and expressed mathematically. Indeed, a student of Galileo's, Borelli (1608–1679), is considered to be the "Father of Modern Biomechanics" for having done just this when he argued that the human skeletal system functions as a system of levers. Borelli studied equilibrium, center of gravity, angles of muscular pull, and is the originator of kinetics (Wilkerson, 1996). Sir Isaac Newton (1642–1727), a mathematician, developed his Laws of Motion, which continue to be studied and applied in biomechanics:

1. Inertia: An object at rest tends to stay at rest, and an object in motion tends to stay in motion.
2. An object will move only if it is affected by another and will be affected with the motive force impressed.
3. Every action causes an equal and opposite reaction.

Nineteenth-century contributions to biomechanics include the use of photography to study the human body as it moves, an advance that allowed for the quantification of movement. Eadweard Muybridge (1831–1904) took a series of photographs in a manner that reproduced movement in two dimensions (picture form), an advance that would lead to the graphing of human movement. Etienne Marey (1830–1904) of France took Muybridge's idea and put the pictures on a "ribbon," the predecessor of film. Both of these advancements are central to contemporary biomechanics research.

Throughout the 1900s biomechanics developed its methods of research and disseminating information. In the 1930s Wallace Fenn published the first biomechanical research studies and, in so doing set the standard for analysis in the subdiscipline (Wilkerson, 1996). Fenn worked with Eastman Kodak company to develop the technology to calculate certain human performance variables such as velocity, kinetic energy, and muscular power. The collaboration between Fenn and Kodak facilitated the development of the use of motion pictures to understand movement.

The 1940s witnessed the growth of the study of biomechanics in colleges and universities. Along with this growth came a number of textbooks for use in these courses of study. During the 1950s researchers in biomechanics began using electromyography, the study of electrical activity in the muscles. This approach allowed researchers to understand how and why muscles contract, and how these contractions affect movement.

The 1960s were the "Biomechanical Era," a time when biomechanics was institutionalized through the development of professional societies and journals, an emphasis on scholarly techniques, and the use and development of research instrumentation such as digitized moving pictures and computer technology. This was also the time when the term "biomechanics" came to be used with increasing frequency, distinguishing the specialized subdiscipline from the growing field of kinesiology. The incorporation of the digital computer in biomechanical analysis and the advancement of the 16mm high-speed motion picture significantly improved the quality of research. These improvements in technology made research much less time consuming: Calculations that once had to be done by hand could now be done electronically, speeding the analysis of data immensely.

The first professional associations devoted to the study of biomechanics were created in the 1960s. The International Society of Electromyography (ISEK) was formed in 1965, and the current name of this association's journal is *Electromyography and Clinical Neurophysiology*. In 1968 the first issue of the *Journal of Biomechanics* was published. Both of these publications anticipated the tremendous growth that occurred in the field in the 1970s.

Contemporary biomechanics is now central to the study of kinesiology. Virtually all degree-granting programs require students to study biomechanics and many require courses in physics, algebra, calculus, and human anatomy as prerequisites. Still, researchers in the field argue that biomechanics is in its adolescence in that it is still growing at a rapid rate. The utility of biomechanics for understanding the human condition is appreciated by many other fields, including medicine, aviation, the automobile industry. This appreciation is causing the boundaries of once distinct disciplines to blur as other disciplines utilize the techniques of study that were once unique to biomechanics. From any perspective, biomechanics is an area of study that will continue to be central to the study of kinesiology.

Motor Behavior

Perhaps the area of research that is most unique in kinesiology is *motor behavior*, along with its sub-areas of motor learning, motor control, and motor development. Motor behavior blends biomechanics and psychology into a coherent area of study, and the manner in which this is done makes motor behavior a truly unique area of study. Karl Newell argued that motor behavior is the only true area of disciplinary study in kinesiology, and that all other areas of study are merely spin-offs from the parent disciplines (Newell, 1990). Whether one agrees or disagrees with Newell, motor behavior has defined itself as a legitimate area of study in its own right.

The four names listed above can be confusing, and even experts in the field agree that distinguishing these names is sometimes unproductive.[2] What all these names have in common, though, is the word "motor." Motor in this context means the "engine" that moves the human body. As such, "motor" means "movement," or the causes of that movement.

Motor learning and control is defined as the subdiscipline concerned with the understanding of processes that lead to human movement (Shea, Shebilske, & Worchel, 1993). Motor learning is concerned with the processes that *facilitate or inhibit development*. Motor control is concerned with the *execution of the processes* that lead to skilled movement. In a sense, motor learning is the "input," while motor control is the "output." This statement oversimplifies these fields of study, but serves as an introduction to this unique area in kinesiology.

Motor development is an area of study that is closely related to sport pedagogy. In short, motor development is concerned with motor learning and control, but looks at that area and how the human body changes over time. It is easy to see why sport pedagogists and physical educators would be interested in motor development: Professionals are interested in how students learn and grow with respect to movement as they go through their school years. Older, more advanced students should be able to do more complex motor skills than their younger counterparts. Motor development would look at the changes that occur as children learn more complex motor skills.

Motor behavior is the total of all of these fields and is becoming the common name for the course of undergraduate study. To do research in this subdiscipline one must be familiar with other disciplines, but primarily the methods of psychology, physiology, engineering, and education. One can see that motor behavior is, like kinesiology, a composition of other disciplines. Depending on a person's particular area of interest in motor development, he or she will focus on one or the other of the "parent" disciplines listed above.

Motor control is closely related to the discipline of physiology. Sir Charles Sherrington studied the role of reflexes in the control of voluntary movements, and to do so he did research on nerves, muscles and their interactions. Sherrington was not concerned specifically with movement, but his work provided much of the understanding that leads to movement (Shea, Shebilske, & Worchel, 1993).

Motor learning is closely related to the discipline of psychology. Scholars in motor behavior find it convenient to define psychology as the scientific study of human behavior. We say "convenient" because psychology, literally defined, is the "study of mind," and "behavior" is quite a different thing than is "mind." Since no one has ever seen a "mind," it is helpful to think of psychology as an area of study that is concerned with behavior and to assume that mind controls behavior.

The founder of modern scientific psychology is often considered to be Wilhelm Wundt, who established the first modern research laboratory and wrote the first textbook in the field. Prior to Wundt, the study of psychology was the domain of philosophy, where concepts like "mind," "self," and "thought" were debated endlessly and, to many, without much insight. Wundt began to use the methods of science to systematically investigate the processes of mind. His studies included the nature of sensation, perception, and attention, and he studied reaction time to assess the speed of mental processes.

The disciplines of physiology and psychology were used by Franklin Henry, the University of California professor who became famous for the argument that physical education has an academic, disciplinary aspect. Henry applied these disciplines to human movement and helped found the subdiscipline that we now know as "motor development." By the early 1970s scholarly societies were formed, most importantly the North American Society for the Psychology of Sport and Physical Activity (1973) and the Canadian Society for Psycho-Motor Learning and Sport Psychology (1969). The first journal in the subdiscipline, the *Journal of Motor Behavior*, was first published in 1969. Like many other subdisciplines in kinesiology, this area was formed because more traditional disciplines like psychology and physiology failed to examine the nature of human movement. Today, however, the advances in this subdiscipline are recognized by many scholars in more traditional disciplines, and there appears to be some movement toward joining the subdiscipline of motor development and the parent disciplines. As one textbook noted, "the arbitrary distinctions between disciplines seem to be on a decline" (Shea, Shebilske, & Worchel, 1993, p. 9). It remains to be seen if this prediction comes to pass.

The Social Sciences

Sociology is related to psychology in that both are social sciences. However, psychology is concerned with the individual psyche or mind, whereas sociology is concerned with humans in groups situations and the institutions that are formed by groups. Psychology and sociology are like two sides of the same coin: On one side is the individual, and on the other is the group. Any given person can be understood from one perspective or the other, and that same person is influenced by both individual and social forces.

These two social sciences exist in kinesiology as sport and exercise psychology and sport sociology. Both subdisciplines are relatively new, dating back to the 1960s, but both have had a significant impact on the contemporary world. The names of the two subdisciplines have changed somewhat to reflect the changing nature of their areas of study, and both continue to change even as you read this text.

Sport and Exercise Psychology

While the sciences have added tremendous amounts of information to the understanding of human movement from an empirical (measurable) perspective, the social sciences have added to our understanding of how the individual and groups relate to human movement. The social sciences began with psychology and sociology, and, in this age of the blurring of disciplinary distinctions, new social sciences like anthropology, exercise psychology, and social psychology are being formed. The first subdisciplinary social science that we will discuss is that of sport and exercise psychology.

Sport and exercise psychology is the subdiscipline of kinesiology that focuses on how the mind affects human movement. Often the relationship of mind or psyche to human performance is overlooked, but it can be argued that it is in this area that some of the great performances of all time seem to be best understood. For instance, Charles (1994) has argued that

> Phenomenal performances that seemed to transcend and even defy the technological and physiological parameters of the times, such as Bob Beaman's 1968 Olympic long jump, have added credence to claims that psychological territory is the final frontier in performance enhancement. (p. 105)

As Charles notes, Beaman's performance far exceeded any previous long jump ever made— by over one foot!—and technological (biomechanical) and physiological (exercise physiology) explanations could not predict or explain this incredible performance, at least not until after it was accomplished. No one in 1968, using scientific methods of analysis of human movement, anticipated that such a jump could be made. So what area is left to explain such an incredible feat? Sport psychology can be used to understand and explain certain aspects of performance that seemingly defy explanation: Why do we believe we have certain limits on our performances? What is a "habit" and how can one break or create a habit in performance? What is "optimal" performance? How can one train for and predict optimal performance?

Sport and exercise psychology is concerned with these and many other questions, and the answers to these questions help us understand and better experience human movement. Sport and exercise psychologists are interested in various motor performance factors such as motivation, arousal, anxiety, and personality theory. By understanding these aspects of the human condition experts hope to improve the quality of performance.

Like motor development, sport and exercise psychology has as its basis the discipline of psychology. Unlike motor development, though, sport and exercise psychology has remained relatively true to its parent discipline. Psychology, as we noted earlier, is defined as the study of mind. More specifically, psychology is "the study of the mental life and activities of animals and men" (Peters & Mace, 1967). Originally, psychology was a part of philosophy known as "mental philosophy," because it was understood that "mind" and philosophy were two closely related aspects of the same area of study. Philosophers such as Plato and Aristotle contributed to the understanding of mind, and this tradition continued into the nineteenth century and still goes on today in the discipline of philosophy.

During the nineteenth century, however, psychology began to use the methods of science to investigate mind. While philosophers like Rene Descartes and Thomas Hobbes tried to understand mind in a more systematic way, as did Galileo and Newton in physics, their efforts clearly were not "scientific" as we understand the concept of science today. Early psychologists such as Wilhelm Wundt, John Watson, B.F. Skinner, Sigmund Freud, and William James used scientific analysis to form different psychologies to investigate the nature of mind. The work of these pioneers was initially influenced strongly by philosophy, but as the discipline developed its own body of knowledge and investigative techniques, psychology began to mark out its own territory.

Wilhelm Wundt (1832–1920), as we noted earlier, developed the first laboratory and wrote the first textbook on psychology. As a result, Wundt achieved worldwide fame. He is credited with founding the science of psychology, and he had much to do with developing the methods of research in this discipline. He was also known in his own time as a philosopher, and he was trained in physiology, which partly explains why his ideas had such a wide impact—they influenced three different academic disciplines (philosophy, physiology, and psychology)! Wundt's research was heavily influenced by physiological principles, and he influenced psychologists with his work on perception and sensation. His ideas are obviously important to us in kinesiology, where our understanding of perception and sensation helps us teach people how to perform better by using this information.

John Watson (1878–1958) and B.F. Skinner are known for the psychology of behaviorism, an approach to this discipline that emphasizes behavior and de-emphasizes the study of "mind." We cannot stress enough the change that this psychology represents. Behaviorism argues that one cannot directly study the mind. This makes sense: One cannot see a mind, weigh it, or directly measure it in any way. Watson and Skinner argued that psychology should not focus on mind, but instead should be considered a *biological science*. Watson and Skinner argued that, at best, psychologists can only make inferences regarding the workings of the mind. Behaviorial psychology, especially Skinner's work, focuses on the *causes and effects* of behavior, and as such is very important to kinesiology. If one can control the causes that guide behavior, then one can control the learning process in human movement.

The subdiscipline of sport and exercise psychology has become increasingly important as the theories that this subdiscipline has generated seem to have had significant and positive results in the world of sport. "Clinical" sport psychologists use the theories of this subdiscipline to enhance sport performance. Similarly, sport and exercise psychology argues for the well-being of all people and provides some of the specific techniques for doing so. The benefits of activities like tae kwon do, a traditional Asian martial art, can be explained by using the methods of this subdiscipline. The concepts of flow, peak moments, and of being "in the zone" are the areas of study that are of most interest to kinesiologists.

The growth of this subdiscipline is one of the most explosive in kinesiology. The professional organization known as the North American Society for the Psychology of Sport and Physical Activity (NASPSPA) was formed in the late 1960s and has grown to a current membership of thousands of members by the late 1990s. NASPSPA's focus is the academic study of sport and exercise psychology. Graduate programs in this subdiscipline are still being formed, although not as quickly as they were during the 1980s. One of the more interesting aspects within this subdiscipline is its division into *applied sport psychology*, which is "clinical" in the sense that it attempts to use the theories of the subdiscipline, and the area of *academic sport psychology*, which attempts to build theories that explain changes in performance that are related to psychology. One of the scholars who contributed to this argument was Rainer Martens, who argued that the traditional methods of science have little to say about the important work of improving performance (Martens, 1987). Both divisions are important, but practitioners in this subdiscipline continue to battle over which is more so.

Other journals and scholarly works that have been created recently include *The Sport Psychologist* and *Contemporary Thought on Human Performance*. Both of these journals emphasize the applied dimension of sport and exercise psychology. This subdiscipline is still growing, and the quality of the research being done by these scholars is having an impact on the parent discipline of psychology. Like motor development, this may be an area of kinesiology where the subdisciplinary boundaries are being eroded as the quality of the scholarship improves.

Sport Sociology

Most generally put, *sport sociology* is the study of sport from the perspective of social interaction. The structure of sport institutions, how these institutions function, and how these institutions affect and are affected by human social behavior are all areas of study of sport sociologists. The sociology of sport is a relatively new area of study in kinesiology that arose in part because of the growth of modern sport in the latter half of the twentieth century (Charles, 1994). The origin of the scholarly societies that study sport sociology explains much about this subdiscipline.

During the 1950s a growing number of scholars became interested in the social forces that surround the sport experience. Primarily physical educators, but also more traditional sociologists, began to examine the types of questions that are central to the subdiscipline. As Charles (1994) noted, these issues include, but are not limited to, the following:

- To understand sport as a social institution and its linkages with education, religion, politics, economics, and the legal system.
- To analyze socialization into and through sport.
- To study social stratification issues such as the relationship between sport and social class, social mobility through sport, and equal treatment revolving around gender, race, and age. (p. 105)

While these issues are of critical importance to understanding the role of sport in society, they were not discussed frequently prior to the 1950s as were those questions that dealt with strictly physical performance. Perhaps because of the difficulty of answering questions that deal with society, as well as the idea that sport was considered to be primarily a physical phenomena, physical education research concentrated mainly in the sciences: exercise physiology and biomechanics. It was not until the 1950s that such types of thinking were abandoned for answers to the pressing questions of how sport fits into society.

During the 1950s European researchers began to examine the social role of sport. In the United States, however, sport sociology began almost a decade later. In 1965, Gerald Kenyon and John Loy published their classic article "Toward a Sociology of Sport," an argument for the development of research and scholarly bodies into how sport fits into society.

Since then sport sociology has grown steadily, with several scholarly societies and publications developing. Scholarly societies include the North American Society for the Study of Sport (NASSS), the Sport Sociology Academy in the National Association of Sport and Physical Education division of the American Alliance of Health, Physical Education, Recreation, and Dance (AAHPERD), the Center for the Study of Sport in Society at Northeastern University, and the American Sociological Association. Scholarly journals include the *Sociology of Sport Journal, Journal of Sport and Social Issues*, the *Journal of Sport Behavior, Quest*, the *Arena Review*, and the *International Review of the Sociology of Sport*.

Sport sociology can be understood from three perspectives, each with its own approach to the study of sport in society (Charles, 1994). The first perspective is acknowledged by almost all sport sociologists and includes the desire to understand sport as a social construct. By "social construct," sport sociologists mean that they see sport as an activity that people participate in purposefully, an activity in which we consciously share rewards and responsibilities, an activity that we make important in our lives, and an activity that is central to our social existence. Sport is said by many sociologists to be a microcosm of society, meaning that all of the problems, values, social hierarchies, and values that are evident in society in general are also evident in our sports institutions. For instance, a sport sociologist could compare the institution of professional football to comparable institutions in American society. In general, are football players more or less educated that their nonsporting peers? Are their religious and political affiliations comparable? Does sport enjoy unusual legal freedoms? (Major league baseball, for instance, is unique among professional sports in that it is exempt from federal antitrust legislation.) These and other questions could be asked and researched by sport sociologists.

The second perspective utilized by sport sociologists has to do with the possibility of social change. Many times the perspective provided by social science research lends itself to working toward desirable social change. This social activism has been evident in a variety of situations. Harry Edwards, a sociologist at the University of California-Berkeley, worked in 1968 to inform black American athletes participating in the Olympics in Mexico City how they could use sport as a political forum. The ideas that Edwards promoted were derived from his research in sport sociology.

The third perspective seen in sport sociology is known as critical theory. Critical theorists argue that sport is a microcosm of society, but that sport sociology serves as a tool to understand social inequality. For the most part, critical theorists have argued that sport is one of the problems in society and not one of the solutions. Furthermore, it is argued that sport does not foster pluralism (an acceptance of difference in individuals), but instead promotes hegemony (the acceptance of cultural ideas without conscious reflection). For instance, it has been argued by critical theorists that many of the negative attitudes that men have toward women are formed and reinforced in the locker room, even though many of the participants in that sport are unaware that they are being "conditioned" to accept certain attitudes toward women (Messner & Sabo, 1994). Critical theorists also argue that these same environments can be used to foster change if the participants are made aware of how sport is an institution that socializes the participants into these attitudes.

While sport sociology may be a relatively new subdiscipline, it is an becoming an increasingly important area of study. At one time, scholars did not believe that play, games, and sport could reveal much about a society. Now, however, contemporary scholars see the value of examining sport as a social institution and will continue to utilize the techniques of the parent discipline (interviews, statistical analysis, questionnaires, and surveys).

The Humanities

The humanities are what most people think of when they are asked to name the "liberal arts." Philosophy, history, literature, and language are the traditional liberal arts. What makes these disciplines "liberal" is that it is believed that the study of these bodies of knowledge literally "liberates" one from the traditions of the past and provides ways of understanding the world that never would have been possible had the study of the humanities not been conducted. These disciplines are the "humanities" because they examine what it means to be human: Is one only a combination of chemicals, or is one a thinking being? Philosophy provides answers to this question. How have the events and people throughout history shaped our understanding of the human condition? History answers this question. What are the great narratives that have described the human experience? Literature answers this question. What are the oral traditions that have been used to express the human experience? Languages have been used to do this.

Kinesiology has a place for these disciplines, although "sport language" has not been developed well unless one considers movement itself a language. This possibility is an interesting one, though, and more will be said about dance and the latest human movement expressions in Chapter 14 when we discuss the nature of human movement. The other sub-disciplines are well developed, though: sport philosophy, sport history, and sport literature.

Sport Philosophy

The first area of study in the humanities that we describe is *sport philosophy*. Philosophy is often defined as "the love of wisdom," as well as the "wisdom that is sought." Another definition that is helpful is that philosophy concerns itself with the systematic investigation of what is real, what knowledge is, the nature of values, and logic. While reality, knowledge, and values may be familiar to students, logic is an area of study not often approached by kinesiologists (Zeigler, 1995). Logic concerns itself with the study of ideas and their relationships to one another.

The philosophical terms that describe the nature of reality, the nature of knowledge, and the nature of values are defined below. It is our argument that kinesiology students should become familiar with these terms because understanding them can have a significant, positive impact on how students understand the ideas with which the field of kinesiology concerns itself. And of most importance to kinesiology students is the area of philosophy that examines the nature of knowledge, epistemology.

The history of the subdiscipline of sport philosophy goes back to the late 1800s and the early 1900s. Scott Kretchmar (1997) divided the history of sport philosophy into three rough periods, the first an educationist approach, the second guided by competing philosophic systems, and the third by the categories and methods of a parent discipline. Each stage was a reaction to, and in some ways an improvement upon, its predecessor. Furthermore, it appears that sport philosophy is moving into a fourth stage as we move toward the twenty-first century.

The educationist approach of sport philosophy was closely related to the progressive education movement that lasted from the late nineteenth century and into the mid-1900s. Philosophers such as William James and John Dewey attacked old teaching methods and assumptions and argued for improved methods that would prepare Americans for life in the twentieth century. Students of James and Dewey used the developing philosophy of pragmatism and new theories about the education of children to create the first foundations textbooks in physical education (Jewett, Bain, & Ennis, 1995).

Some of the most famous philosophers of physical education were Jesse Feiring Williams, J.B. Nash, and Charles McCloy, whose philosophies were described in the classic article by Ellen Gerber (1971a), "The Ideas and Influence of McCloy, Nash, and Williams." Williams argued for the development of citizenship through physical activity, a position that came to be known as the "through the physical" philosophy of physical education. Williams argued that one acquired virtues like citizenship, leadership, teamwork, respect, and responsibility through physical activity. Charles McCloy, in contrast, argued that the purpose of physical activity was to develop the physical body itself, and that this type of education was enough in and of itself. McCloy argued against Williams, stating that one did not need to justify the profession in terms of idealized virtues. J.B. Nash differed from Williams and McCloy in that he argued for the quality use of leisure time through skilled movement. The purpose of physical education, argued Nash, was to teach students how to use their leisure time safely and efficiently. In so doing, the student's life would be better throughout adulthood.

Williams was probably the most influential sport philosopher of the period, although Nash and McCloy had their own vocal supporters. These sport philosophers debated extensively the mission of physical education, and while it appears that they differed significantly, Kretchmar argued that, in fact, they did not differ as much as it would appear. As Kretchmar noted,

> They all saw human beings as wholly biological organisms; they all promoted education for responsible citizenship; they were all aware of the pressing societal needs of their times and felt that education should respond to them; they all honored individual differences; they all saw great value in sport, dance, and games—not just rote exercise; they all believed in physical activity settings as powerful laboratories for learning; and they all saw themselves as non-dualists. Most importantly, they were all engaged in the same project—an attempt to describe physical education as an integral part of overall human education. (1997, p. 5)

While all of these early sport philosophers were familiar with the writings of James and Dewey, they were more "educationists" than philosophers. Their passion was for the improvement of teaching, and not for the acquisition of philosophical insights (Kretchmar, 1997). As a result, they committed certain philosophical errors and, in the long run, produced little knowledge about the nature of human movement. Kretchmar summarizes the philosophical errors these writers committed, and the consequences of these errors that the field of kinesiology has to live with to this day:

> A common contemporary criticism of these writers is that they promised too much; they raised expectations about the benefits of physical activity far beyond the profession's ability to produce and document them. While there is surely more than an element of truth to this charge, this problem arose largely from an empirical miscalculation, not a philosophic one. From a philosophic standpoint, the complaint about these writers is more fundamental. It is not that they promised too much, but that they did not skillfully argue for what they were promising. Thus, they may have been promising the wrong things. (Kretchmar, 1997, p. 9)

The "comparative systems approach" lasted from roughly 1950 to 1970. Kretchmar argues that this approach was similar to the educationist approach in that it had as its goal the identification of physical education as an important element in general schooling (Kretchmar, 1997). Two philosophers, Elwood Craig Davis and Earle Zeigler, argued for the "isms," or schools of philosophical thought. These schools of thought were memorized by generations of physical education majors: naturalism, realism, idealism, and pragmatism. Each of these schools of thought had specific advantages and disadvantages for physical education, and depending on one's goals as an educator, one would select one system over another.

The comparative systems approach used four basic steps: (1) the main elements of a system well described; (2) the basic concepts were discussed in terms of their impact on education; (3) deductions were drawn relative to the field of physical education; and (4) the strengths and weaknesses of each system were discussed in light of their impact on physical education. The advantage of the comparative systems approach was that it focused on philosophy, and thus the errors of McCloy, Nash, and Williams were avoided. However, this approach was difficult because students had to memorize whole systems of philosophy, and this "encyclopedic" approach was clumsy. Furthermore, students were left asking a simple question: Which system was right? Debates regarding the merits of one system or "ism" over another evolved into emotional arguments where physical educators argued for their own favorite system (Kretchmar, 1997).

The "disciplinary approach" began around 1970 and continues to this day. Sport philosophers began using the tools of philosophy—logic, induction, and deduction[3]—insights about such topics as sport and games and their "relationship to human development, liberation, and achievement, and happiness" (Kretchmar, 1997, p. 15). The disciplinary approach can be compared to the educationist and systems approaches:

> In contrast to the eclectic educationists, (the disciplinarians) took their primary cues from the discipline of philosophy, not science. In contrast to the philosophers of the comparative, systems approach, they attempted to do actual research much like many scholars in the parent discipline. Merely to copy, borrow, translate, apply, or deduce from already completed analyses of "real philosophers" was no longer enough. (Kretchmar, 1997, p. 15)

Furthermore, attention shifted from movement in education to movement itself. It was no longer necessary to justify scholarship only in terms that were educational. Instead, scholars examined every aspect of human movement using the tools of philosophy.

During the 1970s scholarly societies were formed to promote research into the subdiscipline of sport philosophy. One society was the Sport Philosophy Academy in the American Alliance for Health, Physical Education, Recreation, and Dance. Another is the Philosophic Society for the Study of Sport (PSSS), formed in 1972, and this society met in 1973 for the first time. Its journal, *The Journal of the Philosophy of Sport*, was first published in 1974. The mission of the society "is to foster interchange and scholarship among those interested in the scholarly study of sport" (Kretchmar, 1997). The majority of the members of PSSS have worked toward a type of scholarship that is more like that which is found in the parent discipline of philosophy.

While this final approach toward sport philosophy, the "disciplinary approach," may have promoted the quality of scholarship in the subdiscipline, it has also led to criticism from members of professional teachers in kinesiology. In short, many professionals argue that scholarship published in sport philosophy is too technical and removed from what teachers need and as such is not usable. As a consequence, many of the humanizing questions that can be asked about human movement are not asked at all, and as a consequence too many people accept or participate in human movement without thinking about it and their experiences. This condition would explain why critical theorists are upset with sport: Some contemporary problems, such as discrimination and violence, may be traced back to sport experiences. An understanding of sport philosophy might minimize this problem.

Perhaps because of this conflict, sport philosophy remains on the margins in the field of kinesiology. There are very few graduate programs that support this subdiscipline. Still, as Kretchmar argued, changes in attitudes toward the virtues of science, a healthy skepticism among many Americans toward athletes because of their poor behavior, and a desire on the part of many Americans to have an understanding of character in education may lead to a change in the status of sport philosophy. All of these changes may indicate that, perhaps, sport philosophy will become more central to the field of kinesiology in the twenty-first century.

Sport History

Another of the sport humanities is *sport history*. Narrowly defined, history is the study of change and continuity over time. What makes sport history unique is that it is concerned with how and why human movement has changed over time, or has not changed over time. Nancy Struna (1997) argued that the history of human movement should be considered in its most expansive form:

> We all explore the human agents of movement, movement as cultural performance or social practice, and the various forms of movement, even of animals, that were meaningful to human beings. (p. 1)

It may be surprising that human movement encompasses all of these areas, but upon reflection, the inclusion of sports like horse racing, bull fighting, and other blood sports is necessary to understand how play and sport have changed over time.

Most students, when they think of history, think of memorizing names, dates, places, and events. These types of information are part of history, but they are not the only part—nor are they the most interesting part. There are two different types of histories: descriptive and interpretive (Mechikoff & Estes, 1998). Descriptive histories are those that literally describe, as objectively as possible, what happened in the past. The questions of who, what, when, and where are answered with respect to the area of study of interest to the scholar and student. By being "objective," one hopes to remove the possibility of bias on the part of the researcher. Bias can occur either on purpose or by accident. In either case, descriptive histories hope to avoid this problem and present an accurate picture of change over time.

An interpretive history is one that seeks to explain how and why change occurred over time. The advantage of this type of history is that it provides some context or perspective as to why the change occurred (or did not occur). The disadvantage is that the context that is provided is both delimiting and biased. By "delimiting" we mean that the history usually examines only those historical data that are relevant to the questions being asked. The nature of the bias is the type of interpretive device that is used to explain how and why change occurred.

An *interpretive device* is a set of rules or guidelines that are used to select which data will be examined. For instance, one can study where people lived and how their living arrangements affected their attitudes toward play and sport. One will find that people who live in the city will have different attitudes toward play and sport than do those who live in the country. During the nineteenth century many Americans moved from the country to the city, and this demographic change coincided with changes in attitudes toward sport and play.

Done in this way, the set of rules is known as a *heuristic device*, a framework upon which the history is built. Heuristic devices that are helpful in the study of sport history are industrialization and urbanization theory (Betts, 1974), modernization theory (Adelman, 1986; Guttmann, 1978), and ontology (Mechikoff & Estes, 1998). Perhaps the biggest advantage of this type of history, though, is that it is more fun to read than the descriptive history. In our opinion, memorizing dates and people is, at best, informative, but is often downright boring.

Interpretive histories also have their limitations. While interpretive histories are more interesting and provide perspective, they are also limited by their perspectives. Histories that focus on the criteria of modernization, for instance, minimize the amount of information that is related to, say, demographic changes. In the end, no one type of history is better than another. Rather, each type of history is like looking in a different window of the same house: The house is always the same, but one sees different rooms. One can examine the same event with different heuristic devices and learn about that perspective of the event being studied.

Both descriptive histories and interpretive histories get their information from two different types of sources: primary and secondary sources. A primary source is usually an eyewitness account and includes the historical artifacts that were generated during the time period being studied. Pottery, art, poetry, newspaper accounts, film, video, music, and other artifacts that correspond to the time period being studied are primary sources. Even oral histories and anecdotes can be considered primary sources in that they provide information about the attitudes of the people who experienced the events being studied.

For instance, one of the best primary sources of ancient Greek sport are Homer's *Iliad* and *Odyssey*. Homer's epic poem about the Trojan War and the hero Odysseus was written 400 years after the Trojan War occurred and was a compilation of stories that were passed orally from one generation to the next. While the information in the *Iliad* and *Odyssey* is not verifiably accurate in all cases, it still provides the best information regarding attitudes of Greeks toward participation in athletics, when the events should be held, and how the athletes should think and behave when they compete.

A secondary source is historical data that is at least one person removed from the eyewitness. Good examples of secondary sources are academic journal articles, history texts, and history teachers. In almost all cases, secondary sources were not eyewitnesses. However, a good secondary source provides excellent information about how change occurred over time. Because a source is secondary does not mean that it is not a quality source of information.

In summary, both descriptive and interpretive histories as well as primary and secondary sources are the tools of historians. These tools are used to help understand how change has occurred over time, and applied to the study of sport and physical education one can see where the field has been and why. And this information can be used in a variety of ways. As the saying goes, "Those who do not know history are bound to repeat its mistakes."

Early sport histories concentrated were descriptive in nature, focusing on the "who" and "what." An example was Frederic Paxson (1917), who argued that organized sport was the "new frontier" once the West was populated. As Struna noted, the limitation of these descriptive histories is that they "ordered activities over time but did not explain them in time" (Struna, 1997, p. 4). In the 1950s Johan Huizinga published *Homo ludens*, a classic in the field of sport philosophy as well as in sport history. Huizinga argued that play is a foundation to civilization. In so doing Huizinga made two contributions. First, he made a powerful argument that play is not an "extra," but instead is a central part of culture. Secondly, it is arguable that Huizinga is the first to break from the tradition of merely describing the sport and play activities in culture. Clearly, Huizinga made a powerful case for using play to *interpret* culture.

During the 1890s the first histories were written to describe the development of physical education. Basically, these first histories were descriptive, discussing past movements in exercise, gymnastics, and other physical training activities (Struna, 1997). However, the first history of any significance was written in 1926 by Emmett Rice, *A Brief History of Physical Education*. The organization and development of historical works about physical education, however, did not gain acceptance until after World War II. The first major work of history was the classic *A World History of Physical Education* by Deobold Van Dalen, Elmer Mitchell, and Bruce Bennett (1953). The contribution of this history was that it connected sport to physical education, discussed the origin of "amateur" athletics in ancient Greece, and discussed the institutional nature of organized sport. Van Dalen and colleagues' perspective emphasized what many physical educators argued, and still argue today: Sport should be a part of physical education, and that sport experiences taught American values of

> prowess, habits of industry, and the positive effects of democratic living. . . . Moreover . . . participation in sport "taught" long-standing American ideals: fair play, team work, industry, and personal and social discipline. (Struna, 1997, p. 13)

In the 1960s and 1970s a new type of sport history was written: the interpretive history. The first scholar to do so was J.R. Betts, who argued that there exists a relationship between demographic patterns and play. Betts' urbanization and industrialization theory remains one of the classic heuristic devices in sport history. In short, Betts argued that modern sports were the products of America's urbanizing and industrializing that began in the 1850s. The use of the heuristic device continued with Allan Guttmann and Melvin Adelman, who argued that sport *modernized* during the nineteenth century. Modernization theory argues that culture tends to move from a premodern state to a modern state, and in so doing sport modernized as well (Table 4-1).

TABLE 4-1 Modernization Theory

Premodern Sport	Modern Sport
1. No formal organizations	1. Sport formally organized
2. No written rules	2. Rules written down
3. Local competition only	3. Competition is natural
4. No specialized roles	4. Highly specialized
5. No public information	5. Highly publicized
6. No statistics and records	6. Statistics and records kept

From Adelman, M. (1986). *A Sporting Time: New York City and the Rise of Modern Athletics, 1820–1870*. Champaign: University of Illinois Press.

Another example of using a heuristic device is ontology, the study of the nature of being. As a culture's view of the human body changes, so does that culture's view of sport and physical education. For instance, both Plato in ancient Greece and Vittorino da Feltre of the Renaissance argued that both mind and body are "real" and exist to support each other in a state of harmony. With this ontological position, both mind and body need development, and it was the role of education to make sure that this development occurs. Consequently, both literary education and physical education were considered by Plato and da Feltre to be central to human development.

Using the same interpretive device, one can see that the scholastics of the Middle Ages did not believe in the harmony of mind, spirit, and body. Instead, spiritual and intellectual development were considered much more important. In such an environment, sport and physical education were viewed with suspicion at best and were often condemned. In both situations—that of the balanced ontological view of Plato and da Feltre or that of the scholastics—ontology is helpful in seeing how attitudes toward the human body, sport, and physical education have changed over time.

The attitudes of scholars toward historical studies in sport and physical education have changed over time as well. Interestingly, during the early and mid parts of the twentieth century, scholars were not particularly interested in sport history because of biases many scholars had toward play. Sport and play were not considered "worthy" of study because they were not "serious," or worthy of the time of "serious" scholars. However, in recent decades scholars have changed their attitudes toward play, perhaps because of the insights of sociologists and anthropologists. The contemporary belief that play is "a window into the soul" has led the *Journal of Sport History* to be the seventh most heavily cited history journal in the discipline of history (Struna, 1997). The *Journal of Sport History* is the scholarly journal published by the North American Society for Sport History (NASSH).

Founded in 1973, NASSH has become the focal point for the study of sport, and since its inception the body of knowledge in the sport history has grown significantly and been shaped substantially. Other professional societies have contributed as well, including the Sport History Academy of the American Alliance for Health, Physical Education, Recreation, and Dance; the American Studies Association; and the American Historical Association. However, NASSH has been the central force in promoting and shaping the subdiscipline.

For a variety of reasons, however, sport history is not a central area of sport studies or kinesiology. Usually sport history is part of an introductory course to studies in kinesiology or physical education and is not taught in the same manner, nor with the same quality, as are the sport sciences. The reasons for this are varied, ranging from the dominance of the scientific paradigm in the field of kinesiology, to the small numbers of those trained in sport history and who are qualified to teach it, and to the poor understanding of the virtues of the subdiscipline by other professionals in the field. Among the subdisciplines in the humanities, though, sport history appears to be the most well established and is the subdiscipline that will provide a humanistic understanding of movement to kinesiology undergraduates.

Sport Literature

Sport literature is one of the newest subdisciplines in kinesiology. The Sport Literature Association was founded in 1980 by a small group of faculty at San Diego State University and East Tennessee State University who had an interest in how sport narratives have been expressed in literature. The first issue of *Arete: The Journal of Sport Literature* was published in 1981, and the twice-yearly journal has published critical articles, poetry, and short stories since that time.

Begun primarily by physical educators, the majority of scholars now reside in departments of English and American Studies. Still, the use of the study of narratives to understand culture appears to be growing. As Michael Oriard argued, "As Malamud taught us so well, sport may be the sole repository of myth in a nearly mythless society" (1980, p. 212) Our point is that the stories that we tell each other are central to our understanding of sport and physical education, and sport literature is the subdiscipline that concentrates on this type of knowing.

Summary

This chapter has focused on the basic subdisciplines that are studied in undergraduate kinesiology programs. There are other subdisciplines that we did not discuss that should at least be mentioned here: Sport art, sport anthropology, and exercise epidemiology are new additions to the subdisciplines that may, over time, come to be part of the studies of contemporary kinesiology students.

But the subdisciplines that we described are certainly here to stay for some time to come. How they evolve in the next century is anyone's guess, but it is certain that for the next generation kinesiologists will need to know at least the basics of what constitutes the body of knowledge in the *discipline* of kinesiology.

Discussion Questions

1. What are the subdisciplines in kinesiology?
2. What makes each of the subdisciplines unique?
3. What are the methods of scholarship used in particular subdisciplines?

References

Adelman, M. (1986). *A sporting time: New York City and the rise of modern athletics, 1820–1870.* Champaign: University of Illinois Press.

Bain, L. (1996). Sport pedagogy. In J. Massengale & D. Swanson (Eds.), *The development of the subdisciplines in physical education.* Champaign, IL: Human Kinetics.

Barham, J. (1966). Kinesiology: Toward a science and discipline of human movement. *Journal of Health, Physical Education, and Recreation,* (October), 65–68.

Betts, J. (1974). *America's sporting heritage: 1850–1950.* Reading, MA: Addison-Wesley.

Charles, J. (1994). *Contemporary kinesiology.* Englewood, CO: Morton.

Gerber, E. (1971a). The ideas and influence of McCloy, Nash, and Williams. *Proceedings of the Big 10 Symposium on the history of physical education and sport.* Chicago, IL: The Athletics Institute.

Gerber, E. (1971b). *Innovators and institutions in physical education.* Philadelphia: Lea & Febiger.

Guttmann, A. (1978). *From ritual to record: The nature of modern sports.* New York: Columbia University Press.

Huizinga, J. (1955). *Homo ludens: A study of the play element in culture.* Boston: Beacon.

Jewett, A., Bain, L., & Ennis, C. (1995). *The curriculum process in physical education.* Madison, WI: WCB Brown & Benchmark.

Kretchmar, S. (1997). Philosophy of sport. In J. Massengale & D. Swanson (Eds.), *History of exercise and sport science.* Champaign, IL: Human Kinetics.

Martens, R. (1987). Science, knowledge, and sport psychology. *The Sport Psychologist, 1*, 29–55.

Mechikoff, R., & Estes, S. (1998). *A history and philosophy of sport and physical education.* Dubuque, IA: Brown and Benchmark.

Messner, M., & Sabo, D. (1994). *Sex, violence, and power in sports.* Freedom, CA: The Crossing Press.

Newell, K. (1990). Physical education in higher education: Chaos out of order. *Quest, 42*(3), 227–242.

Oriard, M. (1980). *Dreaming of heroes: American sports fiction 1868–1980.* Chicago: Nelson-Hall.

Paxon, F. (1917). The rise of sport. *Mississippi Valley Historical Review, 4*, p.143–68.

Peters, S., & Mace, C. (1967). Psychology. *The encyclopedia of philosophy.* New York: Macmillan & the Free Press.

Rice, E. (1926). *A brief history of physical education.* New York: A.S. Barnes.

Shea, C., Shebilske, W., & Worchel, S. (1993). *Motor learning and control.* Englewood Cliffs, NJ: Prentice Hall.

Siedentop, D. (1994). *Introduction to physical education, fitness, and sport* (2nd ed.). Mountain View, CA: Mayfield.

Struna, N. (1997). Sport history. In J. Massengale & D. Swanson (Eds.), *History of exercise and sport science.* Champaign, IL: Human Kinetics.

Van Dalen, D., Mitchell, E., & Bennett, B. (1953). *A world history of physical education.*

Wilkerson, J. (1996). Biomechanics. In J. Massengale & D. Swanson, (Eds.), *The development of the subdisciplines in physical education.* Champaign, IL: Human Kinetics.

Zeigler, E. (1995). Competency in critical thinking: A requirement for the "Allied Professionals." *Quest, 47*(2), 196–211.

Endnotes

1. Kinesiology, as we defined in early chapters, includes the scholarly study of human movement from all scholarly perspectives. As we noted in Chapter 1, this name confusion inspired the American Academy of Physical Education, an organization dedicated to research, to change its name to the American Academy of Kinesiology and Physical Education. The change in the name of this organization occurred because it was recognized by its members that the term "kinesiology" includes both the teaching of sport pedagogy and the scholarly research into the subdisciplines that is distinct from the teaching of sport pedagogy. Both types of activities are considered important and appropriate to the field of kinesiology.

2. As Shea, Shebilske, and Worchel (1993) argued, "the two subfields are so closely intertwined that it is often unproductive to separate them. Factors that influence the control of a motor skill often influence the learning of that skill, and vice versa."

3. More will be said about these tools in Chapter 9 when we discuss the epistemology of rationalism, or a way of knowing that emphasizes thought.

Chapter 5

Professional Responsibilities and Opportunities

Chapter Objectives

Upon completion of this chapter, the reader will be able to:

1. Understand the role of the professional in modern society.
2. Understand the need for certification and various issues surrounding certification.
3. Understand why it is necessary that a profession must achieve legitimate professional recognition and public respect.
4. Understand the process of earning professional recognition and respect.
5. Identify professional standards that mature professionals must demonstrate.
6. Identify national issues concerning professional leadership.
7. Identify selected professional opportunities and career paths available to kinesiology majors.
8. Understand the role of technology and the benefits of developing technological skills.

As we noted at the beginning of this textbook, most students enter college with the idea of preparing for a career although there are some who are "undeclared" and investigating various potential career paths. Perhaps these undeclared students will be fortunate enough to enroll in a kinesiology course and discover "the joy of human movement." The field continues to expand, which in part reflects the interest that health professionals and the American public have with enhancing our overall health and well-being through education and exercise. Students who elect to major in kinesiology and related areas will soon discover how personally rewarding and gratifying this profession can be.

By reading the previous chapters, the students should understand why the traditional designation that identifies our field—physical education—has been gradually replaced by new names that seem to more fully reflect the content of the profession. Exercise Science, Kinesiology, Sport Science, and Human Movement are academic and professional titles that identify the field and the professional expertise we claim by formal education and training. Rigorous preparation and the desire to become a recognized and respected profession has been the goal of our field for over a century. The quest to become a mature and respected profession is an important concern that has a direct relationship to career development. We will discuss this issue and related ones throughout this chapter. In so doing we are able to take the issue of the "professionialization" one step further and demonstrate how it directly applies to your career aspirations.

Establishing Professional Credibility and Integrity

Recall that the profession of physical education in the United States was born on November 27, 1885. Dr. William G. Anderson, a gymnastics instructor who taught at Adelphi Academy in Brooklyn, called a meeting of prominent physicians and educators who were seriously involved in the study and promotion of exercise and fitness activities. He presided over this landmark gathering that brought forty-nine aspiring professionals together. Twenty-eight of those in attendance were physicians; the rest were teachers. One result of this meeting was the formation of the American Association for the Advancement of Physical Education (AAAPE). Elected as the first president of AAAPE was Dr. Edward Hitchcock of Amherst College. Among the most important goals of the AAAPE was to initiate the process that would distinguish physical education as an emerging profession and to determine professional standards for the new field.

The original founding members of AAAPE recognized the importance of establishing the credibility and integrity of this newly emerging field. It was critical to the founders that physical education embody the concept of professional responsibility and the standards that go along with any profession. The founders of the AAAPE were part of the growing number of professionals who believed that it is crucial to insure the public that *professionals* have the requisite knowledge and competencies to deliver a service and advice to the public.

Professionalization is the benchmark that distinguishes a professional from the ordinary rank and file workers. The concept and importance of becoming a professional began to take shape in the nineteenth century as American society began to establish a middle class. This may not appear very relevant at the moment, but an appreciation of the values and goals that this newly emerging middle class identified with actually set the stage for most of the professional opportunities and competencies we have come to expect. In fact, this is one of the reasons that you are in university today: By obtaining an undergraduate degree, your university *certifies* that you have learned about your discipline and your profession. In a sense, a college degree is a "license," one that states that its owner has knowledge.

Until the election of Andrew Jackson as President of the United States in 1823, professional status was accorded primarily to three select careers. The clergy, physicians, and lawyers retained the exclusive right to be identified as "professionals." Jackson ran on the platform that advanced the agenda of the "common man." He was against the traditional professional monopoly that physicians, lawyers, and the clergy enjoyed by right of an elite education or legacy.

These three expert professions had been able to promote themselves as the "arbiters of truth" and set the social and political agendas of nineteenth-century society. President Jackson fought against their arrogance and their belief in exclusivity that worked against the common worker and the growing middle class who wanted their children to have the same opportunities as the children of these elite professions. At the same time that this political and social upheaval was occurring, science was making astonishing discoveries that held the promise of medical cures and the restoration of health. The combination of professionalization, the development of science, and the birth of the modern American university led to the process of professional certification that we use today.

Developing Professional Expertise: The Emergence of Specializations and Certifications

Health was a major concern to nineteenth-century Americans and Europeans alike. Even though physicians attempted to "practice" medicine, they were not very successful. Medical training could be obtained by serving as an apprentice for six months as well as attending a "school of medicine" for a year or so. Many people distrusted doctors and relied on alternative treatments that were supposed to promote or restore health in order to prevent disease. Disease was rampant. Cholera, tuberculosis, mumps, smallpox, polio, and deadly strains of the flu would devastate cities and rural America. Poor medical training and quack cures peddled by doctors with dubious qualifications did not inspire confidence. Americans had good reason to be suspicious and wary of medicine and related health enhancing techniques during this era.

As the emerging middle class grew, so did their access to higher education. This new middle class was the product of the industrial revolution. Technology and science were the fields that held the promise of a better future. Colleges began to respond to middle-class demands that the education of their sons and daughters be relevant and prepare them for professional careers in business, science, and industry. The traditional liberal arts and humanities curriculum that had been the domain of the clergy, physicians, and lawyers was augmented by major courses of study and professional preparation that focused on the sciences and the training for a professional career.

Since disease was a serious problem during the nineteenth century, Americans were serious about maintaining and improving their personal health. As the population grew and access to formal education expanded, people became more sophisticated in their understanding of science. Popular magazines were published that presented information about science and medicine that captured the public eye. The collective nineteenth- and twentieth-century social conscience that reflected middle-class values helped shape the social, political, and professional agenda that was on the horizon. This acted as a "professional" catalyst that transformed the once elitist halls of medicine and law into professions that became highly responsive to the demands and needs of the populace.

The newly educated and increasingly affluent middle class wanted access to the best educational and professional expertise available. As a result, specializations and certifications began to be established in these new emerging fields. Specializations reflected the advances in science. Certifications reflected the need for professional competencies. The study of medicine and law underwent major changes to reflect the demand for high-quality training and the establishment of standards and minimal competencies. Professional organizations emerged that would determine educational standards, codes of ethics, professional competencies, licensers, and the authority to discipline or remove members who did not adhere to established professional conduct. This was especially evident in medicine.

Physicians were determined to elevate the practice of medicine to such a status that society would indeed value their knowledge and expertise. Gaining admission to medical school became exceedingly difficult. The training became long and difficult, and only the best bothered to apply. The profession of medicine became based on reliable and documented scientific fact. Many specializations began to emerge as advances in science and medicine created new areas that required specialized training. Many Americans believed that the relationship between "a sound body and a sound mind" was of critical importance. This mind-body link as it related to optimum health and well-being was one of the main focal points of the membership in AAAPE.

The AAAPE was a newly emerging profession and a sub-specialization of medicine. Over time, the AAAPE underwent many changes (leadership, orientation, goals, growth of membership) as did the profession. The historic link between a sound mind in a sound body coupled with the goal of achieving a quality lifestyle through play, games, scientific exercise and lifetime sports became the crown jewel of our profession.[1] The original AAAPE evolved into the American Alliance for the Advancement of Health, Physical Education, Recreation, and Dance (AAHPERD) with over 20,000 members. AAHPERD represents an alliance of six national associations (these will be described later in this chapter) that claim to have closely related interests.

The relationship that was established long ago between exercise, health, and quality of life (prevention of disease and health and wellness) remain as strong as ever. To address this specialized area, physicians and university academics with the doctor of philosophy degree (Ph.D.) and the doctor of education degree (Ed.D.) who are interested in sports medicine and the medical aspects of exercise science and related research formed the American College of Sports Medicine (ACSM) in 1954 to regulate and promote professional growth in this high profile area. Professional competence and the regulation of membership standards are ideals that must be adhered to if a professional field is to gain the public trust and respect.

Sports Medicine: The Need for Professional Regulation

The establishment of the ACSM illustrates the process of developing professional maturity, sophistication, and advancement in both exercise science and medicine. The benefit of regular exercise in achieving optimum health unites our profession and the medical profession, and professional organizations like ACSM and the American Medical Association (AMA) advance this cause. Professional career paths in the field broadly known as sports medicine appeal to many professionals (coaches, athletic trainers, sport psychologists, exercise physiologists) and the allied medical areas (physicians, nurses, physical therapists, chiropractors, and podiatrists).

The subject of sports medicine as an actual therapeutic agent is a frequent question of journalists, parents, and most everybody with an interest in sports, exercise, and health. As a profession, we believe that regular exercise is one of the first steps people can take to reach optimal health. The famous Cooper Clinic in Dallas, Texas has generated significant research in this area. The medical director of the Cooper Clinic, Dr. Larry Gibbons, believes that for every hour we exercise, we extend our life for two hours.[2] Proper exercise can reduce the risk for heart disease, hypertension, and some cancers. People who are overweight by 40 percent or more are at greater risk of developing colon cancer, breast cancer, and ovarian cancer. In addition, the Centers for Disease Control (CDC) in Atlanta reports that every year there are 250,000 deaths in the United States that could have been prevented through regular exercise.

Recent research indicates that exercise and related fitness activities remains the best and cheapest health insurance available! The professional bodies of the CDC, ACSM, and the AAHPERD are working in concert to educate the public that regular exercise is among the best medicine there is. Education in the form of providing information that is in the public interest is an important role of every profession.

Injury is part of athletic participation and the number of trained professionals with an interest in serving the population of athletes who are injured grows larger every year. The ACSM and the National Athletic Trainers Association (NATA) are leaders in injury prevention and in providing the necessary medical treatment when an athlete does become injured.

The American Psychological Association (APA) has a group of clinical psychologists who practice sport psychology (refer back to Chapter 4 for details on this subdiscipline). The APA is responsible for licensing in psychology, and membership is available only to trained psychologists. Educators and psychologists who claim expertise in sport psychology, also called performance enhancement, usually hold membership in the North American Society for the Psychology of Sport and Physical Activity (NASPSPA), founded in 1966 for the Association for the Advancement of Applied Sport Psychology (AAASP). AAASP offers certification as a "consultant" in sport psychology. Physical injury is debilitating experience. Experts in sport psychology research how to help injured athletes recover psychologically from injury. Interestingly, many college professors identify themselves as professionals in the area of sport psychology, but do not qualify for membership in the APA and may not have the qualifications to obtain AAASP certification as consultants. One can hold membership in AAASP but not necessarily be certified. This situation undermines the integrity of the profession of sport psychology and will have to be remedied before the public accepts this profession unconditionally.

The field of sports medicine is largely unregulated by the AMA, which would seem to be the appropriate professional body to oversee this area. No board-certified specialty in sports medicine is offered by the American Medical Association. Membership in ACSM is not exclusively limited to physicians, as anyone with an interest in sports medicine can apply for membership. The truth of the matter is that, in most states, almost anyone who wants to claim expertise in some area of sports medicine can do so, whether it be in sports nutrition, sport massage, chiropractic sports medicine, sport psychology, performance enhancement, orthopedic sports medicine, and sport scientists with some claim to sports medicine.

The NATA, as well as a number of physicians, physiologists, and psychologists, is concerned with this lack of regulation of the field and is taking steps to remedy this situation. How can the public be protected from less than qualified professionals in this area? One way is to determine whether the certification in question is approved by the National Commission for Certifying Agencies (NCCA). The NCCA is based in Washington, DC, and sets standards for certification and licenser programs in the United States. While the NCCA is a professional body that assures that certifications meeting its rigorous criteria reflect high professional standards, it is a voluntary process. This simply means that an organization that wants to offer certification can either comply with NCCA standards or ignore them and set their own.

Although selected professional organizations in the field will be presented later in this chapter, it is important to point out that the tremendous proliferation of professional associations in the 1990s illustrate the myriad of needs and interests that are desired by individuals in the field. Some of these associations are affiliated with AAHPERD, and some have no affiliation at all. A number of associations have emerged that offer services that rival and in some cases appear to exceed those offered by AAHPERD.

The professional opportunities available in our field are numerous and exciting. The purpose of this chapter is to provide you with relevant information so that you will understand the significance of professional development and the corresponding professional responsibilities. We will address obvious areas of concern (sports medicine has already been used as an example) that are identified with becoming a professional. We will pay close attention to the rapidly expanding fitness and health industry as well as the more traditional profession of teaching and coaching. Information about the various professional opportunities, also called career paths, that are available will be discussed. Of particular importance is to recognize the reality that career paths and advancement in the late 1990s and beyond will depend on your ability to earn legitimate professional credentials and exhibit behavior consistent with that of a highly educated professional; society in the twenty-first century will accept nothing less.

Establishing Professional Status and Recognition

To achieve professional status is a symbol of maturity and recognition, an achievement that means one has become an "expert" in a field that is consistent with recognized academic standards and enjoys strong public support. Yet kinesiology does not have the same status as does law or medicine. It is hard to explain why the field of kinesiology has not sought the benefits of professional licenser to any significant degree. Perhaps it is the culture of our field that explains why it has not pursued licensing with the vigor and aggressive posture that physicians, attorneys, and other well established professional groups have. Does this present a problem? Let us examine this situation by illustration.

Dwight Eisenhower served as President of the United States from 1953 to 1961. He, like President John Kennedy, was concerned about the lack of fitness that the young people of this time lacked. This noticeable "lack of physical fitness" that earned President Eisenhower's attention may have been due to his concern that the Cold War between the United States and the former Soviet Union would "heat up" (it did), and the armed services of the United States would be better prepared to respond to a war if the nation's young men were more physically fit. Eisenhower called upon individuals whom he believed to be experts—professionals, if you will—in the field of physical education. He summoned to the White House Joe Louis, former heavyweight boxing champion of the world and a "professional" prize fighter, a "professional" basketball player, and a former Olympic diving champion. Physical educators were not invited to give input. What does their absence suggest?

President John F. Kennedy was equally concerned with the nation's apparent lack of physical fitness and created The President's Council on Physical Fitness and Sports. The formation of this council was an improvement over what Eisenhower did. However, more often than not individuals selected to head the President's Council were high-profile public figures who did not have a degree in physical education or kinesiology. It should be noted that over the years there was some success in bringing some physical educators into the President's Council. Ash Hayes was a prominent physical educator from California who spent a number of years serving on this prestigious body.

Recently, the high-profile Chair of the President's Council was movie star and "professional" body builder Arnold Schwarzenegger. Although some members of the profession hailed his appointment, including the National Association for Physical Education in Higher Education (NAPEHE), many were deeply disappointed. Schwarzenegger's appointment was an indication that the appointment of a president from the field of kinesiology was still in the future and that American presidents and American people seem to more easily relate to a body builder than kinesiology professionals. To his credit, Schwarzenegger did surrounded himself with professional educators such as John Cates, former head of the California Alliance for Health, Physical Education, Recreation, and Dance. Still, it is apparent that much work remains to be done with respect to the education of the American public about the professional status and integrity of kinesiology.

Why is it that our profession appears to lack the credibility of other professional organizations such as the AMA, the American Bar Association (ABA), or the National Educational Association (NEA)? Why did two presidents ignore some of the best expertise available? True, there are kinesiologists on the President's Council. But do you know who they are? Are they in the public eye?

It should be apparent why it is crucial that professional credibility and high-profile professional status be attained. With it comes influence, respect, and competence that is achieved through the hard work necessary to earn professional certification. The need for kinesiology to become a full-fledged profession, just like those represented by the AMA, ABA, and NEA, becomes apparent.

This issue has been discussed many times for over a century, beginning with an article titled, "Physical Education: A New Profession" written in 1890 by Luther H. Gulick (1865–1918). Gulick was the consummate professional. He was in attendance at the landmark meeting called by Anderson in 1885, and he served as the Secretary of AAAPE from 1892–1893 and President from 1903–1907. The AAHPERD honored Luther H. Gulick by instituting an award named after him. The Luther H. Gulick Award is the highest award that can be bestowed by AAHPERD.

Another argument for professional standards was written by William G. Anderson (1860–1947), who published "The Founding of the American Physical Education Profession" in the American Physical Education Review over fifty years ago. Dedicated professionals have labored for over 100 years to earn the respect accorded professionals, but most indications are that we may well have fallen short of our goal. The question is not so much what happened but why it happened.

Our field appears to be in a perpetual state of "emerging" as opposed to the full-fledged status of profession. There have been numerous definitions of what a profession is supposed to encompass.[3] Everett C. Hughes, a sociologist at Brandeis University, said that "a profession considers itself the proper body to set the terms in which some aspect of society, life or nature is to be thought of and to determine the general lines or even the details of public policy concerning it" (Bucher & Goldman, 1969, p. 12). The definition by Hughes seems to be a reasonable and worthy goal to strive for.

There are a number of professional groups that have done so, and we have already pointed out that medicine and law "reinvented" themselves over a century ago to claim exclusive domain over these two areas. Since then accountants, engineers, scientists, psychologists and other university-educated individuals with common backgrounds and goals have joined to form professional organizations. In so doing they have met the criteria that all professions must meet:

- Advancing their professional agenda
- Regulating and controlling professional development of the field
- Setting professional standards and goals that are highly regarded by the general public
- Having the authority to punish or remove members who act in an unprofessional manner

Once these standards are described, how successful has our profession been in uniting under one powerful entity and retaining control and regulation over sport, exercise, and fitness/health promotion? AAHPERD, our oldest professional and academic organization, has not been as successful as the AMA or ABA in controlling and regulating the field of kinesiology. As a result, other organizations have emerged and stepped forward to offer certification rights in exercise and related areas. Perhaps the most visible example is in the area of the thousands of "professionals" without a degree who market themselves as coaches, personal trainers, fitness instructors, and aerobic dance instructors. Many of these individuals are "certified."

The Issue of Professional Certification

Health clubs and fitness centers employ thousands of "fitness instructors," trainers, councilors, and dance teachers. Tens of thousands of people work out at these fitness clubs and gyms every day. Is a degree in kinesiology, exercise science, physical education, or related area mandatory before a "professional fitness instructor" is employed in this business? In most cases the answer is no. Most fitness instructors do not belong to AAHPERD, and AAHPERD does not offer a program to certify fitness instructors, personal trainers, aerobic dance instructors, and other fitness and exercise professionals.

The decision by AAHPERD to largely ignore regulation and certification of the thousands of individuals working in the fitness and health industry in order to maintain professional quality continues to perplex many in the field of kinesiology.[4]

This loss of credibility in the status of professional certification may be due to the apparent decision by AAHPERD to focus more on instructional activities in K–12 programs. In addition, there are a number of professionals in the field who identify more with the subdisciplines (sport psychology, exercise physiology, athletic training, etc.) that are taught in colleges and universities who believe that AAHPERD has done little to benefit their professional growth. Clearly, there is a perception that a vacuum exists relative to the need for a strong professional organization that can regulate and enhance the professional growth opportunities of the entire field.

This regulation and certification vacuum has been filled by organizations that recognize the opportunity to certify movement professionals. There are numerous examples that can demonstrate this situation. The International Dance Exercise Association (IDEA) is a professional organization of fitness instructors that publishes *IDEA Today* and IDEA *Personal Trainer* magazine. In their 1996 products catalog, IDEA promotes itself as, "the world's leading source of credible fitness information, education, and training." The American Council on Exercise (ACE) was founded in 1985 and is in the business of certifying aerobics instructors and personal trainers. In 1995 it began to offer certification for Lifestyle and Weight Management Consultants. The Aerobics and Fitness Association of America (AFAA) also issues certifications in the fitness area. The American College of Sports Medicine (ACSM) has several levels of certifications, and because of its scholarly background, it may be the most prestigious of the above mentioned non-AAHPERD certifying organizations.

The failure of AAHPERD to address the needs of teaching professionals led to a challenge by a rival professional organization. The United States Physical Education Association (USPE) was formed to respond to the needs of professional teachers in the field that were not satisfactorily addressed by AAHPERD. USPE was developed with the help of Human Kinetics Publishers. Human Kinetics publishes books in health, physical education, and recreation and offers certifications in teaching and related areas. USPE went "head to head" with AAHPERD in an attempt to represent and reflect the views of physical education, especially in the K–12 area and in the education of coaches. The USPE largely failed to achieve most of its goals and after a few years folded. However, the message to AAHPERD was clear: There is a need for a viable professional organization that will EFFECTIVELY represent the interests of the profession of kinesiology and its related subdisciplines in the United States.

While professional certifications and specialized training are highly encouraged, understand that the source of any certification should be viewed with a healthy skepticism. The following questions should be addressed when considering investing your time and money in an effort to obtain certification(s):

1. What professional organization is acting as the certification authority?
2. What qualifies the certifying body to issue certification?

3. Is there integrity in the certification process? In other words, is the process done through the use of videotapes that are viewed when time and energy permit or are their structured workshops and assessments conducted by professionals in the field?

4. What are the entry-level educational standards that need to be met in order to enroll in the certification process?

5. What does the content/subject matter of the certification process actually reflect? Example: If you are a football coach and attend a coaching clinic-coaching certification course, is it specific to football or is it a general overview that is supposed to "have something for everybody"? A cardiologist is not going to attend a workshop for physicians specializing in orthopedics or a medical meeting that will make little, if any, contribution to his or her medical specialty.

6. How will certification be attained—how will you be evaluated? Through assessments? Practicums? Formal papers/presentations? Will you have the opportunity to evaluate the instructors?

7. What is the fee?

8. What percentage of the applicants pass the certification test?

9. For how many years is the certification valid?

10. What must be done to become recertified?

11. Do other organizations offer certification in the area?

12. Is the certification approved by the NCCA?

Some of these professional certification programs are as short as one week. A written exam may be the only requirement, and there may be no demonstration of appropriate skills. Many certifications do not require a bachelor's degree in kinesiology or a related field. It has been observed that it takes seven to eight years of college and veterinary school to restore the health of a pet hamster or cat, but a person can become a certified physical fitness professional in about a week and counsel human beings in matters of exercise and health.

It is not unusual to attend a certification workshop and find that the instructors do not have a degree in kinesiology or a related field. These "professionals" (Are they really professional? We think not.) supposedly "certify" people to become fitness and aerobics teachers over the course of a few hours or a few weeks. Many of these certifying agencies sell home study materials that prepare individuals to pass the certification exam. Sometimes even students with a kinesiology degree attend these programs. From our standpoint, it is very disconcerting to see a highly trained and highly educated graduate in kinesiology become part of a process that certifies instructors in a single weekend/day or in a few weeks instead of years of rigorous study. This practice demeans and tarnishes the significance and expertise of a bachelor's degree in the field.

The certification process is best understood relative to the issue of professional preparation and professional standards by examining several of the more visible organizations that offer certifications in our field. An examination of the certification requirements of the American Council on Exercise will help to illustrate the wide range of certification requirements of one organization.

American Council on Exercise

Among the certifications offered by the American Council on Exercise (ACE) are Group Fitness Instructor, Personal Trainer, and Lifestyle and Weight Management Consultant. The ACE pamphlet titled "Get Certified by the American Council on Exercise" has two requirements that must be satisfied before any of the ACE certification exams are administered:

1. Be 18 years of age or older.
2. Have current CPR certification.

As of November 1998, the "Early-Bird" cost to take any of the ACE certification exams was $175 in the United States, $187 in Canada or Mexico, and $212 International. ACE certification exams have 175 multiple-choice questions that must be completed within three and a half hours (ACE, personal communication, November 10, 1998). We have selected the Personal Trainer Certification to illustrate basic content areas covered on the $3^1/_2$-hour exam.

This certification may be appropriate for individuals who provide one-on-one exercise instruction. This certification exam is structured around four areas. The content of the examination by percentage is: client assessment 24%, program design 22%, program implementation 37%, and professional responsibility 17%. Study materials to prepare for the Personal Trainer certification are available. The *Personal Trainer Manual* costs $44.95 as of November 10, 1998. *Master the Manual* is a workbook and costs $24.95, *Sample Tests* cost $14.95, and the *Exam Content Outline* costs $5.95.

ACE has developed its own Code of Ethics. Ceritification is good for two years. In order to maintain ACE certification after the initial two-year period, the individual must earn 1.5 continuing education credits through an ACE-approved course. ACE makes the claim that it is the world's largest certifier of fitness professionals.

National Strength and Conditioning Association

As noted at the beginning of this chapter, there are several organizations that certify health and fitness professionals. The National Strength and Conditioning Association (NSCA), founded in 1978, offers certification as a Certified Personal Trainer. The examination is designed by the Certified Strength and Conditioning Specialist (CSCS) Agency, which acts as the certification body for the NSCA.

Certified Strength and Conditioning Specialist Agency

The Certified Strength and Conditioning Specialist certification was initiated in 1985 and is accredited by the National Commission for Certifying Agencies (NCCA). The Certified Strength and Conditioning Specialist (CSCS) Agency identifies professionals who have demonstrated an adequate level of competence in designing and implementing safe and effective strength and conditioning programs. In 1992 the CSCS became an separate agency that is administratively and financially independent of the NSCA. The new CSCS Agency is the exclusive certifying body for the Certified Strength and Conditioning Specialist examination. To apply for certification, the applicant must hold at least a bachelor's degree from an accredited institution or must be a currently enrolled college senior.

American College of Sports Medicine

The American College of Sports Medicine (ACSM) has various certification programs. All individuals who desire to seek any level of ACSM certification must have a current certification in cardiopulmonary resuscitation (CPR). Once the certification has been earned, each individual is required to document currency by earning continuing education credits (CECs) or earning continuing medical education credits (CMEs). Current CPR certification is mandatory.[6] A bachelor's degree in kinesiology or a related area is expected.

Review

A strong argument could be made that a "mature" professional organization would have the desire to set and maintain appropriate standards and professional training. Certifications, some of which may be suspect, and the fact that just about anybody can call him- or herself a "fitness" or "exercise" expert without fear of legal action, suggest that the field of kinesiology has *not* achieved the same status accorded medicine, law, engineering, or psychology. Alternative associations usually come about because the professional needs of a significant number of people are not being met. It remains to be seen if kinesiology can create a unified set of professional standards that will both help its clientele as well as provide for high professional status of its members.

Coaching Certification: The Double-Edged Sword

The issue of mandatory coaching certification has been intensely debated for decades. In the past two decades it has become more and more difficult to secure enough coaches to meet demands. Title IX was one of the recent changes in the schools that significantly increased the demand for coaches. Coaching involves a serious commitment and long hours. Stress levels are frequently high and originate from a number of sources; the pay is not particularly good (often coaches work an entire season for less than $1000); and the community, parents, and athletes place demands on coaches that were unknown to most people until recently. Many coaches report that their personal life is affected as a result of these stresses and eventually leave their positions as coaches. This loss results in more demand for coaches, and the cycle is begun again.

As we mentioned above, coaches at the middle school and high school level do get paid, but more often than not it works out to less than a dollar an hour. The demand for professionally prepared coaches at the middle school level and high school level often exceeds the available supply. Even more problematic, coaches involved in youth sports volunteer their time and energy, and often receive no financial remuneration at all. On many occasions, there are not enough volunteer coaches to accommodate all the youngsters who want to participate in organized athletics, whether baseball, softball, soccer, hockey, football, swimming, gymnastics, or other popular sports.

In order to field sports teams, a significant number of middle schools in California (grades 6–8) and high schools have come to depend upon "walk-on coaches." These men and women are not professional educators, but live in the community, are employed in other occupations, and enjoy athletics and coaching. The vast majority, like their counterparts in youth sports, have little or no formal education as educators and have little if any legitimate training as a coach.

It is not unusual to find that many coaching staffs rely upon unpaid volunteer coaches as an integral part of their organizations. No one would argue against the concept that requiring all coaches to earn professional certification would be of significant benefit to the athletes they serve. However, insisting that these unpaid volunteer coaches pay for certification and attend the necessary workshops may effectively remove this resource and consequently eliminate a very popular and desirable program.

As an example, California has a population in excess of 37 million people. There are not enough qualified coaches available, and even though coaching certification has been discussed for years, it has never been implemented. The fear is that, were it to be required, high school sports would have to be drastically curtailed or eliminated if the coaches were required to fund their own certification.

In spite of the problems we listed above, coaching can be a highly rewarding endeavor for both the coach and the athlete. There are not many activities that embody the authority a coach enjoys and provide the opportunity to help a group of young people as much as coaching. These are just a few of the benefits that draw many to coaching. Yet coaches must be qualified, or problems will result from the errors that can result because the coach simply does not know how to respond. The physical and emotional stress that is part of competitive athletics must be understood lest serious injury occur. Coaching is a science as well as an art. Appropriate coaching education and quality certification programs will insure that, at the very least, a minimum level of understanding and competency has been demonstrated.

As it stands now there is no national certifying examination, required in all fifty states, in order to become a coach. States that do require coaching certification draw up their own standards or may utilize an existing coach-education program. It is our belief that coaching education should become mandatory at all levels. In addition, adherence to National Standards for Athletic Coaches, developed by the National Association for Sport and Physical Education (NASPE) should receive strong consideration.

National Standards for Athletic Coaches

The National Standards for Athletic Coaches are the result of a project entered into by NASPE and AAHPERD.[7] The standards are intended to provide direction for administrators, coaches, athletes, and the general public relative to the skills and knowledge that a coach should have. The National Standards provide increased opportunities for athletes, trainers, administrators, and coaches within the population addressed by the Americans With Disabilities Act to have greater levels of participation. These standards were designed to attract the entry of additional individuals, especially women and minorities, into coaching.

The National Standards are not intended to be a certification program or act as the basis of a single national assessment for all coaches. The standards are offered to help organizations and agencies who are involved in (1) certifying coaches, (2) providing coach education/training, (3) evaluating selected coaches, and (4) designing programs to meet the needs of prospective and practicing coaches. The standards are not sport-specific, but were developed to ensure the enjoyment, safety, and positive skill development of the several million athletes who participate in sports each and every day.

American Sport Education Program and Program for Athletic Coaches Education

The American Sport Education Program (ASEP) is a multilevel educational program that claims to have provided relevant resources and educational programs to more that 400,000 coaches since 1981. ASEP is operated by Human Kinetics and is built around three curricular areas: SportCoach, SportDirector, and SportParent. Each of the curricular areas is divided into three levels:

1. Volunteer Level: For adults who help children in community-based sport programs.
2. Leader Level: For coaches, parents, and administrators who are involved in interscholastic or competitive club sports.
3. Master Level: This level represents the opportunity for additional professional development for coaches and administrators who have completed the Leader Level.

In addition to ASEP, there is the Program for Athletic Coaches Education (PACE). PACE was developed at the Institute for the Study of Youth Sports at Michigan State University. ASEP and PACE represent serious efforts in an attempt to establish professional competency in the coaching arena. Several states, notably Colorado, Texas, and Minnesota, require coaching certification for employment. Colorado passed its coaching certification law in 1989. Coaches can renew their coaching certification by completing continuing education coursework that is directly related to their coaching duties and by maintaining successful performance evaluations.

We have presented some of the more important issues and concerns that the profession is working to resolve. It is essential that professions in kinesiology and the associations within the field continue to mature in order to serve our clients and to raise the status of these kinesiology professions. In the next section we will identify the criteria of a mature profession, and, more importantly, discuss how kinesiology can meet these criteria.

Criteria for a Recognized and Respected Profession

Several experts have addressed the criteria for professional status, and Abraham Flexner, Bernard Barber, and Myron Liberman are among the most recognized. We know that the concern about the current and future status of our field has been an important issue for decades. Dr. Charles A. Bucher, a highly respected physical education professor at New York University, attempted to point out this problem to colleagues over thirty years ago. His comments and analysis were illuminating and are just as pertinent today. Bucher (1969) studied the accepted rationale for establishing professional criteria and placed them under four headings:

1. Rendering a unique and essential social service.
2. Establishing high standards for the selection of members.
3. Providing a rigorous training program to prepare its practitioners.
4. Achieving self-regulatory status for both the group and the individual.

How well does kinesiology meet these four criteria that are representative of a recognized and respected profession? The following analysis of each of Bucher's four professional criteria will help this question.

1. *What is the unique and essential social service we deliver to the public?* Having a unique service means that only professionals trained in kinesiology provide professional services utilizing the methods of science and the tools of technology. Having the expertise and capability to deliver a unique service also means that the public clearly understands the function of this profession and defers to its exclusive expertise. Does it appear that the general public and the schools believe we have a unique and essential social service? Can you identify the unique and essential social services that professionals in kinesiology are expected to provide?

2. *Is the necessity for establishing high standards for gaining admission to study and practice kinesiology a high priority?* If kinesiology desires to become a respected and honored profession, it must become very selective about who it admits into practice. According to Liberman, "A profession cannot in good conscience or in good faith with the public gain respect and have full fledged status unless it is willing and is able to undertake the onerous task of weeding out the unethical and incompetent practitioner" (Bucher, 1969, p. 14). Bucher elaborated on this idea when he argued that "Our goal. . . [is to] direct our organized efforts toward the end that those who can teach physical education will teach and those who can't teach physical education will be guided into business or some other career" (Bucher, 1969, p. 14).

What justification can be been made by our profession to permit thousands of pseudo-fitness and exercise "buffs" who have not earned degrees in kinesiology or related fields to obtain professional certification? This practice does not reflect the criteria for selectivity or the requirement for rigorous academic preparation. What steps could our profession take to remedy this practice?

3. *Rigorous training programs must be provided for those selected to perform the unique and essential social service that kinesiology lays claim to.* This criterion is strongly supported by the recommendations contained in a report issued by the Holmes Group Consortium. This group consisted of 28 college deans who serve as chief administrators of colleges or schools of education. Their task was to raise the quality of the professional preparation of teachers at their own institutions. The Holmes Report (1986) became a model for other institutions as well. Since the reform and attendant improvement of teacher education is a continuing process, the Holmes Report was followed by similar report issued by the Carnegie Forum Task Force on Teaching as a Profession (1986). Both reports found the need for significant improvement if future professionals in the teaching field were to adequately trained for professional careers in education. Among the suggestions were:

- Higher entrance standards.
- More emphasis on an undergraduate area of study (kinesiology) as opposed to making students take coursework in the area of teaching methodology.
- Professional preparation of teachers and relevant course work should be assigned as a fifth year of study, after the bachelor's degree in a specific area of study (kinesiology in this case) has been awarded.
- Prospective teachers should undergo appropriate assessment tests to determine their suitability for the profession.
- The need to develop uniform national certifications and national standards of professional preparation to replace the existing model of 50 different state credential programs.[8]

The Holmes Group Report, along with the Carnegie Report, had a positive impact upon the professional preparation of physical education teachers. Some of these suggestions have been seriously studied and are in the process of becoming implemented. The National Council for Accreditation of Teacher Education (NCATE) has established standards for the professional preparation of teachers. Membership in NCATE is voluntary, as is adhering to their curricular models that are designed to assure that a standard of minimum and essential competency has been adequately demonstrated.

While national education standards are desirable and meet the criteria of a strong profession, they may never become a reality. The reason is that the Constitution of the United States makes education the responsibility of the states. As a result, the certification requirements for teachers are the responsibility of each state, and it seems unlikely that the states will defer their credentialing process to a national body. As of this writing, President Bill Clinton is working with the Congress to develop national education standards, but he is meeting much resistance.

This does not mean, however, that educators are resigned to the fact that national standards will never become a reality. Professionals who prepare teachers in grades K–12 continue to explore the possibility of developing this recommendation. The concept of a national K–12 physical education curriculum that would provide a common foundation and common experiences was proposed in 1988, and it has surfaced once again in a different format through NASPE and AAHPERD (Berg, 1988).

In order to respond to the question, "What should students know about and be able to do as a result of physical education," the Outcomes Committee of NASPE (1992) developed and published a benchmark report titled the *Outcomes of Quality Physical Education*. This report identified twenty outcomes for physical education as well as providing sample benchmarks in grades K–12 that were based on two-year intervals. After developing the *Outcomes of Quality Physical Education*, the NASPE Standards and Assessment Task Force was created to developed content standards and assessment material based on the findings reported in *Outcomes of Quality Physical Education*. The work of the task force eventually produced a blueprint for developing quality physical education programs in grades K–12 titled, *Moving Into The Future: National Standards for Physical Education* (NASPE, 1995). NASPE argued that publication of *National Standards* is a guide for developing a quality physical education curriculum and not a curriculum. However, as a guide, it can help physical educators create their own curriculums at the local level.

Another obstacle to a national curriculum is that physical educators still do not agree among themselves as to what should be taught in physical education in K–12. Some professionals argue for the traditional approach of teaching play, games, and sports in K–12 physical education, while other professionals use scholarly research to create curriculum that emphasizes health, wellness, and the prevention of disease through proper exercise. The standards and assessment model developed by NASPE may not appeal to all professionals and is certain to be a subject of interesting debate.

There is a concerted effort to implement national standards in K–12 physical education that will help insure that teachers are competent, professional, and sensitive to the needs of their students. The work of NASPE and AAHPERD in this area is a significant professional endeavor. These activities and other related efforts will help the field continue to reform and mature. However, as much as NASPE, AAHPERD, and other professional associations work and strive to bring the field into the "mainstream professional ranks," these voluntary standards that are thoughtfully developed do not carry authority and regulatory capability that are associated with the mature professions.

Along the lines of establishing a set of guidelines for a national curriculum, NASPE has worked to establish minimum standards and competencies that all first-year credentialed physical education teachers should be expected to demonstrate. The following nine proposed standards and content reflect what professionals in the field should know and be able to do. In these standards you will see the influence of professional standards discussed by Bucher earlier in this chapter.

- **Content Knowledge**. The teacher understands physical education content, disciplinary concepts, and tools of inquiry related to the development of a physically educated person.
- **Growth and Development**. The teacher understands how individuals learn and develop and can provide opportunities that support their physical, cognitive, social, and emotional development.

- **Diverse Learners**. The teacher understands how individuals differ in their approach to learning and creates appropriate instruction adapted to diverse learners.
- **Planning and Instruction**. The teacher plans and implements a variety of developmentally appropriate instructional strategies to develop physically educated individuals.
- **Management and Motivation**. The teacher uses an understanding of individual and group motivation and behavior to create a learning environment that encourages positive social interaction, active engagement in learning, and self-motivation.
- **Communication**. The teacher uses knowledge of effective verbal, nonverbal, and media communication techniques to foster inquiry, collaboration, and engagement in physical activity settings.
- **Learner Assessment**. The teacher understands and uses formal and informal assessment strategies to foster physical, cognitive, social, and emotional development of learners in physical activity.
- **Reflection**. The teacher is a reflective practitioner who evaluates the effects of his or her actions on others (e.g., learners, parents/guardians, and other professionals in the learning community) and seeks opportunities to grow professionally.
- **Collaboration**. The teacher fosters relationships with colleagues, parents/guardians, and community agencies to support learners' growth and well-being.

4. *In order for physical education to become a mature and respected profession, it must become self-regulatory.*

The American Bar Association (ABA) determines who will be admitted to the bar, as well as which law schools will receive accreditation. Similarly, the American Medical Association (AMA) sets accreditation standards for medical schools and licenses physicians. These professional associations regulate their profession and have the authority to suspend or expel a member from practicing law or medicine. Our profession should strive to regulate and police professionals in the field of kinesiology. We have an enormous responsibility for enhancing the health and well-being of the people we serve. We are trained to employ the most advanced techniques that sport and exercise science has developed. We use the techniques of sport science to teach athletes through the medium of biomechanics, physiology, psychology, biochemistry, and nutrition.

Working directly with individuals in matters of fitness, health promotion, physical and cardiac rehabilitation, restoration of motor control (stroke victim), and the training of athletes is a highly complex process. To permit a poorly trained pseudo-professional to become employed in our area with the distinct possibility of causing serious injury to another is unacceptable.

A code of ethics that has meaning should help to develop responsible professional behavior. Remaining current in the particular area(s) that you work in should be an expectation, not an "elective." We have a professional responsibility to not only regulate the profession but chart our professional destiny as well. The intrusion of for-profit business concerns that have arrived on the scene to form professional associations and issue certifications and specializations does not speak well for kinesiology.

Professional regulation of our field has many sources. We already pointed out that IDEA, ACE, AFAA, USPE, ACSM, NSCA, and CSCS provide workshops and certifications.

The existence of these organizations can be viewed as an attempt to regulate and establish some degree of minimum competency as a profession. All of these certifying bodies require a program of continuing education in order to renew or retain certification. However, given the fact that some of these organizations require only that a person be over the age of 18 and hold a current CPR certificate, it appears that these organizations are not as rigorous and demanding as they could be.

As presented earlier in this chapter, some subdisciplines (like sport psychology) have formed associations that set standards and determine a code of ethics for the express purpose of regulating and certifying practitioners (AAASP in sport psychology). This may have happened because kinesiology could be viewed as too large and eclectic to develop into a profession that could effectively represent the interests of ALL the subdisciplines. AAASP is not the only subdiscipline to form a professional association that is apart from AAHPERD. Another big development is taking place in the subdiscipline of exercise physiology. Professionals in this area have recently formed a new organization, the American Society of Exercise Physiologists, with the goal of professionalizing and regulating the area. For more information about the professional development taking place within this subdiscipline, access their homepage via the Web and search for: http://www.css.edu/users/tboone2/asep/fldr/links5.htm (web addresses are subject to change).

Additional evidence of the professionalization of exercise physiology can be found in the state of Louisiana where there exists a licensure process for the profession of Clinical Exercise Physiologist.

Continuing education is a process that helps regulate a profession and assists professionals in maintaining their currency in the field. Professional associations require that their members attend a certain number of classes to retain their professional status. This process could be implemented in kinesiology. Colorado, for instance, has taken this step by requiring certified coaches to remain current in order to renew their coaching certification(s).

Achieving the status of a "mature profession" is essential to our field. However, you may think, "But I just read that kinesiology may be too big and, as a result, may not be able to effectively represent the professional interests of all the subdisciplines—some have already gone their own way. This seems to preclude kinesiology from becoming a mature profession." At first glance, you could easily jump to this conclusion. However, ask yourself these questions—Do you know how many sub-specialities exist in medicine? Do you know how many specializations there are in the field of law? Far more than in kinesiology! Still, the AMA and ABA have done a splendid job in achieving the status of a mature profession and kinesiology professionals should expect to accept no less.

There have been significant professional advancements that have moved kinesiology much closer to the goal of being recognized as a "mature profession." Although the professional development of our field has been at times "a bumpy ride," the overall professional development of the field has made great strides, especially during the last fifteen years. And in spite of the concerns that we previously presented, the future of our profession is bright. If this were not so, why are thousands of people each year seeking to become "certified" by a number of organizations that seldom require a college degree in kinesiology or related field? It is because the general public's interest in health, nutrition, and exercise has

TABLE 5-1   **The Professional Path**

Credentialing	Certification	Licensure
Features written documentation that a formal course of education and training has been completed.	Individual has demonstrated that he or she has met the minimum criteria of a specific profession.	First and foremost, a legal authorization to practice.

become a very important part of their lifestyle. As a result, the demand for professionals with expertise in this area will, in all probability, continue to increase dramatically. As the public becomes more educated and consumer oriented about the vast knowledge required of professionals in this field, do you believe that people will continue to accept the services of poorly trained professionals? It is to your advantage that the public knows the difference between those "professionals" who attend a workshop or two and take a test and those who are true professionals in every sense of the word.

Professional expertise and advanced training often reflects the modern concept of kinesiology (see Table 5-1). In all probability, Professor Bucher would be pleased with the dedication, energy, and enthusiasm that reflects the momentum in kinesiology to earn professional status and educate the public about our unique and special contributions. At the same time, Professor Bucher would advise the profession to continue working toward higher standards.

Focus 2000: Professional Opportunities for the Next Century

Career preparation is one of the most important reasons for attending college. Majoring in kinesiology or a related field, and augmenting coursework in the major with supplemental courses that prepare you for the job market, is often viewed as an "essential" reason for selecting the major. These supplemental areas in kinesiology include computing technology (discussed later in this chapter), the teaching minor if you plan to go into education, becoming fluent in another language, and earning appropriate certifications that are in demand.

Work experience is very important and one of the best ways of gaining knowledge in the field. There are a variety of opportunities to gain work experience in kinesiology. Take the opportunity to gain valuable work experience by applying for administrative internships if you are going into sport management or athletic administration. Serving as a volunteer in the schools will enable you to gain personal insight about the day-to-day duties and responsibilities of teaching and all that it entails. Settings such as hospitals and clinics will reveal the demands and rewards of working as an athletic trainer, physical therapist, cardiac rehabilitation–exercise physiologist, and wellness counselor. People are living longer than ever and you may be interested in serving the adult fitness population that focuses on men and women over the age of 50. Internships and volunteering your time may just put you in the right place at the right time if a position becomes available with the organization you are working with. It allows you to meet professionals in the field—this is called "networking," and it can be very helpful in securing meaningful employment. At the very least, valuable references and actual work experience can be generated in your behalf.

The ability to utilize computers and a variety of computer-related programs could be the difference between a terrific opportunity and a routine job. Many of the older, established professionals in various job settings obtained their education and job at a time when computers were not essential. A professional with computer skills can bring these people up to speed and at the same time offer instant computer expertise to the organization. Sport scientists and coaches who are preparing to meet the demands of the future must be adept at using computing technology, especially developing and writing software programs.

The following information will assist you in identifying additional professional opportunities and potential career paths among the "clients" that kinesiologists are trained to serve. Many of these career paths will be illustrated by the professions that are represented through AAHPERD and its six specialized associations that form the alliance. In addition to the professional opportunities provided through AAHPERD, information about selected careers in physical education and related areas along with their respective professional associations will be presented.

Careers in Education

The traditional career path for kinesiology majors is in teaching and coaching. However, like everything else in society, teaching has changed. During the 1980s teaching jobs were not as plentiful as they were in the 1950s and 1960s. This was partly because the post World War II "baby boomers" had long since left school. In addition, the birth rate declined in the United States for a number of reasons, among them a poor economy and demographic changes.

Population forecasters predicted, however, that the number of children in school will change radically in the year 2000 and beyond, and there are already indications that this change has begun to take place. Recently, the state of Texas began hiring teachers in grades K–12, and Texas education officials have stated that there is a need for over *10,000* certified teachers in that state. New York state, and especially New York City, has been hiring teachers *without* state-mandated teaching certifications because there is such a teacher shortage. Finally, California recently mandated the maximum number of students in the kindergarten class room at 20 students, and this has created demand for an additional *10,000* teachers. It seems clear that, if Texas, New York, and California are any indication, then there will be demand for licensed teaching professionals.

K–12 Teaching and Coaching

Teaching and coaching remain popular career choices that impact upon the number of available jobs in education. Depending upon the school, teaching can either be a rewarding and wonderful career or one that falls short in delivering professional and personal satisfaction. Factors that determine the quality of the position depend on the community environment, the school facilities, the school administration, and your ability to adapt to a number of situations and predicaments that college never prepared you for. There will always be work for you to take home, and there will be conferences with students, parents, and administrators. Vacations are one of the benefits (teachers, like students, get summers off) and after tenure (usually determined by state law, and coming after three years), earning seniority, and additional college study the salary and benefits are adequate.

Every state requires a teaching credential for employment as a public school teacher. This may require a fifth year of course work normally taken in a college or school of education. Most fifth-year credential programs require course work that can be used to earn a masters degree. There is also the possibility to move to education administration. With this career advancement comes more responsibility, more prestige, and more money.

The service you deliver and the knowledge you impart in the classroom, field, gym, court, or pool put a teacher in the position of positively influencing young people. This opportunity to significantly influence the lives of young children is hard to match. Coaching, which is often a responsibility of professional physical education teachers, has the responsibility for the welfare and safety of dozens of students, and provides for a significant professional responsibility. The teacher of the twenty-first century will be expected to do much more than provide instruction in games and sports. Lifetime fitness and knowledge about the benefits of exercise and health will be an important part of the curriculum.

Technology will provide the professional educator with a number of software programs that assess each student's current lifestyle habits along with an individualized program for change. Nutrition counseling, wellness screening, and weight management are just a few of the computer-generated assessments programs available to teachers. Coaches and trainers can use software programs to personalize weight training and cardiovascular conditioning programs for athletes. Recent world wide web sites such as *PE Central* located at Virginia Polytechnic University make access to these software programs fast and affordable. For teachers and coaches in the future, it will be essential that they be able to access these programs and use them efficiently for the benefit of their students.

Coaches have a long history of taking an active role in social reform and instilling traditional values and building character and self-esteem. This historic role is especially important in today's society since approximately 50 percent of students in grades K–12 live in single-parent households. Thousands of young boys and girls are "latchkey kids," meaning that they come home to an empty house after school. The opportunities for these children to become involved in mischief due to lack of parental supervision is significant. Historically, teachers and coaches have shown that these children can be positively influenced by our field. For many, participation in athletics is the one activity that stands between hope and a life of despair. Teachers and coaches, as the Reverend Jesse Jackson has insisted we all do, work hard to "Keep Hope Alive"!

Dance Education

Dance has been enjoying an increase in popularity. Folk dance, jazz dance, country and western, and popular dances favored by today's high school and college students teach people how to move and engage in personal expression and vigorous physical activity. Dance as a major course of study separate from kinesiology can be found in a number of college and universities. Women make up the predominate student population in this area. More often, though, men are entering this area of artistic and physical expression.

Health Education

An unusual if not predictable change may be taking place relative to the degree designation in our field. Until the mid-1960s, a significant number of the undergraduate degrees awarded were a combination of "Health and Physical Education." The trend towards specialization from the late 1960s to the present separated health and physical education. Physical educators received a degree in physical education, and undergraduate health majors received their degree in health. The direction taken by many financially strapped school districts is to hire those teachers that can provide instruction in more then one subject area. This is especially true in the smaller school districts across rural America.

Some colleges and universities have responded to this trend by returning to the days when graduates were awarded degrees in "Health and Physical Education," although "Health and Kinesiology" designations may be more appropriate. Graduates with the traditional training in both health and kinesiology (physical education) may have a distinct advantage in the job market.

There is a national campaign to promote healthy lifestyles. The federal government has taken an active part to educate the public about behaviors that are detrimental to personal health and to identify and promote those behaviors that contribute to personal health and wellness. This objective is illustrated by the Office of the Surgeon General of the United States, which introduced *Healthy People 2000*. This program identifies goals that will develop personal responsibility to achieve optimum health and wellness.

The high-profile *Healthy People 2000* agenda will provide professional opportunities for both college-educated health and kinesiology professionals. There is a national trend toward managed health care. Part of this approach involves keeping people well so they have fewer incidents of disease. Lifelong exercise and wellness programs are an essential part of managed health care and kinesiology and health professionals are highly trained to provide this service.

Safety Education

It is not immediately obvious that kinesiology contributes to the area of safety education. Historically, however, physical education professionals have performed this service. This specialty area makes an important contribution to enhancing personal health and well-being by providing information about the prevention of accidents. Driver education is the most visible area of safety education, and it is offered by the majority of the nation's secondary schools. Most automobile insurance policies have rate reductions for students who have satisfactorily completed an approved driver education course. Bicycle and personal safety are subjects that are covered in this area as well.

Community Colleges

Professional opportunities exist in community colleges, also known as junior colleges, for professors and coaches. Most of these institutions require a masters degree in the field. Positions usually entail teaching and coaching. It is important to note that many community college departments remain comfortable with the traditional physical education label as opposed to kinesiology. This condition may change, however, in the near future. Teaching assignments can be in professional courses and in the general physical education activity program that provides instruction in sport skills (tennis, basketball, volleyball) and lifetime sports and fitness (jogging, golf, weight training, aerobics). Athletic trainers can expect to teach introductory courses in this area, oversee the training room staff, and care for the athletes. Professional opportunities in the community colleges are coveted because of the maturity of the students, the emphasis on teaching, and prestige.

Recreation

More and more recreation teachers are being hired at the community college level to provide services to students. Intramural sports, supervision of the campus recreation program, and assisting in the area of student clubs and organizations are within the professional domain of recreation services. Other areas include outdoor education, therapeutic recreation, and sometimes occupational therapy and recreation therapy. Kinesiology majors have often discovered that their education and interests have prepared them for a career in this field. Additional employment in this area can be in the capacity as a recreation leader for youth activities, park supervision, therapeutic recreation, recreation for the elderly, and in the emerging field of tourism.

College Teaching: A Tale of Two Academic Environments

Securing a position at a traditional college or university is considered the height of professional and personal success in the teaching professions. However, there are many different types of employment profiles. Small liberal arts colleges require their faculty to wear a number of different hats. A doctoral degree is preferred but may not be required. Faculty often have responsibilities as coaches, and coaching two sports is not unusual. Providing academic instruction to students majoring in kinesiology, health, and recreation is an essential part of the job. Like their colleagues in the community colleges, faculty also teach courses in the general physical activity program.

Professional opportunities at the larger major colleges and universities require a doctoral degree (doctor of philosophy, or Ph.D.; doctor of education, or Ed.D.; doctor of medicine, or M.D.), which is a significant personal and financial commitment. Coaching duties are usually not assigned or expected. Instead, the ability to teach and conduct research is considered essential. The teacher-scholar model is a concept that is in place in most research institutions. This model reflects high professional standards, superior teaching, and a research agenda that brings national and international acclaim to the university. Faculty are hired according to their specialized training in one of the subdisciplines and may teach undergraduate or graduate students depending upon their professional interests and expertise. Leadership in professional organizations and scholarly groups is an expectation. Tenure is earned after seven years of rigorous review by one's peers that examines the areas of teaching, research, and service. In the past decade it has become increasingly important for faculty to attract external funding in the form of grants and other appropriate resources.

College Coaching

The athletic department at larger institutions is run as a business. Coaches do not need a doctoral degree, although some coaches earn the doctorate. The minimum requirement is a bachelors degree with a masters degree becoming more commonplace. Some coaches have "split appointments," meaning that they work as coaches in the athletic department and also teach courses for the kinesiology department.

Coaches in National Collegiate Athletic Association (NCAA) member institutions competing at the Division 1-A or 1-AA level are usually hired because of their coaching expertise and normally will not teach in the kinesiology department. Salaries are quite comfortable, especially for the head coach. In many NCAA Division 1 schools, the head football and basketball coaches earn more money than the university president! Assistant coaches at these schools earn a good salary also, frequently more than the professors.

In NCAA Division II and Division III institutions coaches will usually hold split appointments and could be eligible to earn tenure. Their salary is not as much as their counterparts in the Division 1A and 1AA institutions, but can easily exceed $50,000 to 60,000 (including benefits) per year with financial augmentation through camps and other related opportunities.

Membership in the National Association of Intercollegiate Athletics (NAIA) appeals to small colleges and universities with enrollment between 400 and 6000 students. NAIA member institutions are not the high-profile colleges featured every week in prominent weekly sports magazines or seen on television. Unique to the needs of the small college, the NAIA has a philosophy that encourages a high degree of participation by college students; academics come first and athletics have their place in the college as a mechanism to help students become "well rounded." Most NAIA athletes will never receive a professional sports contract, but, on the other hand, most will graduate from college. Most NAIA coaches are tenured professors in departments of kinesiology or physical education.

Coaches have their own professional organizations that revolve around specific sports. For example, male college basketball coaches can become members of the National Association of Basketball Coaches (NABC), women basketball coaches can join the Women's Basketball Coaches Association (WBCA). The College Football Association (CFA) represents college football coaches. Professional opportunities in high school coaching are available through state associations affiliated with the National Federation of State High School Organizations (NFSHSO). It is important to stay professionally active. Membership in a professional organization provides opportunities for professional growth in the form of coaching clinics where coaches can learn from some of the best in the business. Membership in professional organizations is also an excellent opportunity to earn recognition and meet people who may be in a position to help in establishing your career. There may be several different organizations that appeal to you because of your interests, especially if you will be coaching several sports.

The federal government implemented Title IX in the 1970s to eliminate sexual discrimination in the schools and colleges. Prior to the enactment of Title IX, the resources and personnel needed to provide opportunities in sports were predominantly geared to males. Women and girls were deliberately denied access to the resources routinely provided to men and boys, which was blatant discrimination.

With Title IX came new opportunities for women athletes and women coaches. Recently, the issue of gender equity in athletics has been another catalyst that will provide increased employment opportunities for women coaches. Gender equity means that sports for women are being added in both high schools and colleges. The demand for professionally trained women coaches will in all probability exceed the supply.

The American Alliance for Health, Physical Education, Recreation, and Dance (AAHPERD)

Physical education teachers and coaches who are employed in the public and private schools (K–12) historically have become members the American Alliance for Health, Physical Education, Recreation, and Dance (AAHPERD) and their respective state physical education association. AAHPERD focuses on the needs of teachers and administrators involved with K–12 physical education as well as issues in higher education and related areas. AAHPERD publishes newsletters that address the needs of the elementary, middle school, and high school physical education teacher.

AAHPERD has been receiving attention throughout this text. As a professional organization, it is over 100 years old, having first been established as the AAAPE in 1885. AAHPERD has held dozens of national conventions and has over 20,000 members. AAHPERD has long been a professional organization that sought to provide both K–12 professionals and college professors with an effective national presence. AAHPERD is an alliance of six national associations that represent related professional interests:

1. **Association for the Advancement of Health Education (AAHE)** For health education teachers and health professionals.
2. **American Association for Leisure and Recreation (AALR)** For recreational professionals involved in parks, tourism, and leisure services.
3. **American Association for Active Lifestyles and Fitness (AAALF)** This association consists of twelve councils and the safety society that actually traverse the disciplines of AAHPERD:

    Adapted Physical Activities
    School Administrators of Health and Physical Education
    Measurement and Evaluation
    Aging and Adult Development
    Ethnic Minorities
    Outdoor Education
    Aquatics
    Facilities and Equipment
    Physical Fitness
    College and University Administrators
    International Relations
    Student Action
    School and Community Safety Society

4. **National Association for Girls and Women in Sport (NAGWS)** This association is the leading organization promoting quality and equality in girls' and women's sports. Coaches, teachers, officials, and trainers with a professional interest in this area join NAGWS.
5. **National Association for Sport and Physical Education (NASPE)** There are approximately 25,000 members of NASPE. This association is for professionals who are involved in any and every aspect of physical education—in the public schools, pri-

vate schools, and in colleges and universities across the nation. Members are devoted to improving sport and physical education and include coaches, teachers, sport psychologists, athletic trainers, administrators/athletic directors.

6. **National Dance Association (NDA)** Dance professionals join the NDA to help promote dance and dance education throughout the nation.

All of the six associations of AAHPERD employ full-time professional staff members, publish newsletters, conduct workshops, help with job placement, provide information to politicians that help to advance professional agendas, and provide leadership opportunities and professional representation. NASPE even has "position statements" complete with statistics that can help physical educators promote the educational merits and lifetime benefits of exercise, games, and sports to school boards, administrators, and parents. AAHPERD and the six national associations that reflect the alliance advertise job openings and may present interesting and challenging career opportunities for those professionals who are highly qualified. For more information about AAHPERD or any of the six associations, write to:

> Alliance for Health, Physical Education,
> Recreation, and Dance
> 1900 Association Drive
> Reston, Virginia 22091

Specialists

Athletic Training

Athletic training, also known as sports medicine in some instances, is a very popular major within kinesiology. Indeed, athletic training is probably the most "professional" of all of the professions, probably because of its close association with the medical profession, along with the possibility of negligence that can be associated with medical malpractice. Athletic trainers must be highly trained to avoid the threat of lawsuit, and as a profession athletic training has instituted many of the criteria that Bucher called for in the 1960s.

Students must have a through understanding of anatomy, physiology, mechanisms of sports injuries, therapeutic modalities, and the management, care, and rehabilitation of the injured athlete. Knowledge of strength training and conditioning is an important part of professional preparation. Prevention of injury is a major focus of study. Athletic trainers work very closely with athletes, physicians, and coaches. It is a very exciting profession that demands a cool head in order to attend to needs of an athlete who is seriously injured with a broken neck, heart attack, or other life-threatening injury.

Athletic trainers are involved with the education and counseling of athletes, parents, and coaches. They must know how to administer and organize the athletic medicine program. Athletic training is an allied health profession recognized by the AMA. Athletic trainers work under the direct supervision of a physician.

Students majoring in athletic training must obtain a minimum of 1500 hours in a clinical setting under the guidance and supervision of a certified athletic trainer (ATC). Upon completion of the professional program of study terminating in a bachelors degree. On-the-job training requires more than 1500 hours of clinical practice. After earning the bachelor's and completing the clinical experience, the student can sit for the National Athletic Training Association (NATA) certification exam. The NATA Board of Certification has established that all certified athletic trainers must attain a minimum of 6 continuing education units within a three-year period to maintain their certification. Failure to satisfy this requirement can result in suspension and/or revocation of certification.[9]

Elementary Physical Education Specialists

Training to deliver appropriate skills and developmental activities to this population is a specialization that continues to grow. Specialists in elementary physical education are trained to plan and implement a program of physical education in the school setting. They may act as advisors to classroom teachers who have a period of physical education set aside every day or several days a week and need help. These specialists frequently do the actual teaching and may be assigned to several schools within a district.

Aquatics Specialists

This area is for coaches, teachers, and recreation professionals. Water environments present special situations that necessitate specialized training. Safety is a dominant issue. Most everybody has a liking for water sports and related activities. Accidents can occur in seconds. Aquatics specialists have training to not only provide instruction in swimming, lifesaving, and safety but also know how to design and implement a safe environment. Certifications by the American Red Cross in CPR, Water Safety Instructor, and as a SCUBA instructor by the National Association of Underwater Instructors (NAUI) represent some of the professional training that is needed.

Care and operation of community and college aquatic centers that have several pools is also part of the job. The chemicals that are placed in swimming pools must be monitored every day and when need be, adjusted to provide a clean and healthy environment. Aquatic specialists have training that is very much in demand especially due to the increase in law suits filed claiming negligence and lack of appropriate training as a cause of accidents.

Administration and Sport Management

There are three possible career paths to choose from, professional sports, college, or club-elite teams. Sport management has become a popular major that combines accounting, business, personnel management, labor law, and kinesiology. This career path can lead to a front-office job in professional sports or managing an athletic venue such as a stadium or resort. Preparing for athletic administration at the college level requires similar coursework in addition to learning about the unique rules and regulations that cover the nonprofit, tax-exempt status enjoyed (for now) by colleges and universities. The rules and regulations of the NCAA that govern intercollegiate athletics are so complex that many Division I institutions hire compliance officers to interpret and enforce the rules. Fund raising, which is not an issue in professional sports, and alumni relations are critical areas in which the successful athletic director will have to excel.

Elite club teams with hundreds of athletes and operating budgets in excess of several hundred thousand dollars are becoming more prevalent. This phenomenon has occurred because of the demand for highly specialized coaching and high-level competition and because many schools have dropped sports due to budget cuts. Elite clubs are searching for professionals who can demonstrate sound business practices, assist in some coaching duties, and plan fund-raising events and manage the venues(s) of the club (e.g., pools, gymnasiums, tennis courts, soccer fields, etc.).

Nontraditional Career Paths

Kinesiology is a major that (1) incorporates a significant science component; (2) requires the ability to demonstrate athletic skills; (3) provides students with an understanding of how individuals develop physiologically, sociologically, and psychologically; (4) educates students about the importance, processes, and activities that promote exercise, health, and wellness; and (5) supports the need for competition and the achievement of personal and professional success. The "well-rounded" qualities that reflect the education in kinesiology attract the attention of professional recruiters from a variety of professions:

1. Law enforcement
2. Officer recruitment—Air Force, Navy, Army, and Marine Corps, Coast Guard, and National Guard
3. Pharmaceutical sales representatives
4. Physical therapy schools
5. Allied health areas, clinics, and hospitals:

   Nursing
   Emergency medical technicians
   Therapists
   Physical therapy assistant
   Physicians assistant

6. Chiropractic
7. Corporate health programs
8. Resort services, cruise lines, and health spas
9. Sales representatives for sports supplies and equipment companies
10. Graduates are opening up their own businesses: personal trainers, health and wellness counselors, lifestyle counselors, sports nutrition counselors, biomechanical analysts, exercise physiologists, and private coaches
11. Publishing—Sales representatives for publishing companies that sell textbooks and popular press books in health, sports, and physical education
12. Sports journalism
13. Alternative approaches to healing:

    Massage specialist
    Herbal medicine specialist
    Naturopathic specialist
    Holistic healing
    Certified Rolfer

The Role of Technology in Kinesiology Professions

The need to remain "current" in a chosen profession is a fact of professional life. Not only is this a matter of personal and professional pride, it is an absolute necessity if the service and knowledge that is imparted to students, clients, or other professionals in the field are going to reflect "cutting edge" information.

The information age arrived via technological advancement in data systems and through the introduction of the personal computer (PC) and the Macintosh (another computer to be sure, but not considered a PC). Information that sometimes is only a few days old can be accessed through online databases. Fresh information and new teaching concepts can be brought to your attention and downloaded and implemented with expediency as a result of technology. Information and ideas can be shared with colleagues around the world. Problems or issues that need a solution can be shared with professional groups in our field on-line and most often a solution will appear from a source that very day!

The source may be a group of professionals that have been approached on-line or from an individual who belongs to one of the many groups that share a common interest. Professors have always offered some good advice to young graduates who are about to take positions as a physical educators and coaches: "Work smart, not hard!" is the advice, and technology provides teachers, coaches, and administrators with the ability to "work smart."

Becoming computer literate is essential. Students in grammar school are being introduced to the marvels of the computer and any college student who is not yet computer literate should make this a priority if a career in teaching or any other related professional field is a goal.

Technology is available in every aspect of the kinesiology field. Computer analysis has been used extensively in biomechanics in order to evaluate everything from an efficient running style to throwing a baseball with greater velocity and accuracy. Coaches have used their personal computers to generate information on everything from tendencies of an opponent to providing their athletes with daily feedback in the form of printouts detailing whether agreed upon training goals were met. Administrators schedule by computer and generate personnel evaluations and log equipment inventories with a minimum of work.

Software programs can be easily purchased for less than $20 that will analyze a person's diet and eating habits and create a personal diet plan. This information is printed out and handed to the students in a matter of minutes as opposed to hours. Professional and personal correspondence is greatly facilitated by popular word processing programs on the market such as Word Perfect, Microsoft Word, or Claris Works. The latest editions of these software programs come with easy-to-use pulldown menus or windows that check spelling and grammar for you. Another source of information available on the World Wide Web, Compuserve, or America OnLine is shareware. Most of the time shareware programs can be downloaded at no charge or for a small charge after a certain period of time.

Summary

Plan your career path(s) carefully. Seize the opportunities that a college education provides to develop professionally and personally. Become part of the process that serves our profession interests and promotes the unique service that we provide. Above all, take personal responsibility to earn the respect of your peers, colleagues, and employers through ethical behavior, professional preparation, and superior work product. These professional qualities will provide you with professional opportunities.

Discussion Questions

1. What is the role of a "professional" in modern society?
2. How does certification facilitate the advancement of a profession?
3. How are professional standards evident in certification processes?
4. What professional opportunities and career paths are available to kinesiology majors?
5. How is technology used in kinesiology?

References

Berg, K. (1988). A national curriculum in physical education. *Journal of Physical Education, Recreation, and Dance, 59*(8), 70–75.

Bucher, C. (1969). Nature and scope of physical education. In C. Bucher & M. Goldman, *Dimensions of physical education*. St. Louis: C.V. Mosby.

Bucher, C., & Goldman, M. (1969). *Dimensions of physical education*. St. Louis: C.V. Mosby.

Charles, J. (1994). *Contemporary kinesiology: An introduction to the study of human movement in higher education*. Englewood, CO: Morton Publishing Company.

Corbin, C.B., & Eckert, H.M. (Eds.) (1990). The evolving undergraduate major. *The Academy Papers, 23.*

Hughes, E. (1969). In C.A. Bucher & M. Goldman, *Dimensions of physical education* (p. 12). St. Louis: C.V. Mosby.

National Association for Sport and Physical Education. (1995). *Moving into the future: National standards for physical education*. St. Louis: Mosby-Year Book.

Outcomes of quality physical education. (1992). National Association for Sport and Physical Education. An Association of the American Alliance for Health, Physical Education, Recreation, and Dance. 1900 Association Drive, Reston, Virginia.

Parks, J.B., & Zanger, B.R.K. (Eds.). (1990). *Sport and fitness management: Career strategies and professional content*. Champaign, IL: Human Kinetics.

Physical activity and health: A report of the Surgeon General. (1997). Atlanta: Centers for Disease Control and Prevention.

Endnotes

1. Plato and Aristotle argued about the link between the mind and the body, and the Romans coined the phrase *mens sana in corpore sano*—literally translated to mean "a strong mind in a healthy body."

2. Obviously Gibbons understands that this relationship does not last forever: At some point the benefits of exercise taper off. But Gibbon's work is unquestioned when it comes to the health of most Americans, who exercise so little that their lives are measurably shortened.

3. We defined, in general terms, the *field* of kinesiology in Chapter 3. This definition of a profession provides the detail necessary to explain the problems of professionalization in kinesiology.

4. This fact alone may explain why AAHPERD's size has dropped by one-third over the last decade: What advantage is there to

being in a professional organization that does not offer the criteria that are described earlier in the chapter? The answer is that there is not much advantage to being in such an organization, so its numbers are dropping. We are not arguing against the existence of AAH-PERD. Rather, we are pointing out that as a professional body, it does not meet the criteria for success that other professional bodies have met, so it does not have the same status.

5. Adapted from the American Council on Exercise, "Your Guide To Getting ACE-Certified," 4/95. American Council on Exercise, 5820 Oberlin Drive, Suite 102, San Diego, CA, 92121-3787. (800) 825-3636.

6. Adapted from ACSM pamphlet titled, "When You're Certified by ACSM, You've Reached the Gold Standard of Excellence." By American College of Sports Medicine, 401 W. Michigan St., Indianapolis, IN 46202-3233. Interview conducted on 7-7-95 with Chris in Certification Department of ACSM.

7. Adapted from "National Standards for Coaches, Overview," copyright by NASPE, March 1995. For more information, write:

National Association for Sport & Physical Education
1900 Association Drive
Reston, VA 22091
Phone (703) 476-3410

8. Holmes Group Consortium, "Tomorrow's Teachers: A Report of the Holmes Group," Holmes Group, Inc., East Lansing, Michigan, 1986. Excerpted in *The Chronicle of Higher Education, 32* (9 April 1986), 27–37; Carnegie Task Force on Teaching as a Profession. "A Nation Prepared: Teachers for the 21st Century," Carnegie Forum on Education and the Economy, Hyattsville, Maryland, 1986. Excerpted from *The Chronicle of Higher Education, 32* (21 May, 1986), 43–54.

A Selected Overview of the History of Sport and Physical Activity

Chapter Objectives

Upon completing this chapter, the reader will be able to:

1. Identify basic methods used in historical research.
2. Develop an appreciation and understanding of the cultural significance of sport and physical activity throughout history.
3. Identify and discuss the purpose of sport and physical activity that reflects the practices of the ancient Greeks and Romans.
4. Discuss the ritual significance of sport during the Aztec Empire.
5. Develop an understanding of how the philosophical position of the body influenced the development of sport and impacted physical activity.
6. Identify the individuals, institutions, and movements that influenced the development of sport in America.

The previous chapter addressed several critical issues. One of the more critical issues that has yet to be resolved to everyone's satisfaction is agreement on an appropriate name that accurately reflects the body of knowledge. In the United States and Canada, physical education has historically been the name that the field has identified with and this designation continues to reflect the curriculum in grades K–12 and in many colleges. However, a number of colleges and universities have dropped the name physical education and replaced it with a name that is believed to be more reflective of the body of knowledge and attendant scholarship. As a result, it is not unusual in this day and time to find that college diplomas that once identified the major area of study as "physical education" have chosen kinesiology or another name (human performance, exercise science, human movement, etc.).

The reason that this gradual change (from physical education to other "names" that the field embraces) is brought to your attention at this time is to avoid confusion when presenting the history of the field. This chapter will use the name physical education when appropriate. However, most of the material presented in this chapter will focus on the concept of physical activity as opposed to physical education. This is because most of the societies that are discussed in this chapter embraced physical activity as a significant cultural component but did not necessarily incorporate a formal educational program to teach human movement, with the exception of the ancient Greeks. In the next chapter, the development and reform of physical education and sport in the United States will be presented.

The Significance of Historical Information

History is the study of change over time. The study of the history of sport and human movement provides us with the opportunity to learn how sport and human movement activities changed over time. The historical and social significance of sport and human movement activities throughout the ages have had a significant impact on modern culture. Current civilizations are to a great extent composed of the attitudes, behaviors, and symbols that reflect sport and human movement. To say that sport and human movement have enjoyed prominent cultural status throughout history is an understatement! That sport in our times is central to our existence should not be surprising. Indeed, our attitudes toward sport can be seen in ancient sports stadiums and countless works of art depicting human movement. Modern culture pays tribute to sport by building enormous stadiums and arenas that showcase athletes and pamper fans. The enduring quality of the institution of sport is similar to that of religion and politics. In all of these modern institutions we see spectacular monuments and large numbers of devoted fans.

The impact and cultural importance of sport and human movement is, and will continue to be, significant. As is the case with any important human activity that captures out attention and time, sport and human movement occupy a prominent place in the history of the human race. Not surprisingly, sport and human movement have attracted serious scholarship. Indeed, they still do. If the student is to understand and appreciate the social significance and cultural identification we have with play, games, and sport, it is imperative that we study these activities as they have been practiced and viewed in the past. This chapter will enable students to understand our current attitudes and behaviors in play, games, and sport by understanding how these attitudes and behaviors changed over time.

Historical Methods

There are two basic types of historical research, *descriptive* and *interpretive*. Descriptive historical research is fairly straightforward in that it describes, as objectively as possible, what happened in the past. Essentially, descriptive history is a record of the past without any attempt to impose current ideas, thinking, and values on the historical events of past years. Most of the history textbooks that you have read probably fall in this category.

In contrast, an interpretive history attempts to explain the "how and why" of past events. It does so by putting people, events, and situations in a certain perspective that makes them more easily understood. Common interpretations, or perspectives, that explain how and why sport and human movement have changed over time include modernization theory, urbanization and industrialization, and metaphysics. These interpretations allow historians to select certain historical data over others, and in so doing they reveal certain attitudes and behaviors that otherwise might be lost in the large amounts of information that are available to them.

Both types of history rely on two main sources in order to study history, primary sources and secondary sources. *Primary sources* provide an account of the event by an eyewitness and can be found in a picture, video record, or firsthand journalistic account such as a diary. *Secondary sources* are those that tell the story "secondhand," or those that repeat what a primary source or other secondary sources report. Textbooks, academic journal articles, and magazine articles are examples of secondary historical sources because the authors of these accounts were not at the actual event to record firsthand what happened. For example, later on in this chapter you will read about the ancient Greek Olympic Games. Obviously the writers of this textbook were not around to witness the Ancient Greek Olympic Games, so we rely on secondary sources to tell the story of the Ancient Greek Olympics. We did not visit the ancient sites of the games, read only of the games in other textbooks, and so on. Indeed, many of the sources that we relied on are secondary sources. That the sources of information are "secondary" does not make them less valid. Rather, it merely describes the type of information that is relied on to tell the story.

Cultural Bias

When "doing history," it is useful to keep in mind that many of us are "prisoners of our culture." What this means is that most people think and evaluate information according to the cultural norms that they have been taught. We "know" or evaluate events and opinions that have their origins outside of our culture using the beliefs and values that we find comfortable. By coming to "know" something by relying on *one way* as opposed to *multiple ways*, individuals will limit their understanding of the circumstances that gave genesis to something; it is relatively easy to see that with "what happened," the key is understanding "why it happened." For example, the ancient Greeks competed in the nude. American males in all probability will not wrestle or box in front of 40,000 spectators as did the ancient Greeks.

Greek culture had no problem with athletes competing nude (if television were available in 500 BC, the Greeks would have broadcasted it to males who could not make the trip to Olympia). Would American culture accept this?

Sports and Physical Activity in the Ancient World

Through the efforts of archeology and anthropology, we know that the history of the human race probably began over a million years ago. Written language emerged in approximately 3000 BC with the invention of cuneiform writing and hieroglyphics. The ability of humans to develop a written form of communication marked the transformation from prehistory to history. The invention of writing left behind a record of the historical events that occurred during the civilizations of the Mesopotamians and the Egyptians.

Prior to the invention of writing, historians were able to obtain information based upon the art work of the civilizations they studied. This prehistoric art provided valuable insights into ancient civilizations. As a result, historians, archeologists, and anthropologists based their findings on inference and extrapolation rather than using ancient written records. The art and implements of prehistoric men and women are primary sources and therefore provide an accurate snapshot of how these people lived. However, these artifacts do not come with an explanation of the picture or tool, and therefore our explanations of their lives are, at best, good guesses.

It would be helpful at this point to briefly present a time line of the basic change from prehistory to the twentieth century. The Lower Paleolithic Era (Old Stone Age) was represented by primitive stone chipped tools, and began over a million years ago. The Upper Paleolithic Era began about 35,000 BC and was marked by the use of more advanced tools and ability to shape stone implements. The New Stone Age, also known as the Neolithic era, occurred after 7000 BC when stone tools were finely polished and shaped. The Bronze age began in 4000 BC, followed by the Iron Age that began after 1500 BC. As you can see, prehistoric time lines were marked by improvements in tools and weapons.

It can be argued that the ability to survive during prehistoric times was directly related to what we refer to today as "athleticism." Physical ability in general, and athletic ability in particular, was a requisite for being a good warrior or hunter and having the ability to escape from danger. Skillful human movement was critically necessary for survival, and as such it is of profound historical significance to those who study human movement. Understanding the centrality of movement skills to the development of civilization provides a context for the study of human movement in modern times.

Mesopotamia

Historians have debated if the "Cradle of Civilization" ever existed, and if so, where it was located. However, many historians and archaeologists argue that the geographical area that lies between the Tigris and Euphrates Rivers may be the location of the beginning of modern civilization. Known 3000 years ago as Mesopotamia, this area occupies present day Iraq. One of the powerful ancient city-states that occupied part of Mesopotamia was called Sumer. Its inhabitants were called Sumerians, and it was this civilization that helped develop cuneiform writing. Around 2350 BC the Sumerians were defeated by the Babylonians, who adopted many Sumerian practices. Over the next thousand years Mesopotamia was the site of many ancient kingdoms and battles, and by 1100 BC the Assyrians dominated the area. Eventually, the Assyrians were replaced by the Chaldeans and the Medes, who conquered the Assyrians in 612 BC. We are able to date the later civilizations with more accuracy because of the written records that these civilizations and their neighbors kept.

The first evidence we have of sports and games are found in the Early Dynastic period of the Sumerian civilization, dating from 3000 to 1500 BC. Primary sources include literary evidence and archaeological artifacts, all of which point to the central place that sports, dance, and games occupied in Sumerian culture. Archeologists have excavated numerous musical instruments. Harps, flutes, pipes, lutes, percussion clubs, rattles, and drums were used to make music for dance. Boxing and wrestling are depicted in vase paintings, which is no surprise considering the warfare that was prevalent during this era. There were athletic competitions that pitted boxers and wrestlers against each other to determine who was superior. The use of spears and bow and arrow provided ample opportunity for each man to test his skill in competition. The Sumerians used the chariot in war, and one needs little imagination to picture chariot races between the Sumerians through the desert long before the Romans made it popular.

There is much evidence to support the idea that human beings during this period of time were very concerned with establishing dominance, to compete in order to determine who is superior. Historically, humans have not only gone to war to defend or claim territory, but they have competed against each other for prizes of great value. Not surprisingly, the same argument still holds true today. Human beings go to war to defend territory, whether it be an end zone or a country. We compete for valuable prizes today such as a national championship trophy, a Super Bowl Ring, or a high school conference championship. Our point is that our tendency to compete for dominance and for territory has historical precedent.

Historically, sport and human movement rituals served as prominent cultural institutions and enjoyed universal appeal. Evidence of this is found not only in the harsh deserts of the Middle East but in the tropical rain forests of Mexico.

The Aztecs

The Aztecs of Mexico built magnificent temples and courtyards where they played an early form of basketball that was quite serious and sometimes even deadly! The courtyard resembled a rectangle with round stone hoops attached to the wall, and the object was to put the ball through the hoop. Occasionally, and for reasons that are unknown, the losers were taken to a temple and killed! The ritual killing took place on an altar to one of the Aztec gods. Winning was no guarantee of life, though. During special religious holidays, the victorious athletes were sacrificed to the gods. Their hearts were cut out and burned because it was believed that the Sun God liked the smell of the burning flesh of champion athletes. It could be argued that this was a time when finishing second was not so bad!

The Aztec Empire was conquered by Cortes in 1519, and the Europeans who conquered the peoples of Latin America were not interested in learning the games of those peoples and bringing them back to Europe. Consequently, it is the Ancient Greeks and Romans, and to a lesser extent the Egyptians, who put sport "on the map."

The Egyptians

Everyone is familiar with the Great Pyramids, the monuments to a civilization that flourished in the Nile valley thousands of years ago. Biblical accounts and the archeological treasures that have been discovered tell us much about the Ancient Egyptians. By 1500 BC, Egypt had reached the height of its glory after defeating Ethiopia. In 700 BC, Egypt was conquered by the Assyrians and thereafter a succession of rulers governed Egypt, including Alexander the Great. In 30 BC, Augustus Caesar made Egypt a province of Rome.

During the glory days of Egypt, their citizens made tremendous strides in science, agriculture, and mathematics. They developed hieroglyphics and invented the twelve-month calendar. Egyptians worshipped their king, or pharaoh, as a god and believed in the concept of life after death. Egyptian women enjoyed rights and social status that were highly unusual during this time in history. Women could own property and were not restricted from going out in public. They held important religious posts as priestesses and as a result were very influential in Egyptian culture.

The Egyptians were very religious. There were a number of holidays that were devoted to agriculture, military victories, and religious observances where dance, games, and sports were an integral part of the celebration. The Egyptians were not as health oriented as the Greeks or Romans and did not see much value in exercising in order to enhance health. They were a fairly peaceful people and believed that they had little need for a physical education program that developed military skills. On the other hand, recreation, dance, and entertainment performed by acrobats were quite popular. Swimming was a popular sport and some archeological excavations have uncovered swimming pools on the grounds of large estates. The Egyptians held athletic games in honor of at least one god, promoted wrestling matches and bull fights, and held many religious spectacles, funerals, public festivals, and private parties that featured dances or games. Children played with tops, shot marbles, played board games, played with dolls, and engaged in ball games. It certainly looks as if the children of the Ancient Egyptians enjoyed the same types of sports and games as children of today.

The Ancient Greeks

The birthplace of western civilization is historically identified as Greece. It is the home of the Olympic Games, Plato, Socrates, Aristotle, and Homer's *Iliad* and *Odyssey*, epic poems that describe early Greek civilization. Greece is recognized as nurturing democratic ideals, especially in Athens, and of developing fierce warrior-athletes that both protected the shores of Greece from foreign invasion and competed in the Olympic Games. Ancient Greece evolved through five distinct eras: (1) Homeric dating from prehistoric Greece until the first recorded Olympiad in 776 BC; (2) Spartan, dating throughout the entire history of Sparta and sometimes referred to as Lacedaemon; (3) Early Athenian dating from 776 BC to the end of the Persian Wars in 480 BC; (4) the Golden Age dating from 480 BC to 338 BC; and (5) from 338 BC to the establishment of the Roman Empire by Augustus in 27 BC.

Each of these eras of Ancient Greece is a study of contrasts. The Homeric period, for instance, was a warlike time that emphasized heroes and athleticism, whereas the Golden Age emphasized art and politics. While Greece is often cited as the birthplace of democracy, it was a country that was not united in the same sense as the United States. The Ancient Greeks lived in autonomous city-states that were formed as both military alliances and as economic entities. It was not at all unusual for one city-state to declare war against another. In sum, the Ancient Greeks shared cultural attributes such as language, food, and religious deities, but they did not "get along" all that well.

The Greeks are also considered one of the originators of organized sport, and there are many ancient Greek fables that attest to their love of competition for prizes. Indeed, the word "athlete" in ancient Greek can be translated to mean "one who competes for a prize." The nature of the prize varied from contest to contest and reveals much about the attitudes and behaviors of the ancient Greeks. For instance, in Homer's *Iliad*, funeral games were held to mourn the death of Patroclus. Funeral games pitted athletes against each other in running, boxing, wrestling, archery, and other physical contests. From Homer's story we know that the Greeks of the Homeric period valued cunning, courage, honor, and that they associated winning with excellence.

While these games reveal the values of many aspects of Greek culture, they are especially revealing of the relationships of men and women. According to Homer, the winner of a contest could actually win a woman servant. He noted that the first contest was the chariot race. The victor won a servant-woman and a tripod. Second prize was awarded a mare heavy with a mule. The third-place contestant received a cauldron; gold was awarded to the fourth-place finisher, and a jug was the last prize. By today's standards, the practice of giving another human being away as a prize would be considered barbaric, but we find that this practice existed throughout history. Athletic competition and winning prizes was central to the status of men in Greek culture in particular. One Greek king held a "son-in-law" contest that lasted for over a year. He entertained a number of suitors to determine who would win the hand of his daughter. The primary criterion was for winning was first an appropriate dowry and second, athletic ability measured head-to-head against other potential son-in-law candidates. Both of these stories illustrate how athleticism was important to social status, winning valuable prizes, and determining a social order.

Other values of ancient Greek culture are evident in their attitudes toward athletic competition. Many ancient competitions and games were developed to pay homage to the gods, and eventually athletic competitions came to have religious and mythical symbolism. Human sacrifices, funeral games, and ceremonial games were primitive forms of worship that relied on games and competition to appease the gods. For instance, all of the ancient athletic contests were dedicated to Greek gods. The Olympic Games were dedicated to the supreme Greek god Zeus, while the Isthmian Games held at Cornith were dedicated to Poseidon, God of the Sea. Indeed, there was an entire athletic circuit in which Greek athletes competed for both religious and economic purposes.

Gradually, the city-states of Ancient Greece consolidated into twenty leagues. The dominant city-state in each league would assume the primary duties of government. The two most famous city-states in Ancient Greece were Athens and Sparta, and these two city-states competed with each other politically, athletically, economically, and in war. Athens was a city of magnificent architecture and a center of cultural activities that included the arts, sciences, government, and of course sport. Athens progressed farther than any other city-state towards democracy, even though a rigid social hierarchy was firmly in place. The citizens of Athens had to take turns participating in local government. If your name came up in the "draw," you had to serve in some governmental capacity. In this fashion, every citizen had an equal opportunity to participate in governing the city. Interestingly, the famous philosopher Socrates was an opponent of democracy, as was his pupil Plato. Nevertheless, when his name came up for service as a member of the Prytanium, the Athenian governing body, Socrates served his appointed term. Apparently few, if any, of the Athenians were able to avoid public service.

Sparta, in contrast, was a totalitarian city that was short on democratic ideals but long on absolute authority and discipline. It was not at all uncommon for cities to have substantial slave populations. The Spartans were so successful at winning wars and taking slave that at one point in time Sparta was home to 9000 citizens and 250,000 slaves. The fact that a quarter of a million people did not dare challenge 9000 Spartans gives us an idea of how good the Spartans were at military matters.

The Spartans were not particularly interested in the cultural refinements and philosophical discourse that were common in Athens. Indeed, compared to Athens, Sparta was a cultural desert. Athens and Sparta were bitter enemies and went to war against each other numerous times, most famously in the Peloponnesian War where the Spartans emerged victorious. In this respect Sparta and Athens were not unique: The Greeks were often at war with each other. However, when one of the city-states was invaded by a foreign army or navy, it was not that unusual for the city-state to appeal for help from another Greek neighbor to drive off the foreign aggressor. Often the help would come, the foreign army and navy would be defeated, and the city-states would once again turn on each other.

Another characteristic of the Greeks can be seen in their art. Their love of beauty is clearly represented in museums throughout the world. The human body came to be a symbol of individual excellence and beauty, and has never been replicated. Greek sculptors, painters, poets, and architects left testimonials and monuments to their love of the male human form and athletic prowess. Individual excellence was symbolized in their art, especially their statues, and was expressed through the achievement of *arete* and the process of *agon*. *Arete* is the Greek ideal of striving for excellence, a quality that was only obtainable if the individual was a unified whole—mind, body, and spirit. *Arete* was the mark of a man who continued to pursue excellence; if an individual proclaimed himself to have achieved *arete*, it was invalid. *Arete* was bestowed by your peers, not yourself. The process to achieve *arete* was *agon*, which is the origin of the word agony. The agonistic process represented the grueling discipline and dedication that only athletes could relate to. *Agon* was the struggle for excellence, the path to *arete*.

The passion for athletic competition among the Greeks is legendary. Countless gymnasiums and palestras, the wrestling arenas, were constructed in city-states all across the land. Some of these facilities were very exclusive and very private, others were operated by the local government and open to the public. Athletes, old and young alike, would come to the gymnasiums and palistras on a daily basis to train, talk, and generally keep fit. Clothing was not allowed during athletic competition or training. After all, the body was beautiful and the Greeks placed great value on a beautifully developed body. A man with a flabby, fat body was likely to avoid the gymnasium as he would be scorned. Wrestlers, boxers, and pancrationists—athletes who competed in the pancratium, the most brutal of the Greek contests—would apply oil and fine sand to their bodies before competing under the watchful eye of coaches, officials, and peers. Athletic training for men began at a young age.

In Sparta, boys left home at the age of 7 and went to the public barracks where they were indoctrinated into the mighty Spartan military. Obedience to authority was the hallmark of Sparta. Boys were purposefully underfed, thus necessitating that they become resourceful and courageous. They would steal food and do anything to survive, no matter what the conditions. Once in the public barracks, if and when the boys were caught stealing food or other things necessary for survival, they were severely beaten, not for stealing but for getting caught. This was seen as preparation for battle and the hardships every Spartan was expected to endure.

Women were expected to bear strong healthy children, especially males. Mothers were not encouraged to nurture their children but instead to prepare them for the hardships and pain they would experience soon enough. Every newborn was taken before a council of elders who would determine whether the infant would live. If the baby appeared strong and healthy, he or she would live to serve the state. Those infants deemed to be undesirable by the elders were placed on Mount Taygetus, exposed to the elements and left to die.

Between the ages of 7 and 20, the males trained to be soldiers, Spartans. At the age of 20 the young warrior swore allegiance to Sparta and was inducted into the army. There he stayed until he was killed in battle or reached 50 years of age. At the age of 30, he was supposed to marry, gain full citizenship, and become a man of some distinction. Even though the Spartan men married, they spent the majority of their time living in the public barracks with their fellow warriors, not their families. The Spartans, as was the case of the Athenians and other Greeks, were superb athletes and were eager to test their physical skills against others.

The first recorded evidence of the Olympic Games dates from 776 BC when Corebus, a cook from Hellas, won the Stade race. The origin of the Olympic Games remains uncertain. However, in all probability, the games were initiated by the inhabitants of Olympia as an offering to the gods for prosperity. The Greeks saw their gods existing in human form with human qualities. When the Greeks depicted their gods in art, they were magnificent physical specimens that were truly beautiful. The Greeks were very religious and one way to get close to their gods was to resemble them in a physical sense. Thus, since the gods are portrayed as magnificent physical specimens, the Greeks sought to develop a harmonious and beautiful body to compliment the gods. It would not be incorrect to say that the "cult of the body" as defined by the Greeks was closely tied to religion. The Greeks believed that the gods liked to be entertained and worshipped. It is for this reason that in addition to traditional religious ceremonies that worshipped the deities, athletic competition was held in honor of the gods. Interestingly enough, each city-state had gods that were specific to that particular locale. However, all the Greeks, no matter what city-state they lived in, worshipped twelve major gods. Zeus was the chief deity of the Greeks and he and the remaining eleven gods were said to have formed the Olympic council that was located atop Mount Olympus in Northern Greece. The Olympic council controlled the destiny of all the Greeks.

As the most powerful god, Zeus was worshipped intensively. When the small village of Olympia instituted the Olympic Games, it did so to honor Zeus. Gradually, the games held at Olympia grew in stature to the premier athletic festival of the ancient world. The first athletic contest that we have record of was the Stade race. The stade or pole was set a certain distance from the starting line and the athletes would run around the pole and cross the finish line. It is quite probable that the word stadium originates from the Greek word *stade.* By the Fourteenth Olympiad in the year 724 BC, the Greeks expanded the athletic program to include the Diaulos or double stade race; two laps around the stade!

The athletes were probably separated into "heats" and gradually the final race was run to determine the champion. In 720 BC a long distance race of 4800 meters was added. Pentathlon and wrestling were added in 708 BC, followed by boxing in 688 BC, and chariot racing in 680 BC. The mortal combat event known as the pancration was added in 648 BC.

The pancration was an event that combined boxing and wrestling and had no time limit. It was brutal in that rules were almost nonexistent. The breaking of an opponent's bones, dislocation of joints, and the ability to disembowel the challenger were all within the "rules." Blinding your opponent by gouging out his eyes was sometimes permitted. In order to protect themselves and cause considerable damage to the opponent, pancrationists would cure leather until it was as hard as iron, embed the leather with sharp metal, and cover their forearms. They could then slash and rip the flesh of the opponent and protect their arms at the same time.

During the early years of the Olympics, facilities were primitive. In 550 BC an ambitious building period began that culminated in a stadium that sat 40,000 spectators, a gymnasium, palestra, and hippodrome. A temple dedicated to Zeus was erected along with a treasury that housed all the gifts bought to honor Zeus. Every fourth year, three heralds departed Olympia to travel all over Greece announcing the upcoming Olympic Games. It was said that a sacred truce was ordered by the oracle at Delphi that insured the safety of all those who were traveling to Olympia. If the Greeks were at war, the sacred truce would prevail and warrior-athletes put down their swords and shields and traveled to Olympia. The Olympic Games were open only to male citizens of Greece, whether spectator or athlete. No women were allowed to observe the competition other than the female representatives of the Priestess Demeter.

The men competed nude, which had the effect of excluding women as spectators. If a woman was caught at the Games, the punishment could be death. However, there is an exception to this rather harsh rule. It seems that a woman named Callipateira had a son who was competing in the Olympics. She disguised herself as a trainer and jumped over a fence and was immediately recognized as a woman. She was not put to death because her father, son, and brothers had all been victorious in the Games. After the failed attempt of Callipateria, all of the trainers, like the athletes, had to appear nude.

There is scant information pertaining to women athletes in Greece. We do know that even though women were forbidden to compete or spectate, there was no rule prohibiting women from owning the chariot teams that competed in the Olympics. In the chariot race, it was the owner, not the driver, who was declared the victor. Cynisca, the daughter of the Spartan King Archidamus, was the first woman to "win" at Olympia because she owned the horses that pulled the winning chariot. Periodically, after the end of the Olympic Games, there took place the Heraean Games for women, although we don't know very much about these athletic contests. Hera, wife of Zeus, was honored by the women athletes. The Heraean Games were held in the Olympic Stadium. The women were divided into three classifications for competition that was based on age. The Heraean Games were administered by sixteen married women and the victors received a crown of olives and part of a cow that was sacrificed in honor of the goddess Hera. Their races were not as long as the men's and evidence suggests that the women competed in at least three races.

The rules of the Olympic Games were quite explicit. Athletes and their coaches had to arrive in Olympia no later than a month prior to the start of the Games. Athletes could have no criminal record, swore an oath to Zeus that they had trained for at least ten months prior to the start of Olympic competition, and swore that they would compete fairly.

Those athletes who were caught cheating lived in disgrace. Their likeness was sculptured into a bust and was shamefully displayed in the row of Zanes (cheaters). Each Zane had the name of the cheater, town, and description of the scandal. In 472 BC, the Olympics were organized into a five-day program and stayed that way for the next 800 years.

The Ancient Olympic Games started from humble beginnings that revolved around worshipping Zeus. Victorious athletes were crowned with an olive wreath and given an amphora of olive oil from a sacred olive grove. Over time the Olympic Games lost their original intent and grew into a carnival-like atmosphere amid social and moral decay. The Games would eventually become a spectacle that included souvenir sellers, prostitutes, pimps, fortune tellers, and a place where important business deals were made. The Games rapidly slipped into a gaudy carnival atmosphere after the Roman conquest of Greece. The Roman Emperor Theodosius, who had converted to Christianity, declared the Olympic Games to be a pagan spectacle and put an end to them in 394 AD, 1170 years after the first Stade race was run. Can you identify a present day sporting event that seems to have gone the way of the Ancient Olympics, having deteriorated into a carnival atmosphere where the actual athletic event no longer seem to be the primary attraction?

There is no question that the Olympic Games were the premier athletic festival in Ancient Greece. However, there were three other major athletic festivals in addition to numerous local athletic competitions of lesser importance. The Pythian Games, held in Delphi, were the second most popular athletic festival. The Pythian Games began in 582 BC and were held in honor of the god Apollo. The winners were crowned with a laurel wreath. In the same year that the Pythian Games began, the Isthmian Games held their first competition as well. Cornith was the home to the Isthmian Games, which were dedicated to the god Poseidon; the victors were crowned with a wreath of pine. The great philosopher Plato won the Isthmian wrestling competition as a youth. The Nemean Games held at Nemea began in 573 BC to honor Zeus. The winners were crowned with a wreath of celery.

The Olympic Games, Pythian Games, Isthmian Games, and Nemean Games were collectively known as the Crown Games and were the four most prestigious athletic festivals in Greece. When the move to professionalism in athletics began, Greek athletes would often compete for large monetary and material rewards. The Crown Games "paid" the most and it was not unusual for athletes to represent one city during a particular athletic festival and show up at another athletic festival representing yet another city. It depended upon which city paid the most.

The Romans

Rome evokes pictures of the Coliseum, the Forum, gladiatorial combats, Ben Hur, and Spartacus. The monuments and symbols that were part of the cultural fabric of this legendary society provide an enormous amount of information with regard to Roman values, beliefs, and purpose. Like the Greeks, the Romans were a religious people. The Romans were quite utilitarian and did not care much for the abstract philosophy that fascinated the

Greeks. The Roman way of thinking required that everything must have a purpose or utilitarian goal. Their purpose was to rule the known world, which they eventually did. They adopted many of the practices of their vanquished enemies and brought back to Rome and the surrounding areas tens of thousands of slaves who did everything from menial work to acting as physicians and teachers. Greek physicians were especially prized by the Romans.

When Rome conquered Greece, the victorious Romans left Greece pretty much intact as long as the Greeks paid tribute and taxes to Rome. Roman governors were spread throughout the conquered territories, and, if need be, a Roman garrison was also established to protect the interests of Rome. Perhaps the most recognized Roman governor is Pontius Pilate, the Roman procurator of Judea (26 AD to 36 AD?) who was the final authority who had a hand in the crucifixion of Christ. The Romans never could accept Greek athletics, although they did appreciate the exercises that promoted health used by the Greeks. The nudity bothered the Romans as did the Greek quest for individual excellence. The Romans demanded obedience and allegiance to the Emperor. Therefore, a unified and utilitarian program of physical education was required, not the physical education practices of the Greeks that strove for *arete* and individual excellence.

Rome was not a loose federation of city-states as was the case in Greece. Rome was a singular government that was powerful and, when need be, merciless. The Roman legions were the backbone of the government and were among the most feared warriors in that part of the world. The physical training required to be a warrior in Rome was severe. There are two distinct historical periods in Roman history. The Roman Republic was founded in 509 BC after the defeat of the Etruscans. The Republic lasted until 146 BC, which just happens to be the year that Rome conquered Greece. Between 146 BC, and 27 BC, Rome went through a period of unrest and political turmoil. The Roman Empire was established in 27 BC and lasted until 476 AD. It is during the Empire that most of the "athletic spectacles" with which we are familiar occurred.

During the early days of the Roman Republic, the Romans actively participated in games and sports. The Romans, as did the Greeks, held festivals to honor the gods. During these festivals games and sports were conducted as both a form of worship and for general entertainment. Gradually participation was replaced with the move to spectator status. By the end of the Republic, Rome was known more for its rabid fans and spectators than for the population's inclination towards actual athletic participation. Unlike the Greeks, the Romans believed it to be undignified if a Roman competed as an athlete. However, Nero and Caligula, two emperors of infamous reputation, participated in chariot racing. Frequently slaves, Christians, and criminals were the source for both the athletic talent and entertainment. These were the unfortunate victims we have come to associate with the brutal carnage and slaughter that were the fate of men, women, children, and animals who were doomed to death in the Coliseum and other similar venues throughout the Empire.

Ever utilitarian, the Romans would often subject individuals convicted of criminal activity to take part in the "blood sport" that the Romans conducted. These criminals and other victims of Roman jurisprudence were taken to the Coliseum where they would be pitted against each other or thrown to the lions or other savage beasts to be torn limb from limb before tens of thousands of spectators. In this manner the Romans were able to provide both entertainment and justice at the same time.

During both the Republic and the Empire, the government proclaimed numerous official holidays where athletic festivals were the main attraction. The official holidays were primarily a propaganda ploy by the politicians. Rome was engaged in almost constant warfare in order to fulfill its manifest destiny of ruling the world. The populace was weary of the constant state of war and the drain of resources necessary to support the government. In order to distract the population from their grumblings and possible uprisings, the officials would frequently offer "bread and circus," which meant that an official holiday was declared and everyone was supposed to attend the festivities. The admission was usually free and the officials would give away bread and other prizes to a war-weary population. The people would eat, drink, and watch the various athletic feats and slaughter all supplied by the government. The Romans essentially used games and sports as a political tool. Politicians seeking votes would stage athletic combats in order to attract a crowd and deliver a campaign speech; buying votes is what they attempted to do. By the year 173 BC, 53 public holidays were in existence, by the year 300 AD, there were 200 days set aside as public holidays with 175 days devoted to sports and games. The Emperor Marcus Aurelius declared that 135 days out of the year were public holidays and at one point had 17 out of the 29 days in April designated as holidays.

Contests featuring animals against animals, men fighting animals, men against men in the case of the condemned, pacifistic Christians thrown to the lions or ordered to fight condemned criminals, and gladiator combats were held on a regular basis. It seems that each time the Roman officials produced a spectacular festival of barbarian carnage where animals and humans fought to the death, it wasn't enough. The spectators would become bored and demand more exciting events. The Coliseum was an engineering marvel and could actually be flooded for the purpose of staging "naval battles" before thousands of cheering fans. Soldiers clad in heavy armor were put aboard vessels that were placed in the flooded Coliseum, where they attacked each other with savage fury. Unfortunately for the spectators, more of the soldiers would drown than be cut to ribbons. Because of the flaws in marine architecture during that time, the ships were highly unstable. The soldiers often lost their footing, fell overboard, and drowned because their heavy armor sent them to the bottom as if they were an anchor.

In general, the Romans were not big fans of Greek athletics; however, there are exceptions to every rule. In 80 BC, the Roman Emperor Sulla transferred the Olympic Games to Rome in the hope of adding another dimension to the popular athletic festivals. The Olympic Games proved to be unpopular and the Olympics were returned to Greece much to the delight of the Greeks who were outraged at Sulla for removing their Games in the first place. Emperor Augustus enjoyed Greek athletics and supported the Olympic Games.

He attempted to introduce new games to the Romans that were modeled after Greek athletics. An egomaniac if there ever was one, Nero called for a "Special Olympic Games" to be held for him so he could race a chariot and be crowned an Olympic Champion. The Greeks were furious over his request but nonetheless complied with the Emperor's wishes. After Nero was dead, the Greeks did their best to erase all evidence that Nero was an Olympian.

The Romans enjoyed the *thermae* or baths. They found these very soothing and believed that light exercise, "working up a mild sweat," prior to entering the baths was good for health. The thermae were very popular and attached to the baths were often gymnasiums that offered the opportunity for a light workout. The Romans enjoyed various forms of ball games for recreation and promotion of health. The Romans, unlike their neighbors in Greece, were not very interested in serious and intense athletic competition. Instead, the citizens of Rome preferred to stroll to either public or private *thermaes* where they could unwind after a day's labor. Some of the *thermaes* were ostentatious and were constructed with expensive materials and pampered their patrons. The larger *thermaes* were able to house art galleries, libraries, lounges, and even dining rooms. The *thermaes* of ancient Rome seem quite similar to the health and fitness clubs that are very popular today.

The Middle Ages: 900–1400

The fall of the Western Roman Empire occurred in 476 AD and with it came what historians call the Dark Ages. The Dark Ages represents a period in history that was truly "dark" with regard to intellectual and artistic discoveries. With the collapse of Rome a void was created relative to guidance, leadership, and government. Indeed, anarchy was not uncommon and resulted in construction of the fabled medieval walled cities that still stand today. The walled cities were erected to protect the population from marauding armies and tyrants who waged war on a frequent basis. Castles and other fortifications were erected and Europe was essentially divided into a series of kingdoms.

The aristocracy and the Catholic Church were the two dominant social institutions, with the Church holding the greatest power. If you were not fortunate enough to be a member of the aristocracy or clergy, life was often grim. Peasants eked out a meager living and frequently worked for members of the aristocracy. The king, queen, prince, or duke who happened to control the land on which the peasants farmed taxed them heavily and in return was supposed to offer the peasants safety from attack. Life was bleak (dark), so the promise of salvation and a better life in heaven was very appealing to the peasants who barely had enough to survive on a day-to-day basis. As a result, the Church was not only a beacon for the downtrodden peasants, it was also very influential and held great power over the aristocracy.

The Dark Ages lasted until approximately 900 AD. The magnificent baths, gymnasiums, and other venues devoted to physical education and sport that were significant cultural institutions in Greece and Rome were neglected and in ruin during the Dark Ages. During this period, little, if any, physical education and athletic competition existed among the common people. Members of the aristocracy would sometimes enjoy the pleasures of regal sporting activities such as hunting, jousting, and horse racing. With the end of the Dark Ages and the dawning of the Middle Ages in 900 AD, the Church and the aristocracy developed closer ties as both parties relied on each other to consolidate their positions and advance their individual agendas.

Members of the aristocracy were very religious and usually deferred to the Church in most matters. In return for the devotion and dedication of the aristocracy, the Church perpetuated the status quo because it had much to gain. Popes were often more powerful than most kings and queens. The crusades of the eleventh, twelfth, and thirteenth centuries were orchestrated by the Church to recapture the Holy Land from the Muslims. Those members of the aristocracy who declined to provide resources for the Crusades faced the wrath of the Church and possible eternal damnation. The Church usually prevailed. The Church dictated values, beliefs, and blind faith and obedience to the Holy Father. Freedom of speech, a free press, and ideas contradictory to Church doctrine were a rarity during the Middle Ages.

Dualism, the separation of soul and body, was the standard of religious belief. This remains the situation today in Judeo-Christian thought. Simply put, dualism places great worth on the soul and not so much value on the worth of the body. The soul will survive the death of the body and reside in heaven, which is the only hope for a better life the peasants had during the Middle Ages. The body housed the soul, but for a great many Christians during the Middle Ages, the body was a source of evil that could corrupt the soul. The Church provided a code of conduct and guidance that was supposed to control those physical "urges" that would lead to sinful behavior. An extreme example were the ascetic views of some of the monks. These monks practiced self-denial and bodily mortification where they would engage in self-inflicted pain and physical punishment that was supposed to inhibit bodily lusts and desires in preparation for entry into heaven. Thus, the philosophical and religious position of the body was of great significance during this era. True, the Bible does say that the body is a temple and should be treated as such. You would think that this would promote physical education and sports in the eyes of the Church. The Scholastics, an order of the Church, believed this to be true but their opinion was in the minority. After all, clergy warned their flocks to guard against evil and the lusts of the body. If there was ever a "lightning rod" for the promotion of sin, so the clergy believed, it was the body. In addition to the general distrust of the body, the plagues that swept across Europe and killed millions of people were interpreted by the Church as punishment from God. The body was seen as a messenger of death and further suspicion about the worth of the body was perpetuated.

The development of physical education and play, games, and sport was repressed because of ignorance. This does not mean that physical education and fitness for health did not occur during the Middle Ages. The Scholastics did promote physical education and development of the body. To be sure, the Scholastics were dualists, but they believed that a healthy body ensures a healthy mind and this is beneficial to the soul since the soul is housed in the body. The greatest medieval Scholastic was St. Thomas Aquinas (1225–1274). He believed that physical fitness and recreation were a positive force in promoting social and moral well-being. In his acclaimed work, *Summa Theologiae*, he states "in order to achieve happiness, perfection in both the soul and the body are necessary. Since it is natural for the soul to be united with the body, how is it credible that perfection of the one (soul) should exclude perfection of the other (body)? Let us declare, then, that happiness completed and entire requires the well-being of the body."

The Scholastics were not alone in their positive view of the body. Orthodox Christians rejected the belief that the body was a magnet for sin. They believed that because God was everywhere, He was in all things, including the body. Therefore, it stands to reason that the body inhabited with God was good, not evil. It should be easy to see how the philosophical position of the body and the related religious beliefs can have a negative impact upon the development of sport and physical education. Students who study human movement believe in the value of the body and tend to look upon their earthly existence as a uniting of mind and body, a unified whole. Students and established professionals believe that they can offer solid developmental opportunities for each and every person through the medium of human movement. How do you think our field would fare if we conducted physical education classes and extolled the virtues of the body during the Middle Ages?

The Development of Sport in America

Factors That Distinguish Sport from Physical Education

The United States is the home of many peoples, ranging from Native Americans to immigrants to, in a dark chapter for the United States, African Americans who were kidnapped as slaves. All of these groups have contributed to the rich heritage that became American sport and physical education. As a social institution, sport and physical education has been, and will continue to be, an agent of social change.

Before we begin our investigation, it will be helpful to refresh ourselves with the distinction between physical education and sport. Physical education is a formal program of learning that is designed to be educational, developmental, and based on a sound theoretical base and associated curriculum. Physical education is found in the schools and conducted by physical education professionals. The purpose of physical education, then, is to help individuals grow with respect to human movement.

Sports and athletics do not need a school to exist and function. Coaches, athletes, serious competition, time commitment, and an organized structure of rules and rewards represent sports and athletics. In the rest of the world, athletics mean track and field, whereas in America we tend to use both interchangeably. The development of sports and the development of physical education share a common foundation—human performance. However, each of them is distinct and unique in regard to its historical development, mission, and popularity. The remaining material in this chapter focuses on sports and games; the next section of this chapter will focus on the development of physical education in America.

Native American Sports and Physical Activities

America's sporting heritage is derived primarily from England, as the English were among the first to colonize the New World. However, prior to the arrival of the British, Native Americans, historically referred to in the United States as "Indians," had enjoyed athletic competition. Among the most prominent tribes were the Iroquois, who lived in the area we call upstate New York and Canada.

In approximately 1600, the Iroquois joined with the Algonquians to form the Iroquois League of the Five Nations. Present-day Florida was home to the Cherokee Nation and the Seminoles. The Cherokees were forced to relocate to Oklahoma by the federal government, resulting in the much publicized "Trail of Tears" because of the cruelty, hardships, and many deaths that befell the Cherokees by the time they arrived in Oklahoma Territory. Northern Oklahoma was already home to the Pawnee. In addition to the relocation of the Cherokees, the Shawnee tribe moved from the east central United States to Oklahoma as well. The areas of New Mexico and Arizona were home to the Hopi and Navajo, while the Apaches roamed parts of southwestern United States. While the Sioux lived in the Dakotas, the Blackfoot and Nez Perce lived in the Rocky Mountains. As you can imagine, there was and still is a great deal of cultural diversity among the Indian Nations.

Lacrosse, which the Indians called *Baggataway*, was invented by the Indians and was very popular with the Iroquois and other tribes, especially in the northeast. The Indians were quite religious and many of the early explorers brought back stories of the elaborate rituals and dances that were sacred to their religion. Apart from religion, dance was and is a significant component of Native American culture. Ball games were popular as were races and contests that tested bravery and "manhood." A form of basketball was played by Florida Indians and a court used for ball playing that was constructed in approximately 800 AD was discovered in Arizona. Archery was popular because it was not only an opportunity to compare ability but its utilitarian value also put food on the table and provided a means for defense. After the introduction of horses in North America, the Plains Indians developed a reputation for their equestrian ability. Hunting, hiking, fishing, canoeing, and kayaking were other "modern day" sports in which the Indians excelled.

Perhaps the greatest American athlete who ever lived was Jim Thorpe. A member of the Sak and Fox tribe from Oklahoma, he enrolled at the Carlisle Indian School in Pennsylvania. He caught the eye of one of America's greatest coaches, Glenn "Pop" Warner, who immediately made him a member of the track and field team where he was nothing less than spectacular. He broke record after record and was front page material in the nation's newspapers. He played football and was named to everybody's All-America team. He was a member of the United States Olympic Team and was an Olympic Champion at the 1912 Stockholm Olympiad. The King of Sweden proclaimed him the world's greatest athlete during the Olympics. Sadly enough, he had his Olympic medals stripped after it was discovered that he had played for a minor league baseball team and thus was classified a professional athlete. He received less than $100 for playing minor league baseball. Other "amateurs" had played professionally but never used their real names—this was Jim Thorpe's downfall, he used his real name. He later went on to play professional football but then fell into despair and died penniless. Years after his death, his daughter was successful in persuading the International Olympic Committee to restore his status as an Olympic Champion.

The Puritan Influence on the Development of Sport and Physical Activity

The Puritan influence upon the development of sport and physical education was extensive. These English immigrants, as is the case for many of America's immigrants, left their native country seeking freedom of religion and escaping political persecution. They landed in New England and made Massachusetts their home. Staunchly conservative and stoic, they symbolized the "Puritan work ethic," which was a capacity for a productive life based on hard work and the teaching of scripture. The Puritans feared the devil, as the tragedy known as the Salem witch trials of 1692 symbolizes. The adage "idle hands are the devil's playground" originated with the Puritans, which once again demonstrates their belief in hard work and a purposeful and directed life. The attitude of the Puritans in conjunction with the harsh New England winters effectively slowed both the acceptance and development of play, games, and sports. Frivolous activities, which is how the Puritans viewed play, games, and sports were not productive and could be contrary to their religious beliefs. The body was once again viewed with suspicion as it was thought to be a weak moral entity (if not prepared for salvation) that could be tempted by Satan. The Puritans were ever vigilant and admonished their followers to beware of the temptations of the flesh. Sunday was a day devoted to worship, and the remaining six days of the week were devoted to prosperous activities. Ironically, the activities that the Puritans, Indians, and frontier settlers engaged in to put food on the table and survive, we now look forward to doing as a means of recreation and stress reduction. Camping, hunting, fishing, hiking, and related outdoor pursuits that were necessary for survival a little over a century ago have know evolved into a multi-million dollar recreation industry where we pay large sums of money to live like our forefathers for a weekend or two.

Jamestown was the first permanent settlement in North America. Located in Virginia, the British settlers had little time to devote to games and sports. Like their brethren in Massachusetts, the British colonists had to work very hard from sunup to sundown just to survive. Their daily work amounted to considerable physical activity. We would have to believe that with proper nutrition, which frequently was not the case in the New World, some of the colonists were very physically fit. For the first two centuries of North American history, physical education as we know it was not a viable option or an issue of concern to the immigrants.

You can imagine the physical and mental ability necessary for immigrant populations to survive in a foreign environment that we now call home. Athletic ability, endurance qualities, and the daily need for big muscle activity demanded, and provided for, physical training out of necessity. The athletic ability of the Indians and their knowledge of hunting, fishing, farming, and general survival ability became a model for many of the early pioneers who settled the country; for these people, life itself often amounted to a form of physical education, day in and day out. As you can see, the legacy that our nation has with regard to various forms of physical education (sometimes called manual-physical labor) and our historic appreciation of physical talents span the centuries. The body, like the mind, needed care and feeding. Even the Puritans and the Quakers recognized that the body was not to be neglected and must be nourished if they were to survive and prosper; physical health was coveted. Nonetheless, they still guarded against the "pleasures of the flesh."

*The Development of Sport in the South**

While the Puritans were settling New England and the Quakers were in Pennsylvania, the southeastern section of the New World developed an appreciation for games and sports that sent the Puritans and Quakers into shock. Florida was settled by the Spanish, and the Carolinas, Maryland, and Virginia eventually became home to British immigrants who brought their games and sports with them. Unlike the Puritans and Quakers, the Catholics and other Protestants who settled in this part of the country did not share the belief that play, games, and sports were possible tools of the devil. Horse racing became popular, along with ball games, fox hunts, hounds and hares, boxing, marksmanship contests, and other competitive and recreational pastimes. The climate in the Southeast was nowhere near as harsh as New England and this fact was a tremendous factor in the popularity of play, games, and sports. Thus, the religious and climatic constraints that were present in New England and served to slow the development of sport and physical education were all but absent in the Southeast.

---

*The Development of Sport in the South was adopted from a lecture and attendant material provided by Bruce Bennett, Professor, School of Health, Physical Education & Recreation—The Ohio State University, Columbus, Ohio, February, 1976.

The "Southern gentlemen," as they were referred to, were very competitive. They came to America to enjoy the political and religious freedom and make money. They built lavish plantation homes and grew a very lucrative export crop called tobacco. They purchased slaves, and it was the slaves who not only built the fortunes of the plantation owners but emerged as some of the greatest athletes of the day. Gambling was very big, and wagering on horse races or boxing matches with money and tobacco crops was a favorite pastime. At first, horse races took place in the towns between individuals who wanted to determine who had the fastest horse. This proved to be dangerous because pedestrians were often at great risk when these impromptu to races occurred. Today, some people want to determine who has the fastest car and engage in "drag races" in towns; once again, pedestrians are at risk. We seem to have an innate need to race, whether it be horses or cars.

Fearing loss of life and limb, primitive horse racing tracks were set aside on the edge of town. These tended to be straight tracks about a quarter of a mile long and the quarter horse races emerged. People began breeding horses and sent to England for pure breeds that would build a blood line. Horse racing was serious business and serious entertainment in the Southeast and New York City. In 1665 the British governor of New York, Colonel Richard Nicolls, organized the first official horse race in the New World and named the race after his favorite race track in Britain—Newmarket.

The immigrants, as best they could, attempted to replicate the customs and pastimes of the old world into the New World. The English brought their pubs, the Germans and Austrians brought their beer halls, and soon enough all were known as taverns or inns. It was at the taverns and inns where a weary traveler would find shelter and the local folks would gather to socialize and bet on the horses or some other competition.

The innkeepers would often sponsor shooting contests and other games of chance. This gave the owner the opportunity to sell food and drink and provided recreational and social activities for the patrons, much the same way it was done in the old world. Taverns were not found with great frequency in New England or Pennsylvania but were prevalent in the Southeast and on the frontier, which was not more than 50 to 100 miles away in colonial America.

Boxing was imported from England, and, to a lesser extent, from Germany and France. The English have a long tradition of boxing and the American pugilists, as the fighters were called, were influenced by the British boxers. Eighteenth-century Elizabethan England was the birthplace of modern boxing, which was among the favorite sports of the Southern colonists. The best known of America's boxers was Tom Molyneaux, who was a slave. He gained his freedom by fighting on the Southern Plantation Circuit. He also traveled to England to fight the British champion, Tom Cribb. The fight lasted forty rounds in a pouring rain. Molyneux was beating Cribb but the partisan British officials temporarily stopped the fight. He caught a chill in the rain and lost to Cribb. Boxing was thought by many to be cruel and was banned in many states and territories. When fights did take place, they were often a guarded secret and occurred in barns, barges, and other remote venues.

The Development of Baseball

Ball games remained a popular form of recreation. Early forms of baseball was called rounders, town ball, and "old cat." A myth that is still being perpetuated is that Abner

Doubleday invented baseball at Cooperstown, New York in 1839. This simply is not the case. Robert W. Henderson, author of *Ball, Bat, and Bishop*, conducted extensive research and discovered that the game of baseball actual is traced to early eighteenth-century England where it is described in a book published in 1744, 95 five years before Doubleday "invented" the game. In all probability, baseball came to the United States during the American Revolution, because an entry in a diary of a revolutionary war soldier states that he played baseball.

Prior to the Civil War, children picked up the game, and for the longest time, baseball was looked upon as a game for children, not men. Between 1840 and 1860 there were about a dozen baseball clubs in New York City. These baseball players were primarily middle-class, white-collar workers who lived in the city. By 1860 there were in excess of 100 baseball teams in the New York area, the most popular being the club formed by Alexander Cartwright in 1845 called the Knickerbocker Base Ball Club. They implemented a new set of rules that went a long way toward codifying and standardizing the game. One of the rules they instituted was that throwing the ball and hitting the base runner to put him out was no longer permitted. In 1858 twenty-six teams formed the National Association of Baseball Players (NABP) that governed baseball for the next thirteen years. The NABP was a weak organization, but it did make some progress in settling disputes and revising the rules. The first intercollegiate baseball game took place in 1859 between Amherst and Williams. In a game that took over three and a half hours to play, Amherst "edged" Williams 73 to 32.

Baseball's popularity grew after the Civil War. It was played by soldiers of both the Confederate and the Union Armies. When the end of the war came in 1865, these soldiers returned home or sought a new beginning in another part of the country. These soldiers were the first ambassadors of baseball, teaching people the game wherever they went.

Baseball became the premier sport in Eastern colleges during the later part of the nineteenth century. Although the English sport of cricket was played on the East coast, it never rivaled baseball for several reasons. Cricket was not viewed as a "manly" sport and was quite complicated and slow. Baseball was an American game and was not difficult to play—this was much more appealing to the middle class and blue-collar working class who saw cricket as a sport for snobs. In 1869 the Cincinnati Red Stockings became the first professional baseball team to go on a nationwide tour, losing one time in 56 games. The National League was formed in 1876, followed by the American League in 1900. In 1903 the first World Series was played, and baseball was on its way to becoming America's national game. Today Major League Baseball has teams in the United States and Canada. In Mexico and Japan baseball games draw thousands of fans, and in the 1984 Olympic Games in Los Angeles, baseball was included as an exhibition sport. It has since gained full-fledged status as an official Olympic sport and is played throughout the world.

As an agent of social change and mechanism for integration, baseball has been a very significant force. Before World War II, African American athletes were restricted to playing in the Negro Leagues because of racial segregation. Some politicians and national leaders had for years struggled to promote racial equality and an end to segregation but with little success. In 1947 Branch Rickey, president of the Brooklyn Dodgers Baseball Club "broke the color line" in major league sports when he signed Jackie Robinson. This historic decision by Branch Rickey paved the way for other African American athletes to play in the big leagues.

The Development of Basketball and Volleyball

Although baseball is considered America's favorite pastime, we know it did not originate in the United States. Basketball and volleyball, some would argue frisbee, are America's contribution to sport. Both basketball and volleyball owe their origin to two men who worked at the Young Men's Christian Association (YMCA).

In 1891 James Naismith was an instructor at the YMCA Training School in Springfield, Massachusetts. The director of the school was Luther Gulick. It was Gulick who approached Naismith about the need for a ballgame that could be played indoors during the winter months. Naismith tried several variations of rugby, lacrosse, and field hockey without success. He then devised a game that required that a large ball be passed from man to man. In order to score points, the ball had to be put through baskets that were about ten feet up in the air at each end of the court. The first basketball game was played on December 21, 1891 between two teams of nine men per team. Naismith and the legendary football coach, Amos Alonzo Stagg, were the two captains. Basketball grew rapidly within the YMCAs, colleges, and playgrounds.

However, it was the women physical educators who saw basketball as an excellent sport for women and did the most to promote the sport and write the rules of the game. Senda Berenson, who taught physical education at Smith College, modified the game to suit the women. Her approach was acceptable to some, but not all, women who enjoyed basketball. As a result of the success of basketball, a meeting was called to codify the rules and to discuss modification of the game for women in such a way that all the women playing basketball would play by the same rules. The meeting took place in 1899 in Springfield. The women agreed, among other things, that (1) stealing the ball from an opponent was not allowed, (2) each team could have between six and nine players on the court at any given time, and (3) the court was divided into three zones and players were instructed to play in their specific zones, presumably not to tire out the women athletes.

In the formative years of basketball, the men's version was a rough-and-tumble game that frequently resulted in injury. Gradually, the game became more refined until it resembled the game of today. This is not to discount the physical nature of today's game, as basketball has evolved into a game that features huge athletes sprinting up and down the court with amazing athletic ability and moves that bring fans to their feet cheering. Early basketball was often a game that involved lots of pushing and shoving without the athleticism that is the hallmark of modern-day basketball. Professional basketball teams toured the country in the early part of the century. By World War I boys' basketball was among the most popular sports in the high schools. Indiana, Illinois, Kansas, and New York were home to some of the nation's best teams. There were numerous attempts at establishing professional basketball leagues and until the advent of the National Basketball Association (NBA), they came and disappeared with great frequency.

The Harlem Globetrotters have become an American institution and tour the world as goodwill ambassadors. The Globetrotters were organized by Abe Saperstein in 1927. Before the NBA was established, the Globetrotters, the New York Renaissance—both teams made up of African Americans—and the original Celtics, who were all white, were the most recognized teams in the country. In 1948 the National Basketball League and the Basketball Association of America merged to form the NBA. Ironically enough, the NBA was the last of the professional sports leagues to become integrated.

Collegiate basketball enjoyed increased attention in the 1930s and 1940s. With numerous colleges in the New York metropolitan area and the Northeast, collegiate basketball in this region was second only to football. The National Invitational Tournament (NIT) was founded in 1938 by a group of sports writers who covered collegiate basketball. The NIT was the premier basketball tournament in the country for a long time to come and was more popular than the tournament staged by the National Collegiate Athletic Association (NCAA) for years. Within the last decade women's collegiate basketball has become very popular and enjoys frequent television exposure. This is a far cry from the time when women's high school teams played with six players on a team and had a very short season. Historically, the Iowa State Girls High School Basketball Championships would draw thousands of fans to the arena at a time when many people in other parts of the country had no idea that women's basketball was very popular in some sections of the country.

The YMCA in Holyoke, Massachusetts is the birthplace of volleyball. William Morgan was the physical director at the Holyoke YMCA. He developed the game to provide the opportunity for businessman to get some exercise and fun. The businessman went to the YMCA during their lunch hour to exercise and were in need of a game that could be quickly set up and had a high degree of participation. Originally called minonnette, the game utilized a net that was six feet, six inches high and played with the bladder of a basketball. The ball was hit back and forth with the hands over the net between the opposing teams. The game lasted nine innings, which allowed players to move in and out of the game. An "out" was called if the ball was hit out of bounds or made contact with the floor after more than one bounce.

The game of minonnette was presented to the YMCA conference on sports in 1895. The game was renamed volleyball and became an instant success in YMCAs across the country and in the military during World War I. Today volleyball is played around the world and is one of the premier sports for high school and college women. Professional volleyball draws large crowds and is played on the beach and in major arenas where large sums of money are made by suntanned men and women who have lucrative commercial endorsements just as the professional athletes in tennis, baseball, basketball, and football have. The Olympic Games have allowed volleyball to come into the homes of millions of people around the world via television. This has had an enormous impact on the success of the game.

The Development of Football

Football was the most popular sport on college campuses by the turn of the century. The game was played as early as 1827 with interclass competition at Harvard. By the 1840s football was played at Yale and Princeton. In 1873 Yale, Columbia, Rutgers, and Princeton formed the Intercollegiate Association for Football. During this time, football resembled rugby, not the game we are familiar with today. As is the case today, early football was played with reckless abandon and marked with serious injuries. The faculty at Harvard and Yale banned the game because of the violent nature of the sport.

The Eastern colleges had considerable success when competing against college football teams from the South, Midwest, and West. The United States Military Academy at West Point formed a team in 1890, by 1900 the Army–Navy game was "the" game that captivated the nation. The Rose Bowl, first played in 1902, set the stage for the football mania that sweeps the country every fall. Football coaches became national idols and were treated with the pageantry and attention usually reserved for presidents, kings, and queens.

Glenn "Pop" Warner, Fielding Yost, Knute Rockne, Woody Hayes, George Allan, Lou Holtz, Eddie Robinson, Vince Lombardi, and Paul "Bear" Bryant left a legacy and history that symbolize the nature and popularity of the game. Today, college football is a multimillion dollar business at the Division I level. Bowl games pay out millions of dollars and millions of football fans, from high schools to colleges, live and die with their favorite team every weekend.

The first football game between black colleges occurred in 1892 when Johnson C. Smith College and Livingston College played on Thanksgiving Day. From that time, a large part of the success of the game must be attributed to the black athletes and coaches who took the game to a higher level. Coach Eddie Robinson of Grambling College is among the best football coaches ever. He coached at Grambling for 56 years and was honored during the 1998 Super Bowl in San Diego. The football heroics of Walter Patton, Jerry Rice, O.J. Simpson, Doug Williams, Reggie White, Bruce Smith, and the legendary Jim Brown are recorded in the annals of sport history as among the few who truly stand apart from their peers as a measure of excellence.

Professional football was played as early as 1894 where the teams were drawn from the blue-collar workers and former college players. The mill towns of Ohio and Pennsylvania supplied most of these early pro football players. They would practice a few times during the week and play the game on weekends. Although professional football was slow to catch on with the general public and press, a few pro teams managed to remain financially solvent. If a player was able to sign a contract with one of the three teams, he could make between $400 to $1200 per season. That was a considerable amount of money during this era. The cities of Pittsburgh and Philadelphia were home to the most popular pro football teams. Connie Mack, who was one of the greatest players to ever play the game of baseball, was the manager of the Philadelphia Athletics football team. The first serious attempt to form a professional football league took place in 1920 at an automobile dealership in Canton, Ohio. It was at the Ralph Hays' Hupmobile dealership that eleven teams formed the American Professional Football Association (APFA). The APFA's first president was Jim Thorpe and the charter teams paid a franchise fee of $100. The APFA soon became financially troubled and a new president was named to replace Jim Thorpe. Joe F. Carr of Columbus, Ohio became the new president and changed the name of the league to the National Football League (NFL) and lowered the franchise fee to $50. Green Bay, Detroit, Buffalo, and Cincinnati were added to the new league. The Decatur team was sold to George E. Hallas, who moved the team to Chicago in 1922 and changed the name to the Chicago Bears.

After World War I, college football coaches did their best to discourage their players from turning pro after graduation. At that time, college football was far more popular than professional football and had the admiration and respect of the public, whereas the upstart NFL did not. Two people helped the NFL to gain public support. Tim Mara organized the New York Giants and was able to publicize the team in the New York press and radio. Radio play by play was introduced to Giant fans and the demand for tickets increased dramatically. Red Grange, the "Galloping Ghost" from the University of Illinois, signed with the Chicago Bears and thousands of fans packed the stadium to see him play. However, it was not until after World War II that the NFL began to enjoy great success. The American Football League (AFL) began to play in 1960 and eventually merged with the NFL in 1970. However, debate raged across America about who played better football, the NFL or the AFL. To resolve this highly emotional debate, the Super Bowl was invented.

The first Super Bowl was played in the Los Angeles Coliseum in 1966, where the Green Bay Packers of the NFL, coached by Vince Lombardi, soundly defeated the Kansas City Chiefs of the AFL, coached by Hank Stram. It would not be until Super Bowl III that the AFL would defeat the NFL and win the Super Bowl. During Super Bowl III, quarterback Joe Namath lead the New York Jets to an upset of the Baltimore Colts by a score of 16 to 7. Did you know that a ticket to Super Bowl I cost $9.33 while a ticket to Super Bowl XXXII in San Diego sold for $275!

The Growth of Women's Sports

The 1960s and 1970s were a period marked by social unrest and societal change. There was a clash of cultures, the old established culture was seen by the youth of America as perpetuating the status quo, which meant change would occur slowly, if at all. This was not good enough and America was embroiled in bitter disputes that ended in riots, demonstrations, and in some cases death. Out of chaos came a new order and nowhere was this new order more evident than the women's sports movement.

Title IX of the Educational Amendments of 1972 addressed equal opportunity for women in physical education, sports, and athletics. Title IX created co-ed physical education classes and enabled women athletes in high schools and colleges who received federal funding to receive the same level of funding, facilities, and coaching that the men's teams had enjoyed for decades. Over a short period of time, women's athletic competition achieved a level of athleticism and popularity that begged the question, "Why didn't we do this a long time ago?" The men's programs did not want to fund the women's programs and the National Collegiate Athletic Association (NCAA) filed suit to halt the implementation of Title IX. The NCAA lost the suite and women's athletic competition finally was able to join the twentieth century. It must be noted that, historically, women physical educators opposed intensive athletic competition for women in both the high schools and colleges. They did not want the intense commitment and pressure that went with the highly competitive men's and boys' programs. Such excessive commitment to athletic success was not healthy in the eyes of these women. Title IX was not especially welcomed by these physical educators who also doubled as coaches for the women's teams. The old philosophy encouraged friendship and fun during practice and during actual competition. It was common to finish the game and then socialize with the opposing team over punch and cookies. Passage of Title IX ushered in a new era that enabled serious athletic competition to emerge. Some stayed and coached while many others stepped aside to let the new breed of coaches take over the legacy that was started a century earlier when women's basketball employed six to nine players and divided the court into three zones so frail women didn't have to run very much and risk succumbing to fatigue. How times and thinking have changed!

Summary

An understanding of how people have viewed play, games, sport, and physical education in the past is helpful to our understanding of these aspects of our lives in the present. What we find is that our ideas have been shaped by those who came before us. Indeed, many of the ideas that we use when we play and move can be traced to specific cultures, and this understanding helps us know something of these cultures as well as of our own lives. Knowing what we do helps us understand the richness of these past cultures and helps us appreciate the richness of our own movement experiences.

Perhaps the most important lesson to be learned is that we can view our physical, moving existence from a variety of perspectives. Many cultures have done just this, and the ideas that we will examine in upcoming chapters are based on the philosophies that were lived in the past. In understanding our history, then, we may be better able to plan our future.

Discussion Questions

1. What are the basic methods used in historical research?
2. What was the purpose of sport and physical activity for the ancient Greeks? For the ancient Romans?
3. How was sport used in the Aztec Empire?
4. How has the philosophical position of the body in different cultures influenced the development of sport in those cultures?

References

Bower, W.P. (1922). Seven years of progress in preparing teachers of physical education. *American Physical Education Review, 27*, 64.

Cantor, N.F. (1968). *Western civilization: Its genesis and destiny.* Chicago: Scott, Foresman, and Co.

Henderson, R. W. (1947). *Ball, bat, and bishop* (pp. 182–194). New York: Rockport Press.

Howell, M.L. (1975). *The Ancient Olympic Games: A Reconstruction of the program.* The Seward Staley Address of The North American Society for the History of Sport. Boston, Massachusetts, April, pp. 7–8.

Howell, M., & Howell, R. (1976). *Physical activities of the Sumerians.* Paper presented to the Research Section of the Annual Meeting of the American Alliance for Health, Physical Education and Recreation, April 4, Milwaukee, Wisconsin.

Lucas, J.A. (1992) *Future of the Olympic Games.* Champaign, IL. Human Kinetics.

Mechikoff, R.A., & Estes, S. (1998). *A history and philosophy of sport and physical education: From ancient civilizations to the modern world* (2nd ed.) Madison, WI: WCB/McGraw-Hill.

Palmer, D. (1967). *Sport and games in the art of early civilization*. Unpublished masters thesis, University of Alberta.

Spears, B., & Swanson, R. *History of sport and physical education in the United States* (p. 186). Dubuque: Wm. C. Brown.

St. Thomas Aquinas. (1964). *Summa Theologiae (vols. 1–160)*. New York: McGraw-Hill.

Van Dalen, D.B., & Bennett, B.L. (1971). *A world history of physical education*. Englewood Cliffs, NJ: Prentice Hall.

Philosophy in Kinesiology

Socrates.

Chapter Objectives

Upon completing this chapter, the reader will be able to:

1. Understand the basic definitions used in the discipline of philosophy.
2. Apply basic philosophy terms to the field of kinesiology.
3. Define ontology, the study of the nature of being.
4. Understand the relationship of epistemology, the study of the nature of knowledge, to learning.
5. Be able to relate *being* to *learning*: The process of education means to change the nature of a person from some basic condition to one who is *learned*.

Definitions in Philosophy

Kinesiology, like any area of study, is helped significantly by using philosophy to organize the types of knowledge that are created through research. To understand this process of organization, one must understand some basic philosophical terms and concepts. Students may have "crossed paths" with philosophy in their first two years of university study in what many universities call "General Education." More and more often, however, students do not have to study philosophy at all in higher education. Consequently, we find it helpful to define the most basic of philosophical terms and concepts and then apply these definitions to the study of kinesiology.

A French Enlightenment philosopher, Auguste Comte (Mazlish, 1967), helped categorize some of the questions with which philosophy concerns itself. In a sense, philosophy is concerned with three different types of questions: What is *real*? What is *knowledge*? What is *value*? In turn, these areas can be further divided into more specific areas. The list below defines these areas and describes their relationships:

> **Metaphysics:** The study of the nature of reality
> > **Ontology:** The study of the nature of being
> > **Cosmology:** The study of the nature of the material universe
> > **Theology:** The study of the nature of God
> **Epistemology:** The study of the nature of knowledge
> **Axiology:** The study of the nature of values
> > **Aesthetics:** The study of the nature of beauty
> > **Politics:** The study of the nature of the common good
> > **Ethics:** The study of the nature of right and wrong

Each philosophy that we discuss has specific metaphysical, epistemological, and axiological positions. And each of these positions is logically related to one another. The purpose of our providing information is twofold: (1) to familiarize you with terms and definitions that make possible the discussion of the distinctions of different philosophies; and (2) to show how the metaphysical, epistemological, and axiological positions of a given philosophy provide information about the type of knowledge in a given subdiscipline. In the opinion of your authors, that Americans are not familiar with the different areas of philosophy is a measure of the quality of education, because a good answer to philosophical questions—and, more importantly, an understanding of why they are important—makes possible an entirely different way of understanding how humans live in the world.

Metaphysics: The Study of the Nature of Reality

Why should a student of kinesiology be concerned with the question, What is real? Indeed, why should anyone be concerned with this question? Most Americans never worry about whether an idea is real, whether matter is real, or whether mind is real. Yet even though you may have not asked the explicit question, What is real?, you *do* operate on certain assumptions regarding the nature of reality. And these assumptions have profound implications for the student of kinesiology.

Certain assumptions about the nature of reality organize what we value in the world. For instance, if one believes that "ideas" are real, then one will operate differently in the world. Education in Western culture is very concerned with ideas. Indeed, have you ever noticed how many courses one takes that emphasize ideas? English, mathematics, history, language, social studies—all of these areas of study in your educational career have been concerned primarily with *ideas*. Yet have you ever *seen* an "idea?" Can you weigh an idea? Of course not! Then how do you know that they *really* exist (using the word "really" this way literally redefines it for many students)?

Once one acknowledges that ideas exist, one can compare the nature of an idea to the nature of matter. Does matter really exist? This question seems truly silly to most Americans. Of course matter exists! Yet, is matter fundamentally different than an idea? Again, most students will answer, yes. Matter can be weighed, can be observed, and can be contrasted with ideas as its opposite.

An interesting question can now be asked: Which is more important to you, matter or ideas? Asking this question forces one to make a value judgment. Why, you might ask, must one answer such a question? Let us point out that often this question has been answered for you by the courses that you must study. Referring to the list of subjects that many students take in high school—English, mathematics, history, language, social studies—are these subjects important? More important than other areas of study, such as physical education? Why is it that you had one physical education course per day, and five courses that emphasized ideas? Why did you not take courses that emphasize different types of material reality: physical education, wood shop, metal shop, and dance? Might the answer, or part of the answer, be that your teachers operate on certain metaphysical assumptions about what is real and, therefore, what is more important? Indeed, does it not make sense to have your educational experience conform to basic, agreed-upon assumptions about what is real?

It is our argument that, in fact, the Western educational system has emphasized ideas at the expense of material reality. However, this *exaggerated* claim of ours needs to be put in perspective. Not all of education is solely concerned with ideas. For instance, your science courses like chemistry, biology, and physics all investigate the material world. However, it is our contention that even these areas are studied in terms of the ideas that they provide us, and how these ideas relate to one another. It is the *ideas* of these courses that are important in the Western, modern world.

We make this argument only to show that metaphysical assumptions exist in the modern world, that all of us have them, and that making them explicit allows us to understand why we think and live the way that we do. In addition, these assumptions help us value our educational experiences in such a way that certain courses are more important than others. Physical education programs and courses are eliminated before mathematics courses *because* mathematics is considered more "important" to many people in the modern world. In terms of education, the "ideas" presented in mathematics are more "real." And it is considered more important because of our metaphysical assumptions in the modern world that ideas are "real."

Ontology: The Study of the Nature of Being

An important subcategory in metaphysics is ontology, the study of the nature of being. What is meant by the "nature of being" is the makeup of human existence. Are human beings creatures with a soul? Do we have a mind? A surprising question: Do we really have a body, or is our body an aspect of perception? Is mind really separate from body? Each of these questions represents a specific ontological position, and the answer provides one with a different perspective on what education should be.

If, for instance, we are bodily creatures with a mind, should we educate mind first? Or the body? Or should we be balanced? Or, as most contemporary sport philosophers argue, are the notions of mind and body outdated ideas: Human existence is composed of an integrated composite of mind and body. Depending on one's ontological position, one usually will be emphasized over the other. And in the Western world, with philosophical roots going back to Plato, we are first and foremost "mind" and "soul" and only secondarily "body." The consequence for kinesiology is that it is often viewed with some suspicion because of its close and obvious connection with the body. Regardless of the outcome of this debate, however, one's ontological position often determines the status of any field that deals with bodily existence.

Cosmology and Theology: The Study of the Nature of the Universe and of Religion

Cosmology is the study of the nature of the universe. Different explanations of the origins of the universe can be found in all major religious works and mythologies, as well as scientific explanations like the "Big Bang Theory." These theories have in common the idea that the material universe is real, and as such all material objects are real. The human body would, of course, fall into this category. It is worth noting at this point that one's metaphysical position and one's cosmological position must be consistent: One cannot hold that the material world is not "real" and that the Big Bang Theory of the origin of the material universe *is* "real."

At first glance it would appear that religion does not have much to do with the study of sport. But as Michael Novak (1976) argued, sport is a much more religious experience than it would appear. The clothes the participants wear (referees and athletes, fans wearing the school colors), the way players and fans mark time while engaged in play and sport (the clock, the possibility of a baseball game lasting forever in extra innings, the loss of a sense of time when one plays), the special foods we eat and drink (tailgate parties!), and the way we worship our hero-athletes are very similar to what happens in organized religion.

Sport can be also understood from the perspective of mythology, an area of study often associated with religion (Estes, 1990). In short, a myth is a story that is told and believed to be true by both the teller and the listener. The myth comes packed with emotion and is usually supported by some concrete experience that makes it more believable. Surprisingly, a myth is not necessarily false: "Truth" does not merely rest on concrete and observable data. "Truth" exists instead in the mind of the believer. It is this last characteristic that connects mythology with religion. More will be said about myth in the chapter on narratives.

Epistemology: The Study of the Nature of Knowledge

What do you know about sport, and how did you come to know this "truth"? Epistemology is the area of study in philosophy that seeks to answer this question. As we noted above when discussing ontology, one's epistemological position and one's metaphysical position must be consistent. For instance, if one believes that "mind" does not exist (as some behavioral psychologists argue), it is not logical to pursue knowledge through the development of critical thinking skills. There is no mind with which to think! Instead, in this example, it makes much more sense to acquire knowledge through the senses—through observation, listening, and so on. In fact, this is just what behavioral psychologists do: They change the environment in a manner that will cause the subject to behave in certain desirable ways.

Every philosophy defines its own epistemology, its own "way of knowing" what is true and what is real. Yet, if one follows the logic of this argument, then one is left with the impression that all of these philosophies are "equally" correct. Put differently, one way of deriving "truth" is just as correct as another way of deriving "truth." The "truth" is *relative* to the philosophy in question, to the context of the situation, or to the perspective of the person who is asking the question. Known as *philosophical relativism*, the idea that truth changes depending on the rules one uses is a very troubling one to many people. Can all philosophies be equally correct, yet disagree with one another at the same time? Such a philosophy can leave one with a "might makes right" philosophy, where one can say "I think I am right, therefore I will do what I want."

This question has troubled philosophers since there have been philosophers. Who is to say which philosophy is the "truth" and which is not the "truth?" There is no answer to this question, for if there were we would not be studying more than one philosophy. We would be studying the only "true" philosophy. That there are a number of philosophies to be studied is an indication that no one philosophy has won the "truth" war.

Still, one philosophy *may* be the correct one. The idea that there is one *true* philosophy is known as *absolutism*. Put differently, absolutism argues that the idea that a philosophy is *absolutely* correct, under all conditions, and is beyond question. Several religions take this perspective, most notably the Roman Catholic faith. The Pope makes a statement of "truth," say on abortion, and all followers of the Roman Catholic religion are obliged to follow the edict of the Pope and the dogmas of the Church. The Pope's statements are *categorically* correct: They are true without condition. More will be said about *categorical* or *absolute* truth when we discuss authority in Chapter 8. This textbook, though, does not necessarily endorse any one position. Which philosophy that you will choose, or that philosophers and theologians will choose, will be the subject of debate among philosophers, theologians, and learned people for some time to come.

Like metaphysics, the epistemology one chooses has certain characteristics, and some of these characteristics fit very nicely with kinesiology. For instance, those epistemologies that emphasize the functions of the body such as seeing, feeling, hearing, tasting, and smelling would seem to be very friendly toward kinesiology. The senses are "bodily," and using the senses of the body to know reality is called empiricism.

Using the senses of the human body is not the only way of knowing used in kinesiology, however. There are six that we use in this textbook: *authority, rationalism, empiricism, pragmatism, somatics,* and *narrativism.* All epistemologies provide their unique perspective on how we come to know human movement. What is important to us in this textbook is that you appreciate the differences between various epistemologies and use one that is most appropriate for your needs.

One way of appreciating what epistemology can tell us is to examine a tool used frequently in education to determine academic merit: the Scholastic Aptitude Test (SAT). Many have come to criticize the SAT in recent years, arguing that the test is elitist, narrow, and culturally biased. Perhaps a more insightful method of criticizing the SAT is that it utilizes only one epistemology for constructing knowledge: rationalism. Two ways of knowing commonly used in kinesiology are not evident at all in the SAT: One does not move during an SAT test, nor are the powers of observation (empiricism) tested. We have one question for you here: As a potential professional kinesiologist, are other types of knowledge also essential to your career? If you think that the answer to this question is yes, then you, too, are a critic of this tool. We also note, however, that the SAT *does* test other types of knowledge used in kinesiology. We criticize the test only in that, given what the average kinesiology student needs to know, the SAT is too narrow.

Axiology: The Study of the Nature of Value

What do you value, and why? The answer to this question is found in the area of axiology. Divided into the areas of politics, aesthetics, and ethics, axiology is like metaphysics and epistemology: One's axiological position must be consistent with one's metaphysics and one's epistemology. All three of these areas are evident in kinesiology.

Politics is defined as the study of the nature of the common good. Examples of politics in sports range from the boycott by the United States in the 1980 Olympics, the relationship of players and owners in professional sports leagues, and the exemption of Major League Baseball from federal antitrust laws. All of these examples deal with what is best for all of us as fans, players, or owners in the sport world. Should the United States have boycotted the Olympics? Do you believe that the greed demonstrated by players and owners is wrecking professional sport? Should baseball be treated like a business, or is it something special because it is a game? The answers to these questions fall into the realm of politics.

Aesthetics is the study of the nature of beauty. One does not need to go too far to find examples of sport as beauty in the modern world. Slow-motion videos of athletes performing; the athlete as performing artist; and the scoring of athletes in sports like gymnastics, diving, and figure skating are all examples of sport being viewed aesthetically.

Ethics is the study of right and wrong. Again, examples abound in contemporary sport: Should athletes use steroids? When a professional athlete goes on strike, is it the "right" thing to do? Should very young children begin training for elite athletic performance? How one determines what is right and wrong is determined by one's ethical position.

Summary

While all of the areas of sport philosophy are important, this textbook will emphasize epistemology. As we noted above, however, metaphysics, epistemology, and axiology must be consistent and logical. In other words, to understand a particular philosophy's epistemology, one must understand what that philosophy argues is "real," and consequently one will understand what that philosophy argues is "value." We will then point out all three characteristics of a given philosophy as we examine how we come to know the various subdisciplines in the field.

Discussion Questions

1. What are the basic definitions used in the discipline of philosophy?
2. How is ontology, defined as the study of the nature of being, relevant to the field of kinesiology?
3. What is the relationship of epistemology, defined as the study of the nature of knowledge, to learning?
4. What is the relationship of *being* to *learning*? How can kinesiology be understood with respect to this relationship?

References

Charles, J. (1992). Kinesiology in the liberal arts. *Quest*, *44*(1), 122–126.

Estes, S. (1990). *Sport myth as lived experience*. Unpublished doctoral dissertation, The Ohio State University.

Mazlish, B. (1967). August Comte. *The encyclopedia of philosophy* (pp. 173–177). New York: Macmillan/ The Free Press.

Novak, M. (1976). *The joy of sports*. New York: Basic Books.

Singer, R., Lamb, D., Loy, J., Malina, R., & Kleinman, S. (1972). *Physical education: An interdisciplinary approach*. New York: Macmillan.

Chapter *8*

Knowing through Authority

Chapter Objectives

Upon completing this chapter, the reader will be able to:

1. Define authority in historical, philosophical, and contemporary contexts.
2. Understand the basis for the use of authority in teaching, coaching, and other learning situations.
3. Understand how authority can be abused.
4. Relate authority to being, specifically the idea of *character*.
5. Relate authority to specific teaching and learning situations in kinesiology.

In education the relationship of those in "the know," or teachers, and those who want to "know," the students, is of critical importance. The teacher has knowledge and dispenses it to students in the way he or she feels best. While one can argue that there are many philosophies of education, from the students' perspective there is only one truth to know, and the teacher has it! You, the student, have to learn it. Similarly, athletes and dancers are obligated to respond to their coach or the choreographer. The teacher/coach is in absolute control of all of the ideas that are discussed. Think about it. Can a student "really" challenge what a teacher knows? Can an athlete "really" challenge the authority of the coach?

Sometimes these situations do occur, but in the vast majority of occasions where students and athletes interact with those who guide them, teachers and coaches have absolute authority when it comes to what they know. Indeed, coaches and teachers have authority for two reasons: first, because they have the "knowledge" that students or athletes value. Coaches and teachers are usually knowledgeable about their sport or their subject. Second, coaches and teachers have authority because they have the power to make decisions and student/athletes do not. Therefore, teachers and coaches are granted a corresponding amount of political power over their students in order to promote the learning process. If teachers have all of the knowledge, then they have absolute authority in a political sense.

It has been argued that a relationship between students and teachers or between athletes and coaches that is based solely on the epistemological method of authority is not a healthy one (Brown, 1985; Ravizza & Daruty, 1985). These scholars argue that often there is no check on whether the teacher or coach does, indeed, have access to knowledge. Yet the politics of the student/coach or the student/teacher relationship remains the same as it has been for decades in the United States. In short, students, teachers, athletes, and coaches continue to operate using the epistemological method of authority, a style of learning where it is believed that only the teachers and coaches have the knowledge, and learning occurs when students and athletes accept what their teachers or coaches tell them.

Authority: "I Know What I Am Told"

The use of authority in kinesiology is obvious when described, yet it is often taken for granted: All students at one time or another have been on the receiving end of the authority relationship. If you think about it, we, the authors, have used this method in this textbook up to this point and will continue to do so throughout this chapter. Students are used to receiving instructions from teachers. Athletes feel comfortable when their coaches direct them through their practices and competitions. Lecture is the common method of the professoriate. In fact, to *profess* is to practice the method of authority.

The epistemological method of authority explains why "teachers tend to teach in the same manner as they were taught," an observation Karl Newell (1990) made when he criticized the failure of professional teachers to use knowledge and information generated through other ways of knowing human movement, like the scientific method. Newell argued that most teachers use the methods that were used on them when they were students.

The problem with this approach is that there is little change in teaching and learning techniques over time, even though research and experimentation have revealed that there are now much better ways of getting students to learn and athletes to perform. Interestingly, even professors of kinesiology have a difficult time changing their approach to teaching and learning. When one examines how the type information that this textbook covers has been delivered historically to college physical education students, one can see that the approaches used have not changed *in almost 60 years*.[1] This does not mean, however, that the method of authority has no value. Rather, students should realize that the method of authority is one of many teaching and learning styles (such as the scientific method or collaborative learning techniques) and that it has its good points and bad points just like any other teaching and learning style.

Philosophical Basis of Authority as a Way of Knowing—Plato's Truth

The method of authority is derived from the idea that there is one truth and that this truth does not change depending on who knows it. Put in a common and more humorous way, authority argues that it is, "My way or the highway," meaning that the one in authority determines the truth and all others can leave. Philosophically based on absolutist philosophies, of which Plato's *Phaedo* and *The Republic* are good examples, truth is the same for all concerned—instructor and student. It is the mission of the instructor (who *knows* the truth) to impart truth to the students. Knowing the truth makes one an authority.

The method of authority begins with one simple idea: that "truth" is real. In fact, it is the most "real" thing there is! Yet truth, if one considers the word, is nothing more than an idea. There are aspects of "reality" other than idea, some being more real, some being less real. For our purposes, we will divide all of reality into two distinct parts with which you are already very familiar: matter and ideas. Both are "real," and both are absolutely different from each other. Can you think of an idea that is really "matter," or something that is "material" that is literally held as a thought in your mind? Probably not—philosophers have pondered these questions for centuries.

The philosophical position that matter and ideas are the distinct components of reality is known as *metaphysical dualism*, and the corresponding position that humans are composed of both spirit and body is known as *ontological dualism*. This approach to the nature of reality (metaphysics) and of being (ontology) was perhaps first described in western philosophy by Plato in the *Phaedo*.[2] Plato's arguments influenced decisively the purpose and status of physical education, both in Plato's time as well as in our own.

Both Socrates' and Plato's metaphysical positions divide all aspects of reality into two parts, and of these two parts Socrates and Plato argued that "ideas" are more "real" than "matter." If you have never studied philosophy, this may be the first time you have ever heard of such an argument. Indeed, how can "ideas" be more "real" than something you can see and touch? This argument has a certain logic to it, and it bears repeating here.

Plato argued (we have nothing of Socrates' writings, so we will refer to all of these ideas as Plato's) that ideas are "perfect" in that they never decay, that they last forever, and that they convey a type of knowledge that is pure and perfect. Plato also argued that the material world is "imperfect" in that all matter decays, changes, and does not convey anything that is "perfect." Mountains decay, atoms decay, stars collapse, and, eventually, even the universe will change radically from its present state. Yet, according to Plato, the "idea" of perfect good will never change, whether or not there is a material universe to house it.

Plato's argument is described in the "Simile of the Sun," which argues that the material world we can see is "less real" than the ideal world, which we cannot see (see Table 8-1). However, while we cannot see the ideal world, we can infer (or "figure out") its existence, and in this ideal world dwells what Plato refers to as the "Form of the Good." The Form of the Good is the *essence* of reality, the perfect blueprint for all that exists in the material world. The Simile of the Sun compares the Form of the Good (an idea) to the sun (matter), which can be seen and is part of the material world. The Form of the Good is of a higher order of reality than the sun, and this relationship is set out in Table 8-1.

Plato's "Simile of the Sun" provides an explanation of the distinction between the material (visible) world and the ideal world, which can only be understood through the power of the mind.

Knowledge of the Form of the Good can be had only through philosophical means, meaning that it has to be "inferred" or "figured out." The Form of the Good is the essence of reality and truth, and as the "essence" it is of a higher order of "reality." Plato argued that "the good" gives intelligibility to objects of thought, and that intelligibility is a product of the mind. Therefore, anything that had to do with knowledge of the good, the most perfect and essential part of reality, is of a higher order of reality than anything of the material world. Also, the mind, which understands intelligibility, is superior to the body.

Another way of describing the relationship between the two orders of reality is provided by Plato's analogy of the "Divided Line." This analogy describes reality from a different perspective than the Simile of the Sun, one that leads us into a discussion of ontology, or the nature of being. The Divided Line describes the perspective of an individual trying to know reality. What can an individual know of reality? The analogy is set out in the Table 8-2, where "Mental States, "Reality," and "Being" are understood on the continuum of line ABCD. The content of the line AB is intellectual in nature, and of the ideal world, whereas the content of the line CD is sensory in nature, and of the physical world. The ideal world, known through intellectual operations, is "superior" to the physical or material world, which is "inferior" and known through the senses.

Line ABCD is the first column. The next column categorizes the type of knowledge and its value and argues that intelligence is a higher order of knowledge than illusion. In the third column, ideas are the "most" real, and illusions are the "least" real. Finally, the

TABLE 8-1   Plato's Simile of the Sun

Visible World	Intelligible World
The Sun	The Good ("form of the good")
Source of growth and light	Source of reality and truth
that gives	that gives
Visibility to objects of sense	Intelligibility to objects of thought
and	and
the power of seeing to	the power of knowing to
the eye.	the mind.
The faculty of sight.	The faculty of knowledge.

From Plato, 1987, *The Republic* (p. 300), Desmond Lee (Trans.). London: Penguin Books.

TABLE 8-2   **Plato's Analogy of the Divided Line**

Line	Mental States	Reality (Metaphysics)	Being (Ontology)
A	Intelligence		Character
		Ideas	Mind
	Knowledge	Forms	
	Mathematical		
B	reasoning		
C	Belief	Matter	Body
	Opinion		
D	Illusion	Shadows	
		and	
		images	

Adapted from Plato's *The Republic,* 1987, Desmond Lee (Trans.). London: Penguin Books, p. 310.

mind, which has knowledge of ideas, is superior to the body. This is because the body has only the senses. A human being, obviously in the observable world, is "body." But a person, according to this understanding is also mind, and the mind is more "real" than the body. This division ends when the soul departs the body upon death, whereupon it exists in the "world of forms." Throughout Plato's writings (*Phaedo, Republic,* Books II & III) the practice of philosophy, which Plato and Socrates regarded as primarily intellectual, is always elevated over the training of the body.

While Plato argued that we are composed of both mind and body, he was actually concerned with what he called a person's "character." *Character* is the *most* "real" aspect of a person and is that part of a person that is eternal and perfect.[3] A way to think of one's character is to describe it in religious terms as the *soul.* Plato was not religious in the way that we understand religion today. Rather, he argued for the existence of something like a soul—*character*—in philosophical terms.

Plato went to great lengths discussing how one could develop character and did so in the *Republic.* It is here that Plato articulates how physical education is justifiable: Physical education, as well as intellectual education, exists to develop knowledge of one's character. Keep this idea in mind, because it explains to a great extent why physical education is eliminated or marginalized in modern education: *Physical education was good only insofar as it helped one come to know the eternal spiritual aspects of existence—in a word, one's "character."*

Plato's View of Physical Education

Although the *Phaedo* describes a philosophical position that *appears* to devalue the body, or at least value it less than the mind, do not be deceived. The body does have a place in education, and we find that in fact the body has a *central* place in education. We wish to emphasize this point: Plato understood the body. In fact, he was an accomplished athlete.

Plato won wreaths at the Isthmian Games as a wrestler, and his name, "Plato," was given to him by his wrestling coach! Plato trained hard for competition, indicating that he must have valued the body in some manner.

Yet Plato also argued that the body was a "source of endless trouble" that stands in the way of one coming to know the truth. How can we reconcile these seemingly contradictory positions? The answer can be found in how Plato wanted to *use* the body to train the character, or the soul. Plato argued in Books II and III of *The Republic* that the body is *essential* to knowing one's "character," or one's soul here on earth. Why is this so?

Plato argues in the following passage that there must be *balance* and *harmony* of the minds and bodies of the educated citizen:

> Come then, and let us pass a leisure hour in story-telling, and our story shall be the education of our heroes.
>   And what shall be their education? Can we find a better than the traditional sort?—and this has two divisions, gymnastic for the body, and music for the soul.[4]

In *The Republic*, Plato attempted to construct the first utopia or perfect society in literature. The education of citizens in his utopia was of critical importance to Plato, and gymnastics (physical education) and music (intellectual education) were the two components of the curriculum. Of interest to physical educators is that these components reinforce and perpetuate the dualistic approach to education that continues to remain in place today. One component educates the mind (music), while another component (gymnastics) educates the body.

According to Plato, the purpose of educating both of these parts is *to develop character*. This argument is important to physical education, for the logic Plato used to incorporate physical education into his curriculum makes the body, and its education, important to the community. Although the body will never be equal to the mind or soul, the body is now in a position of importance even though it continues to be "less real" than the mind. In the Plato's *The Republic*, Book III, Plato writes of a conversation in which Socrates states:

> Gymnastic as well as music should begin in early years; the training in it should be careful and should continue through life. Now my belief is . . . not that the good body by any bodily excellence improves the soul, but, on the contrary, that the good soul, by her own excellence, improves the body as far as this may be possible.
>   Then, to the mind when adequately trained, we shall be right in handing over the more particular care of the body.[5]

"Music" is the term the Greeks used to encompass traditional academic subjects. Plato was concerned that the citizens of his utopia, especially its leaders (the philosopher-kings) and the warrior-athletes, receive a well-rounded education. Just as importantly, Plato discussed the problem of excess devotion to either music or gymnastics, which can be seen in the following conversation between Socrates and Glaucon from *The Republic*. Socrates stated:

> Did you never observe, I said, the effect on the mind itself of exclusive devotion to gymnastic, or the opposite effect of an exclusive devotion to music?

In what way shown? he said.

The one producing a temper of hardness and ferocity, the other of softness and effeminacy, I replied.

Yes, he said, I am quite aware that the mere athlete becomes too much of a savage, and that the mere musician is melted and softened beyond what is good for him. . . .

And so in gymnastic, if a man takes violent exercise and is a great feeder, and the reverse of a great student of philosophy, at first the high condition of his body fills him with pride and spirit, and he becomes twice the man that he was.

Certainly.

And what happens? If he does nothing else, and holds no converse with the Muses, does not even that intelligence which there may be in him, having no taste of any sort of learning or enquiry or thought or culture, grow feeble and dull and blind, his mind never waking up or receiving nourishment . . . ?

And he ends by becoming a hater of philosophy, uncivilized, never using the weapon of persuasion—he is like a wild beast, all violence and fierceness, and knows no other way of dealing; and he lives in all ignorance and evil conditions, and has no sense of propriety and grace. . . . And he who mingles music with gymnastic in the fairest of proportions, and best attempers them to the soul, may be rightly called the true musician and harmonist in a far higher sense. . . .

You are quite right, Socrates.

And such a presiding genius will be always required in our State if the government is to last.[6]

In summary, Plato provides us with an argument that justifies physical education, and even demands it in education. Without physical education there can be no development of one's character. It is physical education that teaches certain important virtues, such as honesty, courage, discipline, and friendship. While music, or intellectual education, is critically important, so is physical education. Without both the person is not well rounded.

We have spoken at length about how Plato felt about physical education: He was for it. How did Plato feel, though, about athletics? Athletics was, according to Plato, only concerned with the body. Winning, appearance, trophies, and money are all "bodily" in that these rewards are material in nature. Physical education, by contrast, helped develop character. Therefore, physical education is good, and athletics is not.

This argument is probably surprising to most of you, but it has a certain logic to it. Even in Plato's day, the excessive devotion to athletics led to one being less than well rounded. There are stories of the legendary athlete Milo of Croton, who won four consecutive Olympiads in wrestling and who could outwrestle, outeat, and outdrink any man alive. One story has Milo killing a bull with his bare hands and eating the whole bull in the same day! Plato would not have appreciated Milo's exploits; he would have found them excessive, and would have judged Milo to be "savage" to the extent that he overemphasized the body.[7]

Many of you may have heard of the phrase, "Sport builds character." How would Plato have felt about this statement? To the extent that sport helps modern athletes develop virtues such as discipline, a work ethic, perseverance, and other modern virtues Plato would have been pleased. He would have understood how the body can be used in sport to develop one's character.

At the same time, Plato would have nodded his head knowingly at the excesses of contemporary sport. Just pick up your daily newspaper and read of the excesses of our modern athletes: drug use, shootings, robbery, rape, and other crimes committed by athletes undermine the idea that sport builds character. Male athletes are *six* times more likely to commit crimes on college campuses than are their nonathlete counterparts. Plato would have argued that an excessive emphasis on athletics is the reason for these crimes: The athletes have focused too much on their bodies and not enough on the development of their character. What do you think of Plato's explanation?

Authority in Action

While there is only one truth—at least according to Plato's philosophy (we will discuss five more, so don't be upset if you don't like Plato's philosophy)—there are two types of authority: epistemic authority and moral authority (Adams, 1976). Kinesiology uses both. Epistemic authority refers to knowledge claims made by authorities to those who are less knowledgeable like students and athletes. As Adams (1976) noted,

> To be an authority on a subject is to be in a position to know about it, or in a somewhat stronger sense, to be one whose *business* it is to know about such things, and to have credentials such that others less privileged in relevant ways are justified in accepting this views on the subject, indeed, ought to accept his views, even if they are contrary to their own. (p. 4)

In kinesiology, this argument would mean that teaching credentials, provided through teacher certification programs, are a license that "prove" that what the authority says is "true." Indeed, one must accept what a credentialed authority says even if you do not agree with it. Earning the credential is proof that one has knowledge.

This statement describes what happens in almost every physical education setting or classroom on any given day. Teachers speak, students listen, and knowledge is acquired (hopefully) by the students. In a university, professors *profess*, students take notes, and knowledge is passed from the authority to the student. Similarly, coaches speak, and athletes accept and perform what they say.

The other type of authority, or moral authority, has to do with the area of decision and action. For example, a police officer has moral authority in that the officer has the authority to decide when a law has been broken, and also has the authority to do something about it. The officer's authority is felt by those who are breaking the law. Moral authority means that you have to *do* what an authority says, whereas epistemic authority deals only with knowledge.

Moral authority, then, is especially relevant in the profession of physical education. Often moral authority is based on epistemic authority, where one is given license to *act* because of one's knowledge in a given area. In kinesiology, moral authority is associated with an office or position, such as a teacher or coach, in whom is invested certain responsibilities and rights, and who makes decisions for others. Those others are obligated to comply with the authority, and often there is some agency whose function it is to enforce compliance. For instance, when a coach makes a decision to cut one player from a team to play one athlete instead of another, then that coach's decision is based on moral authority. Adams noted that one who has moral authority has "the responsibility or the right to decide or to act in such a way that commits others or obligates others to commit themselves accordingly" (Adams, 1976, p. 6).

Ideally, the relationship between those in authority and those who must submit to authority is a good one. However, authority can be abused, and the field of kinesiology provides especially vivid scenarios in which students or athletes are subject to the arbitrary use of authority on the part of teachers and coaches. The teacher or coach has authority because students and athletes *allow* their teachers and coaches to tell them what to do. What many students and athletes do not realize is that the relationship between students and teachers, and between athletes and coaches, is a political one. Scholars in kinesiology have debated the merits of the method of authority and have found that students and athletes should be aware of their rights and responsibilities as students and athletes, and that they should speak up when teachers and coaches abuse their authority (Ravizza & Daruty, 1984).

For a variety of reasons, both good and bad, the method of authority is the dominant mode of expressing knowledge in all areas of kinesiology, from elementary physical education programs to graduate departments of kinesiology in colleges and universities (Randall, Buell, Swerkes, & Bailey, 1993). Discussions of teaching and learning begin with the lecture format, where the professor is presumed to be the authority. Scholars in teaching and learning in higher education implicitly recognize that the *norm* is authority and look for new ways that facilitate the acquisition of knowledge by the student such as collaborative learning techniques. From a philosophical perspective, Thomas and Nelson (1990) criticize this method:

> Although (the method of authority) is not necessarily invalid, it does depend on the authority and on the rigidity of adherence. However, the appeal to authority has been carried to absurd lengths. . . . Perhaps the most crucial aspect of the appeal to authority as a means of obtaining knowledge is the right to question and to accept or reject the information. Furthermore, the qualifications of the authority and the methods by which the authority acquired the knowledge also determine the validity of this source of information. (p. 12)

While some scholars have addressed the method of authority from critical and philosophical perspectives, other scholars have discussed how students utilize this method. Perry (1970), in his discussion of how Harvard undergraduates' learning styles evolved through their college experience, noted that first-year students relied much more heavily on the method of authority than their upperclass counterparts. First-year students expected instructors to provide information and answers to questions.

In sum, the learning styles of kinesiology undergraduates are limited to the method of authority more than many instructors realize (Randall et al., 1993). When professors rely on their authority without understanding its limitations, or when students live by the motto "Just tell me what I need to know to pass the test," the limitations of the epistemology of authority are evident.

As kinesiologists, however, we should not eliminate our use of authority. Rather, it is important to understand the method of authority and recognize it for what it is. The obvious exemplars of this method—Vince Lombardi, coach of the Green Bay Packers of the 1960s; Jimmy Johnson, head coach of the Miami Dolphins of the National Football League; and Bobby Knight, coach of the University of Indiana men's basketball team—serve as powerful, successful models of authority. The success of their athletic programs implies that their teaching methods are not only acceptable, but desirable; the ends justify the means. To fail to recognize this method, its good and bad points, and put it in perspective is to risk the loss of credibility in the eyes of students for whom this method had been either successful or the only method of learning they have seen. Even these models of authority, however, have been criticized for their abuse of this method (Feinstein, 1986; Kramar, 1986). Students should be aware both of the advantages (past successes, ease of use, concerned with traditions) and limitations (failure to change, sometimes abuses students, etc.) of this method.

The use of authority as a method of knowing permeates all of the subdisciplines of kinesiology, primarily because at one time or another all students are passive recipients of the knowledge claims of their instructors. Undergraduates headed into the field of pedagogy should be especially aware of how they might use this method to their best advantage, and should understand the epistemological and moral bases from which this method derives its justification. It is an easy concept to grasp and a good point from which to begin a discussion of teaching and learning. From the method of authority one can compare and contrast alternative styles of learning that are better suited to the objectives of the instructor, or more importantly, the student.

Using Authority to Describe the Subdisciplines of Kinesiology

One advantage of the method of authority is that it can be used to clearly describe objects, events, or types of knowledge about which students are learning for the first time. Indeed, up to this point, and through the rest of this chapter, this method is used exclusively. Baldly put, we, as writers of this textbook, have epistemic authority—we are *telling you* about the various of areas of the field of kinesiology. Your trust is based on our ability to impress you with our knowledge. Your instructor may (or may not) hold you responsible for this material. His or her authority, in this example, is "moral authority": Your instructor has the *power* to grade you on how well you know information.

Summary

This chapter has focused on the type of knowing called "authority." Most scholars in the field of kinesiology have relied on this method to introduce students to the field. Instructors have told you what they want you to know, and it is up to you to accept or reject this information based on their authority. While instructors may have authority by position (moral authority), we hope that we have impressed you with what we know as well (epistemic authority). The basis for authority rests in Plato's philosophy—his definition of what is "real" and how we come to know reality. To help you come to know Plato's philosophy and how it would have an impact on how you study kinesiology, we have provided the following exercises in the form of discussion questions.

Discussion Questions

Construct the ideal program of study for a college physical education program using the epistemology of rationalism. Do this in groups of three or four. Everything you have learned in this chapter should be applied. Answer the following questions using only Plato's philosophy—do not use the information that you think you "know."

To facilitate this exercise, you will need some information. Get your university's or your department's advisement manual that describes the courses you must take to complete your kinesiology degree program.

This course summary checklist should include all courses that are required for graduation at your university. This includes your general education program, which often includes your liberal arts requirements, all of your physical education coursework, and any other coursework you may need to take to graduate. Use this checklist and Plato's philosophy to answer the following questions.

1. What is the metaphysical position of Plato?
2. What is the epistemological position of Plato?
3. What would Plato's ideal curriculum (program of coursework) look like?
4. What would be the most important course in the curriculum?
5. What courses would be specific to the physical education part of the curriculum?
6. How would Plato feel about athletics? about intramurals?
7. How would Plato's program compare with the program that is currently in place at your school?

References

Adams, E.M. (1976). The philosophical grounds of the present crisis of authority. In R.B. Harris (Ed.), *Authority: A philosophical analysis* (pp. 3–24). University of Alabama Press.

Adelman, M. (1986). *A sporting time: New York City and the rise of modern athletics, 1820–1870.* Champaign: University of Illinois Press.

Bain, L. (1997). In J. Massengale & R. Swanson (Eds.), Sport pedagogy. *The history of exercise and sport science.* Champaign: Human Kinetics.

Barham, J. (1966, October). Kinesiology: Toward a science and discipline of human movement. *Journal of Health, Physical Education, and Recreation,* 65–68.

Betts, J. (1974). *America's sporting heritage: 1850–1950.* Reading, MA: Addison-Wesley.

Brown, C. (1967). The structure of knowledge of physical education. *Quest, 9* (Winter), 53–67.

Brownell, C., & Hagman, E.P., (1951). *Physical education—foundations and principles*. New York: McGraw-Hill.

Charles, J. (1994). *Contemporary kinesiology*. Englewood, CO: Morton.

Feinstein, J. (1986). *Season on the brink: A year with Bob Knight and the Indiana Hoosiers*. New York: Macmillan.

Gerber, E. (1971). The ideas and influence of McCloy, Nash, and Williams. *Proceedings of the Big 10 Symposium on the History of Physical Education and Sport*. Chicago: The Athletics Institute.

Guttmann, A. (1978). *From ritual to record: The nature of modern sports*. New York: Columbia University Press.

Huizinga, J. (1955). *Homo ludens: A study of the play element in culture*. Boston, MA: Beacon Press.

Jewett, A., Bain, L., & Ennis, C. (1995). *The curriculum process in physical education*. Madison, WI: WCB Brown & Benchmark Publishers.

Kenyon, G., & Loy, J. (1965). Toward a sociology of sport. *Journal of Health, Physical Education, and Recreation. 36*(5), 24–25, 68–69.

Kramer, J. (1968). *Instant replay*. New York: World.

Kretchmar, S. (1996). Philosophy of sport. In J. Massengale & R. Swanson (Eds.), *History of exercise and sport science*. Champaign, IL: Human Kinetics.

Lee, M. (1937). *The conduct of physical education*. New York: A.S. Barnes and Co

Massengale, J., & Swanson, R. (Eds.) (1996). *History of exercise and sport science*. Champaign, IL: Human Kinetics.

Mechikoff, R., & Estes, S. (1998). *A history and philosophy of sport and physical education* (2nd ed.). Dubuque, IA: WCB Brown and Benchmark.

Messner, M., & Sabo, D. (1994). *Sex, violence, and power in sports*. Freedom, CA: The Crossing Press.

Newell, K.M. (1990). Physical education in higher education: Chaos out of order. *Quest, 42*(3), 243–268.

Nixon, E.W., & Cozens, W.C. (1941). *An introduction to physical education*. Philadelphia: W.B. Saunders.

Novak, M. (1988). *The joy of sport*. Lanham, MD: Hamilton Press.

Paxon, F. (1917). The rise of sport. *Mississippi Valley Historical Review, 4*, 143–168.

Perry, W.G. (1970). *Forms of intellectual and ethical development in the college years*. New York: Holt, Rinehart & Winston.

Plato. (1987). *The Republic*. Desmond Lee, Trans. London: Penguin Books.

Randall, L., Buell, C., Swerkes, B., & Bailey, I. (1993). *Learning style preferences of physical education majors: A qualitative analysis*. Association Internationale des Ecoles Superieures d'Education Physique. July 15–19, Trois-Rivieres, Quebec, Canada.

Ravizza, K., & Daruty, K. (1984). Paternalism, drugs, and the nature of sports. *Journal of the Philosophy of Sport, 11*, 71–82.

Sharman, J.R. (1934). *Introduction to physical education*. New York: A.S. Barnes and Co.

Sharman, J.R. (1937). *Modern principles of physical education*. New York: A.S. Barnes and Co.

Shepard, N. (1960). *Foundations and principles of physical education*. New York: Ronald Press Co.

Staley, S. (1939). *Sports education: The new curriculum in physical education*. New York: A.S. Barnes and Co.

Steindler, A. (1935). *Mechanics of normal and pathological locomotion in man*. Springfield, IL: Charles C. Thomas Publishers.

Struna, N. (1996). Sport history. In J. Massengale & R. Swanson (Eds.), *History of exercise and sport science*. Champaign, IL: Human Kinetics.

Thomas, J., & Nelson, J. (1990). *Research methods in physical activity*. (2nd ed.). Champaign, IL: Human Kinetics.

Van Dalen, D.B., & Bennett, B.L. (1971). *A world history of physical education*. Englewood Cliffs, NJ: Prentice Hall.

Wilkerson, J. (1996). Biomechanics. In J. Massengale & R. Swanson (Eds.), *History of exercise and sports science*. Massengale, John, and Swanson, Dick, Eds. Champaign, IL: Human Kinetics.

Williams, J.F. (1959). *The principles of physical education*. Philadelphia: W.B. Saunders.

Endnotes

1. See Jesse Feiring Williams' *The Principles of Physical Education* (1959), which went through at least eight editions and was a model for most foundations textbooks. See also Sharman (1934, 1937), Nixon and Cozens (1941), Lee (1937), Staley (1939), Brownell and Hagman (1951), and Shepard (1960).

2. *Phaedo and the Republic* (1966). *The Dialogues of Plato*, translated by B. Jowett. New York: Washington Square Press. As we discussed in Chapter 1, metaphysical dualism is the position in philosophy that argues that reality is composed of two parts: matter and ideas. With respect to human beings, it is argued that the two components are mind and body. Dualism is evident in the very words "mind" and "body" and is such a tradition in the though and languages of Western civilization that it is hard to think of existing any other way. Can you envision other parts of being that are not included in this philosophy?

3. Christians could define one's character as the soul.

4. *Republic*, Book II, p. 253.

5. *Ibid.*, pp. 258–259.

6. *Ibid.*, pp. 262–264.

7. Legend also has it that Milo was killed in a religious/philosophy uprising in support of Pythagoras, the famous philosopher and mathematician. Perhaps there was more to Milo than his bull killing/eating story, but that part of Milo's history is overshadowed by his eating habits, which is exactly what Plato did not like.

Knowing through Thought

Chapter Objectives

Upon completing this chapter, the reader will be able to:

1. Define rationalism as a way of knowing and relate it to the nature of being.
2. Understand the basis for the use of rationalism in teaching, coaching, and other learning situations.
3. Understand how rationalism is the "dominant" philosophy in modern education.
4. Understand how rationalism has had an impact on all contemporary scholarship.
5. Relate rationalism to kinesiology, specifically areas of biomechanics and measurement and evaluation.

(M)eaningful discourse simply cannot take place unless people know how to think clearly and responsibly and unless people treat the context with sensitivity. . . . Throughout their professional lives, allied professionals will be continually called upon—perhaps more than ever before—to justify and rationalize the place or status in people's lives of developmental physical activity, health and safety education knowledge and practice, wholesome recreational living (i.e., social, communicative, aesthetic and creative, and "learning" aspects), and dance involvement and appreciation. (Zeigler, 1995)

The subdisciplines discussed in Chapter 4—sport pedagogy, the sport sciences (exercise physiology, sport biomechanics), sport humanities (sport history, sport philosophy, and sport literature), sport social sciences (sport psychology, sport sociology), measurement and evaluation, and motor development—constitute the recognized areas of knowledge of kinesiology. At this point it is worth reemphasizing that you, the student, may or may not accept this claim that the above subdisciplines are the recognized areas of knowledge in kinesiology. If you accepted this claim, it is because you acknowledged the *authority* of the teacher, the writer, or your peer.

But how do you know that this claim is true? Interestingly, only through the faith that you have in the writers of this textbook and the claims of your teachers do you *know* that this claim is true. Put differently, and based on the previous chapter, you know because you have faith in our position as *authors*, we are *authorities* on kinesiology. Yet while faith has been a central part of Western civilization, it is not the only way to come to know about kinesiology—or anything else, for that matter.

Throughout history, philosophers have questioned how one comes to *know* anything. However, this may be the first time that you have ever thought about this question. How *do* you come to know something? The method that was used in the previous chapter, authority, is the method used most frequently in education (Randall, 1993). Your teachers speak the truth; the authors of your textbooks write the truth; your friends speak the truth, and this "truth" is "true" because you believe that your source is knowledgeable about that which is expressed as "true."

But these ways of knowing the truth all rest on the same assumption: You believe that each source tells the truth. Is this assumption, however, a correct one? Is it enough to know the truth? Furthermore, who told your teachers? Who told the truth to the authors of your textbook? Who told your friends? And who came up with this information the first time? Someone had to tell the story the first time; the information that was expressed had to be created somehow.

A highly regarded method of creating knowledge, and one of the first methods developed in the history of Western civilization, is that of what Earle Zeigler has called "reasoning." Briefly, "reasoning" is the process of using one's intellectual capabilities to think through a problem, or to arrive at a conclusion regarding some issue. It is our contention that reasoning is a viable mechanism of creating knowledge in kinesiology. Other scholars in kinesiology have also argued that reasoning is used in our field. As Earle Zeigler has argued, "One necessary aspect of personal and professional competency is the ability to reason clearly—to employ natural argumentation" (Zeigler, 1995).

Zeigler notes that, in spite of some hopeful statistics,[1] most people believe that they are already competent in this capacity. In fact, few people ever study the techniques of logic or rhetoric in their high school or college programs. It has been argued by Zeigler and many other education professionals that all individuals will be called upon to exercise critical thinking skills with increasing regularity as we move into the twenty-first century. The emphasis on information, computer technology, and the rapidity of change in the workplace all will conspire to force individuals to analyze and synthesize information much more rapidly and with much more rigor than ever before. These changes will require in each person critical thinking skills that can be taught in the field of kinesiology (Charles, 1993, 1994; Zeigler, 1995).

What then is "reasoning"? Zeigler provides a breakdown of the terms used by philosophers to describe this word as well as the process thinking, and then argues that this process should be used in kinesiology. The first term Zeigler (1995) defines is *logic*. "Logic treats the exact relationship of ideas as a science, . . . (and) is concerned with distinguishing correct thinking from incorrect thinking" (Zeigler, 1995, p. 198). One is being "logical," then, when that person implicitly recognizes the connections between ideas.

There are two types of relationships between ideas that are recognized by philosophers, *induction* and *deduction*. Induction is when one reasons from certain particulars or instances to a general conclusion, "or from the 'individual to the universal' " (Zeigler, 1995, p. 198). One is practicing induction when one defines the "common denominator" of an entire group of ideas. You may have heard the phrase, "the only things certain in life are death and taxes." This phrase states two characteristics held in common by all people: Eventually all people will die, and on their way to death they will have to pay the government for being alive. The latter part of this statement may not be true in all cases and therefore is not a true statement. The first part of the statement can be arrived at by induction: By definition all deceased individuals in the past were, at one time, alive, and are now dead. We have moved from the individual case to the universal.

Deduction is commonly thought of as the "opposite" type of reasoning from induction in that it moves "from general premises to their necessary conclusions, or from the universal to the individual" (Zeigler, 1995, p. 198). The *syllogism*, the most famous type of deductive reasoning, is an "analysis of a formal argument in which the conclusion necessarily results from the given premises. It uses only categorical statements and includes two premises and one conclusion" (Zeigler, 1995, p. 198). An example of deductive logic can be seen in this well known set of statements:

All men are mortal.
Socrates is a man.
Therefore, Socrates is mortal.

In both induction and deduction, then, ideas are related to one another in very specific ways. To deviate from these relationships is to operate in an "illogical" manner. That is, one idea will not logically follow another, and the entire argument breaks down at that point.

The phrase *critical thinking* is used by Zeigler to mean a kind of informed logic. It is one of many types of logic that can be used by kinesiologists, and, as Zeigler notes, "assuming that all people are not all the same, there is the possibility for an individual to find a particular type of logic that suits his or her ability" (Zeigler, 1995, p. 199). However, no matter what type of logic one uses, that logical approach must be grounded in the principles of formal logic. This is where critical thinking enters the picture. Basically, critical thinking is composed of two parts, the first of which is "an approach to thought in which ideas are analyzed and evaluated carefully (and skeptically)" (Zeigler, 1995, p. 200). Are the ideas used in an argument related to one another correctly? Is the process of induction used correctly? The process of deduction?

Secondly, critical thinking is related to argument. While ideas may be related to one another correctly, critical thinking implies that the ideas that are discussed are presented in such a way that *the premises serve as grounds to justify a conclusion*. Critical thinking, then, is used to justify a position and show that one position is better than another. In the paragraph quoted at the beginning of this chapter, Zeigler did just this. He stated that "meaningful discourse simply cannot take place unless people know how to think clearly and responsibly." He then concluded, "Throughout their professional lives, allied professionals will be continually called upon . . . to justify and rationalize the place or status in people's lives of developmental physical activity, health and safety education knowledge and practice, wholesome recreational living (i.e., social, communicative, aesthetic and creative, and "learning" aspects), and dance involvement and appreciation" (Zeigler, 1995, p. 197). In this *argument* Zeigler used *deduction* to argue for the use of critical thinking skills by allied professionals (professional kinesiologists). His argument can be analyzed as follows:

> All people must know how to think clearly and responsibly.
> Allied professionals are people.
> Therefore, allied professionals must know how to think clearly and responsibly.

It is our contention that all kinesiologists should be able to use critical thinking skills to argue for and justify their profession. It is also our contention that too many students of kinesiology are lacking in critical thinking skills. Why do we feel this way? Simply put, our profession continues to need justification, and it often appears that students and professionals in the field fail to argue effectively for the field's existence and prestige. One example emphasizes this point. Physical education programs are often the first eliminated in times of educational downsizing instead of other, perhaps less valuable programs. Physical educators must be able to use critical thinking skills to justify the existence of their programs. Kinesiologists must be able to both explain and argue for their field, as well as refute arguments that inaccurately portray kinesiology as "unworthy" of educational centrality. The arguments made by kinesiologists must be based on sound premises, utilize the methods of induction and deduction, and the conclusions drawn from these arguments must be clear and valid.

Rationalism

While we have argued for the use of critical thinking skills in kinesiology, it is important to note that how they are used, and when, is also very important. Perhaps the best example of the use of reasoning in the modern world occurred during the Enlightenment and is that of Rene Descartes (1596–1650), the famous French philosopher/mathematician of the Enlightenment. Descartes' philosophy had a profound impact on the development of modern education, and consequently, on the role of kinesiology in education. Not all of the

TABLE 9-1   Rene Descartes' Philosophy

Metaphysical position	Dualist
Epistemology	Rationalism
Characteristics of this epistemology	Critical thinking skills, cooperative learning sessions, intellectual development, mathematical descriptions of material reality
Courses that emphasize this epistemology	Measurement, Evaluation Biomechanics

consequences of Descartes' philosophy are beneficial to kinesiology, though. To understand why one must also understand, at least in simple terms, how Descartes' philosophy was created and the premises on which it is based.

Descartes' (pronounced "day-cart") metaphysical position was that of a dualist, meaning that he divided reality into the two components of ideas and matter. The method Descartes used to develop his position was very powerful, and to a great extent still influences philosophers today. In short, the logical, reductionistic steps Descartes used to state his position as to what is real, how we come to know reality, and what we value were, and are, very difficult to disagree with. If one begins as Descartes did, with the questions of existence and certain positions about what we can know, Descartes' logic is virtually flawless. The end product—Descartes' philosophy—is "rationalism," the first philosophy we discuss that is designed to "create" knowledge. Importantly, Descartes creates knowledge through the process of reasoning. Specific to kinesiology, Descartes' philosophy is evident in how we express knowledge in biomechanics and measurement (Table 9-1).

Descartes' Metaphysics

Descartes' philosophy is best described in his *Meditations*. Interestingly, we can learn about Descartes' philosophy just by looking at the title of his treatise. What does "meditate" mean? The answer, obviously, is to think: One comes to know something through some intellectual process. Descartes is famous among philosophers for, among other things, using the power of logic and intellect to come to know reality. In the *Meditations* Descartes does just this. In a very logical and methodical way Descartes constructs an entire argument, broken into six parts, that both describes how one comes to know reality and defines what reality is.

The first meditation is titled "Of the Things of Which We May Doubt." The argument begins with a statement that he must discount his senses of the body because, at one time or another, all of his senses have deceived him. And if the senses have failed him once, then they could not lead him to absolute knowledge because they cannot be trusted to be accurate all of time. This "not trusting" is known in philosophy as "skepticism." In Descartes' own words, "I observed that . . . these (senses) sometimes misled us; and it is the part of prudence not to place absolute confidence in that by which we may have been once deceived" (Descartes, 1995, p. 13).

We learn two things from this statement. First, Descartes constructs his metaphysical position (his position on the nature of reality) on a foundation of how one comes to know reality (epistemology). In a sense, epistemology precedes and determines reality: Descartes argues that, to determine one's metaphysical position, one can proceed logically only from those things that one can know with *absolute* certainty. Since Descartes' time, before philosophers can perform more complex philosophical discussions philosophers must establish the most basic, fundamental principles of what is real and what can be known of reality. Only then can one proceed to answering the questions that concern us about our daily lives.

Secondly, according to Descartes the most important role of a philosopher is the seeking of "absolute knowledge." The connection between knowledge and reality is very important, and Descartes argued that to be "absolute knowledge," that knowledge cannot be disputed or in error in any way. Descartes asks the question, "What can I know for certain, without doubt, that is unquestionable and absolutely unchanging?" (Descartes, 1995, p. 23) Descartes is seeking knowledge that is immutable, unchanging, and absolute. His answers will lead him to a distinct relationship between the lived, bodily world of experience and the intellectualized, spiritual world of ideas.

While this process may "thrill" philosophers, it also has certain consequences for us in kinesiology. In his quest for *absolute knowledge*, Descartes dismisses his physical body and its ability to generate or access knowledge. So much for kinesiology! Our entire field has just been cast aside! Many kinesiologists assume that using the body to generate knowledge is acceptable, and even good. Yet one of the most important philosophers in the Western world argued that what we can know through the body is irrelevant. If philosophy and education are connected in any way, Descartes' arguments, at least initially, do not make kinesiology central to education.

The above, however, is not all of Descartes' argument as to what is real and how we can know what is real. The next step Descartes takes is to doubt his subjective perception of reality, or the thinking process he experiences while he is conscious and awake. He does so by comparing his dreams to his waking state. Descartes notes that in dreams he believes he is awake, and therefore he cannot trust the belief that he is awake at *any* time.

There is a certain logic to this statement. Have you ever had a dream that is so vivid that, while you experienced it, you *knew* for certain that it was "real"? And then, upon awaking, you are profoundly affected by the dream in your wakeful state? Which state is more "real," the dream or the wakeful experience? Apparently Descartes had this experience, and after that experience the *belief* in being awake is not enough to know that one really *is* awake. Consciousness, then, cannot be known with absolute certainty.[2] Descartes goes so far as to say that he is not absolutely sure that he is awake when he writes *The Meditations*! He is not *absolutely* sure of his mental state at any time.

Descartes finally admits that humans are weak and able to be deceived. This position, by the way, was written for two reasons. The first, and most obvious, is to support his argument that he doubts his conscious state or the senses of his body. The second, however, deals with the politics of the time in which Descartes lived and supports the position that God is all powerful while humans are inherently weak.[3] Descartes argued that a prudent man "doubts" because the senses of the body can err and the perceptions of the mind can be inaccurate. If one cannot trust the senses or the perceptions of the mind, then one cannot use either of these mechanisms to come to know reality. Descartes, using the method of logic, has really painted himself into a corner. He cannot trust his body, and he cannot trust his mind. What else is there?

Descartes asks if there is not something different altogether from the points he has discussed—the human body, the universe, the existence of God—that it is impossible to doubt. Since his bodily senses can deceive him and his conscious perception of reality is in doubt, he no longer is sure of his very existence. Descartes is aware that, perhaps, God has played some cruel trick on him, causing him to believe that he exists when in fact he may not. Descartes now doubts everything: his body, God, the Church, being awake, his very existence. Descartes is a mess!

At his point Descartes makes a brilliant leap in his thinking: He notes that, while one cannot prove his or her existence with absolute certainty through the senses or through one's subjective perception of consciousness, one can still suspend judgment, or "doubt." This act of doubting is an act of free will. One can choose to doubt. And by being able to doubt, one guards against agreeing with that which is false.[4]

This leap of Descartes' distinguishes him from ordinary philosophers. He concludes that, since his existence is in doubt, he must exist. Otherwise, he would not be able to doubt his existence! Nothing would be there at all. In Descartes' words, "Cogito, ergo sum." In English, "I think, therefore I am." With every doubt comes proof of his existence. Put differently, the only thing of which he is absolutely sure is that he can "doubt" everything! His ability to "doubt" or to be "skeptical," is constant, unchanging, and immutable. In all conditions he doubts. He concludes that this ability to doubt would not be present at all times if he did not exist.

The Role of the Body in Descartes' Metaphysics

Reviewing the process of Descartes' logical argument with respect to his ontological position, we can see that the proof of reality is exclusively intellectual or "mind"-oriented. There is no point at which the body is a mechanism for coming to know anything, or even that the body is real in a metaphysical sense. We are, at this point in the argument, creatures of pure intellect.

What are the consequences of this type of thinking for those of us who are interested in physical education? Think about it . . . (no pun intended): The body is not a mechanism for coming to know something. Logically, "physical education" is an oxymoron, or a phrase that is internally inconsistent and meaningless. Three points should be emphasized:

1. It is very difficult to prove that the body exists at all. Descartes has doubted its "reality" into nothingness. Descartes does return to the existence of the body in his Sixth Meditation, but the fact remains that the initial argument excludes the mechanisms of the body for coming to know reality. The existence of the body can only be proven by further, extensive argument.
2. Education can only be justified for its inferential and intellectual benefits. Education from a Cartesian (meaning "of Descartes") perspective should be for the development of those skills that allow us to come to know "reality."

3. "Knowledge" is the product of processes that are logical, deductive, and not based on our bodily experiences.

In the Sixth Meditation, as mentioned above, Descartes returns to the role of the body and attempts to prove its existence. His argument is sound, constructive, and logical. If one accepts Descartes' epistemology, then one can accept his argument. Descartes' return to the body emphasizes the fact that his ontological position is that of a dualist. Were he to disregard the existence of the body entirely he would be a "monist," where all of reality is strictly one thing, in this case, mind.

When Descartes does discuss the body in his Sixth Meditation, he does so in a very special way. Descartes discusses the body, and all of material reality, in the context of metaphysics where all of the sensed world can be described in terms of extension and motion. In short, the material world has these two characteristics: extension, which is the ability to describe the material world in grid coordinates, or "Cartesian" coordinates; and motion on this grid (Figure 9-1). Descartes' interpretation of material reality is that the *expression* of reality in mathematical terms is "real," more so than the *experience* of reality that we have. The Cartesian coordinates are "real," the experience of it is not. The consequences of this metaphysical position in kinesiology are very interesting and useful. If the world can be understood in Cartesian terms, what would these terms be?

The answer to this question is that any course in kinesiology that emphasizes the mathematical expression of human movement relies, to some extent, on Descartes' assumptions. Any time we measure a person running by timing him or her, any time we record how much weight is lifted, when we keep score of a game, we are utilizing to some extent Descartes' philosophy.

There are more concrete examples, however. Biomechanics, described in Chapter 4, utilizes Descartes' concepts of extension and motion to graph human movement. High-speed photography, digitally enhanced, allows researchers in biomechanics to analyze cer-

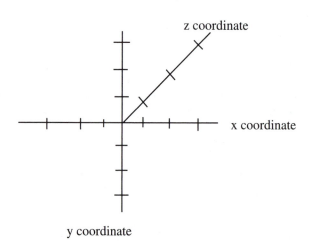

**FIGURE 9-1   Characteristics of the material
world: extension and motion.**

tain motions used in sport. The analysis often yields improved and more efficient patterns of movement.

Another area of study that emphasizes Descartes' understanding of the material world is measurement and evaluation. It has been argued that, if it cannot be measured, then it is not science. Measurement and evaluation relies on the idea that measurement of the material world can and does occur, and that this measurement can be expressed numerically. The "evaluation" occurs with mathematical tools of statistical analysis. The combination of measurement and evaluation is an extremely useful tool in kinesiology, and it is essential that all kinesiology students be skilled in measurement and evaluation techniques. To not be skilled is to not be able to quantify human movement in reductionistic, generalizable terms that are recognizable to all who read them.

Other Consequences of Descartes' Epistemology

Descartes' method of developing knowledge is known as *rationalism*. One comes to know through the process of inference, intellection, deduction, logic, or a whole variety of terms that refer to a "rational" process. We can "deduce" several other characteristics of rationalism from the above narrative. The first principle is known as *reductionism*, a process that is extremely valuable in all walks of life. According to Descartes, to know something with absolute certainty one must reduce all arguments, as much as possible, to the simplest terms. One does this by discarding all irrelevant points and generalizing as much as logically possible the essence of an argument in the simplest of terms. From there one can build an argument based on knowledge that is absolutely indisputable. Conclusions logically derived from knowledge that is absolutely indisputable are also indisputable. Eventually one constructs an argument that is airtight and completely defensible. Complex forms of knowledge thus created are as sound as the most simple statements. This form or method of constructing knowledge has been called the "building block theory of knowledge," where each piece of the argument is indisputable and therefore the conclusions are indisputable.

Can you think of a science in use today that uses this method of generating knowledge? Probably one of the best examples would be the mathematical discipline of geometry, where one constructs geometric "proofs" through a logical process of building upon initial postulates and successive proofs. One begins with a postulate, theorizes a position based on the postulates, and infers the logical conclusion. This method is not limited to geometry, however. The idea that one can build on simple knowledge and move toward the complex permeates all of the sciences, arts, humanities, and social sciences. One begins with simple statements, or courses of study, and moves toward progressively more difficult types of knowledge in logical, step-by-step sequences that are firmly based in the preceding body of knowledge. To skip a step would be like removing a brick from a wall and cause the entire edifice to be suspect. One must stop, go back, reconstruct the argument, fill in any and all gaps, and proceed from there. To do otherwise is to leave one open to charges of poor methodology.

The method of geometric proofs described above leads us to a conclusion that those types of knowledge that easily and clearly express the "simple to complex" relationship will be most able to take advantage of Cartesian methods of knowledge creation. In fact, the creation of knowledge expressed in mathematical form has its origin in Descartes' philosophy.

Descartes' Rationalism and the Value of Knowledge in Kinesiology

What is valuable in Descartes' philosophy? Descartes' axiological position can be deduced from his above argument. Those types of knowledge that are logically determined from simple statements are valued. Those types of knowledge derived from bodily senses and experiences, or those types derived from subjective consciousness, are not valued. What would this rationalist system look like in practice, especially in educational systems?

Rationalism in practice would look very much like what we see in education today. Those types of knowledge that are inferential or intellectual in origin—physics, philosophy, language, the humanities in general—are very highly regarded in higher education. Specifically, "general education," or those courses one takes prior to studies in the major, are assumed to be necessary to the education of the college graduate.

However, those types of knowledge that are "body"-oriented are suspect, and are valued only to the extent that they conform to the model of intellectualism that dominates in higher education. Specifically, laboratory courses, activity courses, methods courses, practicums, and internships are considered less central to the education of the college graduate. For example, how many university credit hours does one get for a course in physics? In philosophy? In history? In literature? Usually three. In contrast, for the same amount of time spent in class per week, how many credit hours would one get for the laboratory experience? Usually only one. There is a valuation process that determines that *theory*, which is a product of intellection and inference, is more valuable than *practice*, which is an experience that is "bodily" in nature. Given this argument, how would one expect to value "physical" education?

Of course, the *logical* answer, based on deduction, is that "physical" education (especially activity courses such as golf, aerobics, swimming, etc.) is not as valued. Historically, programs of physical education were often marginalized and cut when budgets shrank. Using Descartes' rationale, the reason for this decision is that physical education can only be justified as a course of study that supplements the "real" process of education that is intellectual. Similarly, athletes usually receive only one unit of academic credit for the many hours of activity they spend per week (limited by the NCAA to 20 hours per week for Division I level competition).

In any case, bodily activities are almost always described as "extracurricular." In kinesiology, this is usually the activity or performance course. And when money is tight, "extras" are the first to go.[5] While both athletics and kinesiology have tried to justify themselves in a variety of ways, the dominant value system in higher education is clearly Cartesian. Even in programs of physical education one gets three units for a theory class and one unit for a performance or activity class.

Summary

Programs of "physical education" have become considerably more intellectual since the 1960s with the development of the "subdisciplines," or the use of disciplinary ways of knowing that rely on highly structured methods of acquiring and creating knowledge. These structured methods are extremely Cartesian in that they are intellectual, inferential, and theory based. Therefore, as physical education continues to use these methods, it becomes a more "acceptable" and valued discipline. As this change has occurred many have argued that physical education is no longer "physical" education, but is "kinesiology—the art and science of human movement." Think about it: Where is the bodily movement or the subjective experience of movement in this definition? Clearly, at least with respect to what physical education was thirty years ago, these aspects of movement have been marginalized and something else has taken their place. No longer is a program of study in physical education composed solely of methods courses, where one learns how to teach and experience human movement. Rather most programs now require a large number of "theory" courses: history and philosophy of sport, psychology and sociology of sport, biomechanics, exercise physiology, motor behavior, and measurement and evaluation. Can you see the Cartesian influence on kinesiology over the past thirty years? Furthermore, has this change served the field well?

According to Descartes, what courses should one take to acquire a degree in kinesiology? Reviewing Descartes' logic, we can deduce several trends.

1. One would study theory-based human movement. All courses would emphasize theory. Courses that better emphasize theory are valued over those that emphasize subjective experience or the body in action.
2. One would begin with simple theories and move toward the complex. In fact, this is what we do in all courses of study at the university. Even in activity courses one takes beginning swimming before intermediate, and intermediate before advanced. In theory courses, one takes Human Anatomy before Biomechanics or Exercise Physiology.
3. Courses that deal with human movement in terms of extension and motion would be valued over those that deal with human movement in terms of the senses of the body or the subjective experience of movement.
4. Courses that deal with the expression of movement in mathematical terms would be valued over those that do not.
5. Specifically, courses such as Measurement and Evaluation, Philosophy of Sport, and Biomechanics would form the essence of the field.
6. Activity courses, laboratory courses, methods and analysis course would be less valuable.

Discussion Questions

1. Construct the ideal program of study for a college physical education program using the epistemology of rationalism. Do this in groups of three or four. Everything you have learned in this chapter should be applied.
2. Compare your program of study from the perspective of rationalism to the program of study that you developed using the method of authority.
3. Use the collaborative learning session to answer the following questions.
   a. What was the metaphysical position of Descartes?
   b. What was the epistemological position of Descartes?

c. What would Descartes' ideal curriculum (program of coursework) look like?

d. What would be the most important course in the curriculum?

e. What courses would be specific to the physical education part of the curriculum?

f. How would Descartes feel about athletics? about intramurals?

g. How would an rationalist's program compare with the program that is currently in place at your school?

References

Charles, J. (1993). Kinesiology in the liberal arts. *Quest, 44*(1), 122–126.

Charles, J. (1994). *Contemporary kinesiology: An introduction to the study of human movement in higher education.* Englewood, CO: Morton Publishing Company.

College Entrance Examination Board. (1983). *Academic preparation for college.* New York: Author.

Descartes, R. (1995). Meditations on first philosophy. *Classics of western philosophy,* Steven Cahn (Ed.). Indianapolis, IN: Hackett Publishing.

Martens, R. (1987). Science, knowledge, and sport psychology. *The Sport Psychologist, 1*, 29–55.

Randall, L., Buell, C., Swerkes, B., & Bailey, I. (1993). Learning style preferences of physical education majors. *Discipline exchanges: Physical education* (p. 5). The California State University System Institute for Teaching and Learning.

Singer, R., et al. (1979). *Physical education: An interdisciplinary approach.* New York: Macmillan.

Zeigler, E. (1995). Competency in critical thinking: A requirement for the allied professional. *Quest, 47*(2), 196–211.

Endnotes

1. Zeigler (1995) notes that the College Board (1983) stated that critical thinking (or "reasoning" in the words of the College Board) should be one of seven basic academic compencies resulting from formal education. He also noted that philosophy is being taught in over 5000 schools in the United States and to thousands of prospective teachers. However, unless on studies philosophy formally, most students will never formal logic or informal logic (critical thinking) and argumentation.

2. You, like most kinesiology students, probably think that this is the silliest argument you have heard. Of course you are awake! But Descartes' questions, when taken seriously, are very difficult to dismiss. Can you *prove* you are awake? Trust Descartes: It is very difficult to do so.

We can, however, learn something from Descartes' efforts. Why do we think that this is a silly argument? The position that we take—that Descartes' approach to consciousness is ludicrous—tells us much about our own philosophical position. Questions that have nothing to do with our daily lives are easily dismissed by most contemporary Americans. We dismiss philosophical speculation of Descartes and his peers because of our *pragmatic* philosophy. More about the philosophy of pragmatism is in Chapter 11.

3. In the sixteenth century the world was changing rapidly, and the Catholic Church was quite threatened philosophically, politically, and economically. To argue that humans are weak and easily deceived was to accept the argument of the Church that humans are mor-

tal and that God is all powerful. Descartes, a religious man, wrote his philosophy to bolster the political and philosophical position of the Church and to prove the existence of God. It is ironic that, in fact, Descartes undermined the political and philosophical position of the Church. How did he do this? Basically, God is not to be found in Descartes' argument. One comes to know reality *without* God through a process of inference. Once humans can know reality without God, then what purpose does the Church serve in a political sense? Descartes "privatizes" religion in that he sets up an argument that each of us can come to know God through our own intellectual process.

4. This argument was a big one in Descartes' time, and was one used by the Catholic Church. In short, one must have free will to choose not to sin. Otherwise, what is the point of guilt, penance, and the role of the Catholic Church in absolving one of sin? Free will was necessary for the political institution and the theology of Catholicism to work.

5. In the 1995–1996 academic year, the Department of Physical Education at SUNY New Paltz was eliminated. The official excuse was "fiscal exigency," meaning that the college could not afford the program any longer. Using a rationalist perspective, though, the college "valued" physical education less than other programs. Otherwise, funding would have continued for the physical education program, and the college would have been removed funding from some other less valued.

Knowing through Observation

Chapter Objectives

Upon completing this chapter, the reader will be able to:

1. Define empiricism as a way of knowing and relate it to the nature of being.
2. Understand the basis for the use of empiricism in teaching, coaching, and other learning situations.
3. Understand the empirical perspective on cause and effect, induction, and *tabula rasa*.
4. Relate empiricism to kinesiology, specifically areas of sport psychology, motor behavior, sport pedagogy, and all areas where observation is used.

In the last chapter we discussed how one might come to know something—reality, the material universe, or kinesiology—through the use of the intellectual methods of rationalism. So far we have discussed two different ways of knowing: authority, or the method of transferring knowledge from one who is either knowledgeable or has power; and rationalism, the intellectual process of creating knowledge. This chapter focuses on a third way of knowing kinesiology, through the epistemology of empiricism.

Empiricism argues that one gains knowledge through the perception of external objects. This is a fancy way of saying that one can come to know reality by observing it. Right off the bat, students should see that empiricism is a radically different philosophy than rationalism. Indeed, one can view empiricism as the "opposite" of rationalism, especially Descartes' brand of rationalism. In short, whereas rationalism uses intellectual ways of knowing reality, empiricism uses "bodily" ways of knowing reality. Empiricists argue that we *can* learn something about reality by seeing it, hearing it, touching, tasting, or smelling it. Empiricists, then, agree that the material world—the physical world around all of us that we can see and hear—is real. What is interesting about empiricists is how they view *ideas*, or the world of the mind. Each empiricist that we discuss has a different view as to what constitutes an idea.

Empiricism takes a variety of forms; indeed, there are a variety of interpretations as to just how empiricism works. Three proponents of empiricism summarize positions that we use in kinesiology: John Locke, Francis Bacon, and Thomas Hobbes. And while each of these philosophers differs from the other, they all agree with the idea that the body is central to acquiring knowledge.

John Locke

One philosopher of the Enlightenment who had a significant impact on modern thought was John Locke. Locke's philosophy influenced American founding fathers, especially with respect to the Declaration of Independence and the Constitution. Locke's notions of "life, liberty, and property" were used and changed in the Declaration of Independence to read as "life, liberty, and the pursuit of happiness."[1] The framers of the Constitution agreed with Locke that what individuals experience in the world with their senses is both real and important.

Locke's definition of empiricism is easily understood as described by Dewey (1984). Empiricism is based on one's experience of the material world:

> Locke divided experience into two categories—first, sensation, or perception of external objects, and second, reflection, the activity in which the self observes its own state of mind, its own feelings and thoughts. According to Locke all human experience is embraced in these two categories; but the second, reflection, is based in and arises from the first, sensation. (Dewey, 1984, p. 97)

Locke argued, then, that we can observe reality with our five senses. Locke disagreed with Descartes' philosophy, especially with that part of Descartes' argument that dismisses the possibility of using the senses to come to know reality with absolute certainty.

This part of Locke's philosophy has a direct impact on what we do in kinesiology. Knowledge in kinesiology can be derived from (1) one's ability to observe human movement, or (2) from one's reflections of the sensations derived from the movement experience. This sequence distinguishes Locke's philosophy from Descartes': Before one has any experience, there is no knowledge. Without the sensation of movement or of the senses, one cannot know anything. Therefore, with Locke's brand of empiricism, the mind is not the primary mechanism of creating knowledge. The body is.

This position led Locke to make a statement, one that kinesiology students will hear often—especially those who go into teaching. One begins with no knowledge at birth because one has not had any sensations or experiences upon which to reflect. Locke called this condition *tabula rasa,* which is Latin for "a blank slate." The idea that one has no knowledge at birth and acquires knowledge by building upon experiences and reflection of those experiences fits nicely with how many Americans believe that individuals learn. Indeed, the phrase "We learn by doing" is a statement with which empiricists are friendly.

Indeed, students often find it easy to grasp the general concepts of Locke's empiricism (see Table 10-1). As defined above, empiricism is a radical contrast with Descartes' rationalism: Empiricism is what rationalism is *not.* Locke developed his philosophy in order to overcome what he saw as the limitations of Descartes' rationalism, specifically, that knowledge can be had without experiencing the material world. Locke rejected Descartes' position that the existence of one's body was doubtable. He argued instead that it is only individual objects that have the status of real existence. Locke's empiricism, then, unlike the method of rationalism, argued that knowledge claims must be based on one's bodily experience. Certainly this is a position friendly to kinesiology.

Further, empiricism was designed to overcome the limitations of the first epistemology we studied, authority. In Dewey's words, empiricism

> was designed to free men from the tyranny of non-existent universality, and to eliminate the ambiguity which results from the use of undefined or ill-defined abstractions, and to encourage men to concern themselves with individual objects. (Dewey, 1984, p. 108–109)

Locke's empiricism differs from the method of authority in that it "enabled men to subject to critical analysis the traditional institutions, ideas, and superstitions which they had inherited from the past" (Dewey, 1984, p. 105) Being told the "truth" by an authority does not make those knowledge claims reliable or valid. Rather, our material lives can be critically analyzed and examined for "truth."

TABLE 10-1   John Locke's Empiricism

Metaphysical position	Dualist
Epistemology	Empiricism
Characteristics of this epistemology	Observation, reflection,
Courses that emphasize this epistemology	Pedagogy, Coaching

Francis Bacon

Francis Bacon's empiricism, especially his use of induction, is often used in kinesiology (Table 10-2). Bacon argued that one can determine the rules of nature only by observing the facts of nature, and in so doing both legitimized the process of induction and connected it to the material world. If you recall, the process of induction was described as an intellectual one. However, by moving from the particular observations to the general rule, Bacon was able to show that the process of induction is applicable to the material world.[2] Dewey argued that "Bacon's adaptation of traditional methods was to begin with observation of discrete facts, and then from observed similarities in many separate events, to arrive at generalizations" (Dewey, 1984, p. 94).

As much as any field of study, kinesiology uses the method of induction to create knowledge. Pedagogists in particular are expert at observing human movement and inducing generalizations about how to teach certain skills. More famous are coaches, especially football coaches, who view hours of films to determine "tendencies" of both their own players and opponents. Leaving aside the argument that the lives of football coaches were enormously complicated by the invention of videotape, their abilities to induce generalizations from watching many plays, and deduce particular strategies from the "tendencies" they observe, are of the highest quality. Kinesiology students should be made aware of the method of induction and become expert at it, so that they can utilize induction in their own movement experiences either as teachers or as movers.

TABLE 10-2   Francis Bacon's Empiricism

Metaphysical position	Dualist
Epistemology	Empiricism
Characteristics of this epistemology	Observation, reflection, but especially induction
Courses that emphasize this epistemology	Pedagogy, Coaching

Thomas Hobbes

The next philosopher deserves much attention due to his importance to behavioral psychology. The best representative of the philosophy of materialistic empiricism is Thomas Hobbes (1588–1679), the English philosopher of the Enlightenment. A contemporary of Descartes, Hobbes' philosophy could not have been more different. Hobbes argued that the concern of the philosopher is the experienced, sensed world. Everything else should be left to religion. Hobbes, then, sought to separate philosophy and religion. Given that the Church of England believed that everything in this universe, as well as any other universe or reality, was the product of God's will, how do you think Hobbes' philosophy went over? Obviously, not well. Hobbes escaped from England during the English Revolution (c. 1640–1660), in fear for his life, and lived and worked in France during that time. He returned to England after the fall of Cromwell and the Puritans and served as an advisor to

TABLE 10-3   Thomas Hobbes' Empiricism

Metaphysical position	Monist
Epistemology	Materialistic empiricism
Characteristics of this epistemology	Cause and effect
Courses that emphasize this epistemology	Sport Psychology, Coaching, Pedagogy

Parliament. Hobbes attempted to infuse philosophy into the political process and believed that philosophy should be used to improve our lives here on earth.

Hobbes' metaphysical position was that of a *monist* (Table 10-3). He believed that the nature of reality is composed of matter and nothing else. As far as Hobbes was concerned, there was no such thing as an idea. All that is real can be sensed with one of the five senses. If it cannot be sensed, then it does not exist. Hobbes argued that since an idea exists only in our minds, then it must not be real. Hobbes, who argued that all one knows by using the senses is the material world, is a *materialistic empiricist*. Obviously, Hobbes spent quite a bit of time considering the nature of the material world, and some of his arguments anticipate many of the scientific achievements of the twentieth century.

According to Hobbes, reality consists of particles of matter moving through space and time. This argument is not particularly new, even in the seventeenth century. Indeed, it was almost 2000 years old when Hobbes argued for the idea. Hobbes used the word "atoms" to describe the most elementary particles of matter that make up what we sense. This word was first used by the Greek philosophers Democritus and Leucippus (Melsen, 1967) who lived in fifth century BC Athens! Much like Descartes' concept of "extension and motion," Hobbes argued for a definition of material reality that recognized the existence of three-dimensional space (Cartesian coordinates) and motion. Hobbes, however, approached material reality very differently than Descartes. According to Hobbes, the most elementary particles of matter are subject to the principle of cause and effect. Particles of matter move through space and time and affect one another according to the laws of the universe. In Hobbes' philosophy, one merely needed to understand the principle of "cause and effect" to make explicit the laws that govern matter in the universe.

Hobbes' philosophy of materialistic empiricism states that every action that occurs is a function of matter in motion (Hobbes, 1995). All actions are the resultant effects of matter in motion. This philosophy on a cosmological scale can be described as a "billiard ball universe," where all of the material universe is composed of atoms careening into one another, causing specific effects that can be sensed by our sense organs. The best exemplar of this philosophy is the physicist Isaac Newton, whose work in celestial mechanics constitutes the paradigm in which scientists have worked for over 300 years.

With Hobbes' philosophy one cannot emphasize the principle of cause and effect enough. Cause and effect is the principle rule that governs *all* matter in the universe. Now, are our bodies composed of matter? Of course. So the question becomes, "How does the principle of cause and effect have an impact on our physical bodies?"

There are several immediate consequences of Hobbes' ontological position, some of which have philosophical implications and some of which had serious political consequences for Hobbes:

1. The first, and important more to Hobbes than it is to us, is that God is not the concern of the philosopher because he is not of this universe.[3] Since God is considered an "idea" and cannot be directly sensed with our bodies, he does not exist in this reality.

2. Another consequence of Hobbes philosophy is that there is no such thing as "free will."[4] According to Hobbes, the physical universe, in the form of atoms striking one another, causes a chain reaction of events that is not under the control of "mind" or any other word for consciousness. Our physical bodies "react" to the forces of the external environment. Nothing more. The behavior described in this statement is known as *determinism*.

3. Hobbes argued that our sense organs do not reveal reality; they merely transform it so that we can subjectively perceive it. What is perception? It is the impact of particles of matter on the sense organs. Nothing more. Consciousness is the product of atoms knocking around in our brains. There is no mind to interpret the data. This is admittedly an extreme definition of "empiricism," the mechanics of sensing the material world.

To put Hobbes' ontology in perspective, people are considered to be only complicated machines. A quote from Hobbes summarizes his ontology very nicely:

> Seeing that life is but a motion of limbs and organs, why may we not say that all automata (engines that move themselves by springs and wheels as doth a watch) have an artificial life? For what is the heart but a spring, and the nerves but so many strings, and the joints but so many wheels, giving motion to the whole body?

Hobbes, then, argued that the body is merely a complicated machine, and if we know enough about the machine then we can control it. Specifically, by altering the environment in which the machine operates, one can adjust it to operate in any manner. By altering the environment (cause) one can change an individual's behavior (effect). Do you see any implications of this philosophy for education?

Hobbes' Epistemology

Hobbes' epistemology is directly related to his metaphysical position. With Hobbes the nature of knowledge is rooted in matter instead of the soul, as it was with Plato, or strictly inferred, as it was with Descartes. Knowledge from Hobbes' perspective originates in the senses. "Thoughts," or what we call thoughts, also originate there. All activities that are "mental" are really nothing more than sensations.[5]

Does this argument hold up? There is a certain plausibility to this point of view. Think of the brain as a kind of computer. In fact, we have no mind, all we have is "brain." Mental phenomena are the effect of sensory input—chemical reactions along the paths of our nervous system—and interior receptors pick up the stimulus and cause a certain response. Thought is nothing more than the movement of some substance within our brains. Pleasure is the product of endomorphines. Pain could be the complete absence of these chemicals. In sum, knowledge as it has been defined by both Plato and Descartes—something that exists in a mind—does not exist.

If, according to Hobbes, knowledge is not in the mind, then how can one know anything? How can one tell if someone else "knows" something? Hobbes had a very simple answer to these questions. *Knowledge is behavior.* If one knows something, then it will be exhibited by a specific kind of activity that is recognizable to other observers. In a personal sense, I have knowledge if my physical self acts in a certain way that exhibits knowledge. Put differently, knowledge is skilled movement. The more the skill, the more the knowledge. Others can use their senses (to see a dancer, to hear a musician, to smell good cooking, etc.) to witness my knowledge.

How would one acquire knowledge? The answer would be that one experienced an environment that caused a change in behavior. A dancer would observe other dancers, and would then dance and observe his or her own movements for comparison. Similarly, one would listen to music and then play, one would cook (and then eat!), and so on. The key to knowledge, then, is the environment in which one is placed. Does this "key" hold up? There is some evidence that it does. For instance, research indicates that children in a home with no television, lots of reading material, and supportive parents will behave quite differently than students who watch too much television, never read, and are ignored by their parents. The environment causes very different effects in the children. What are the specific effects? The answer, on average, is that in the first situation children are much better students than are those in the second.

Implications of Hobbes' Philosophy: Behavioral Psychology

The most significant consequence of Hobbes' philosophy in practice is that it explains and justifies the psychology of behaviorism.[6] Generally defined, behaviorism is a psychology that reduces "psyche" in an individual to behavior. As in Hobbes' philosophy, in behavioristic psychology there is no such thing as a thought. The terms often used in behavioral psychology to describe the relationship of changed behavior are stimulus-response, cause-effect, and environment-performance.

The beginnings of this psychology have their origin with William James, a pragmatist philosopher who argued that the origins of mind can be found in the senses. His argument was extended by academics who blended the developing field of biology with the academic field of psychology. The beginning of behavioral psychology is credited to the Russian physiologist Ivan Pavlov, who investigated the salivary reflex in dogs and developed the concept of the conditioned reflex. If you recall, Pavlov would ring a bell immediately prior to feeding the dogs. After some time, Pavlov noted that the dogs would salivate at the sound of the bell *rather* than the placement of the food in front of the animals. Behaviorists theorized that the ringing of the bell constituted a change in environment that *caused* the effect of salivation in the animals. The *reward,* or sometimes *punishment,* reinforced the effect. It was the change in environment that was important. What were the dogs thinking? Behaviorists would say this was irrelevant.

Watson believed that psychology could be reduced to the science of physics (Dewey, 1984). Watson wanted to establish psychology as a science and rejected the subjectivism and introspectionist styles of psychology that emphasized something that was not observable (like a "mind"). In short, Watson rejected Platonic and Cartesian psychologies.

Furthermore, Watson argued that one of the goals of science was prediction and control. He maintained that only objective methods enable the achievement of these goals. By objective Watson meant that one could observe the change in behavior of his clients. Furthermore, Watson argued that objectivity promoted the idea that different scientists are able to observe the same objects and events. This notion of objectivity eliminates states of consciousness because they are private, relative, and subjective. Only the objectively observable characteristic of behavior is able to provide the necessary data for scientific psychology.

Behaviorism in Sport and Kinesiology

The psychology of behaviorism has significant implications for the practice of kinesiology, especially for the field of pedagogy (the science of teaching). In short, a behaviorist has very specific views of what a student is, what knowledge is, and how one goes about facilitating the acquisition of knowledge. Behaviorists are a dominant force in the field of sport psychology, for the reason that their psychology often (and by definition should!) achieves observable results.

Behaviorism has had a significant impact on the practice of sport psychology. By manipulating the environment many psychologists (and coaches, athletes, and parents) have been able to achieve significant observable results by altering the environment in which athletes perform and then rewarding, or punishing, the observable resultant behaviors. The virtue of behaviorism is that everyone involved in the performance can tell if the performance has changed. By reducing the number of variables that are changed, one can reduce the change in performance to a cause and effect relationship.

Interval training is one of the best examples of behaviorism. For instance, if one wants to improve the last lap (440 yards) from 65 seconds to 60 seconds in a one-mile race, a behaviorist would argue that the athlete must create the characteristics of a 60-second 440-yard lap in practice. Fatigue levels, pacing, speed, and other criteria that are "subjectively" monitored must be consistent with the last 440 yards of the race. The athlete must perform in practice at the 60-second pace necessary for improvement. Because the athlete in a workout is often fatigued, the distance of each effort is less than the actual length of the race. Specific to our example, an athlete might run a series of 220-yard sprints at 30 seconds per sprint. The pace of 60-second 440-yard sprints is repeated over and over (this is the "cause," or the environment), and eventually the athlete performs at the improved level in the race (the "effect", or the performance).

The Ethics of Behaviorism

While there is considerable research that supports the approach used in behavioral psychology, there are some who argue that there are ethical problems with this method. That this argument exists is fairly easily understood. Ethics, in a sense, do not exist in a universe that does not recognize "mind." However, if one rejects the premises on which behaviorism is built—that mind does not exist, then one will question the right to change environmental conditions to achieve desired results in someone else's behavior. An example might illustrate this premise best.

Steve, who wants to be the best swim coach in the world, knows that to achieve his goal he must create the fastest swimmers in the world. As a confirmed behaviorist, he knows that all he has to do to achieve improved performance is to alter the environment of his swimmers to achieve improved performance. The swimmers, already world class, are subsidized by his club in the form of a small stipend, free workout gear, free meals at local restaurants, and all the ice cream they can eat at the local ice cream shop.

The first alteration in the swimmers' **environment** is the installation of a sound system under the water in the swimming pool. The swimmers enjoy this, and their **response** is to enjoy their practices more. This in turn improves their **performance**. The **reward** is enjoyment, which leads to better attitudes in practice, which translates to more consistent effort.

Their times are not fast enough, however, and Steve resorts to more radical **stimuli**. Steve begins writing the times of the swimmers on a bulletin board in the locker room and puts stars by personal bests. The swimmers, all of whom like the stars by their names, **respond** by working harder to get stars. Again, the **reward** is correlated with performance. Their times improve still more.

After a while, though, the swimmers realize that there is considerable pain involved in getting something as mundane as a star, so they start to let up. The **reward** is no longer serving as a **stimulus**. Steve, needing stronger **stimuli**, alters their **environment** by threatening to cut the swimmers off from their ice cream if they do not step up their intensity in the pool. The swimmers, however, **respond** much differently than Steve thought they would. The swimmers start playing a game with Steve, and learn to measure exactly the effort needed to get their ice cream, but not a bit more.

While behaviorism works, the ethics of the psychology (or what is right or how one ought to behave) are sometimes unclear. Does Steve have the right to use, for instance, a bullwhip if it would improve performance? The issue of intimidation is a big one in sport psychology, yet many consider it dehumanizing. How would you feel about being manipulated because it will improve your performance? What if you just want to have fun? What if you choose to have goals other than those of the person who establishes the environment? Put differently, who has the right to be the creator of the environment?

Often behaviorists are contrasted with humanists, who emphasize the subjective nature of an individual. Behaviorists, however, cannot observe subjectivity, so often appeals to one's "humanity" are incomprehensible. The reconciliation of this contrast often never occurs; each of the parties operates on radically different conceptions of reality. While behaviorists view existence in terms of stimulus-response-reward, punishment, or cause-effect, humanists are talking about means and ends. The humanist position implies that there is something called "mind" in an individual. The behaviorist is not concerned with this aspect of an individual. Rather, behaviorists argue that behavior is all that matters, and how one gets the desired behavior is irrelevant.

We have painted a very extreme picture of behaviorism. To be fair, there are many strains of behaviorism. As long as American culture is concerned with performance, though, this psychology is going to be useful in enhancing performance. The question for kinesiologists is, then, "Can one humanize a very mechanical view of what it means to be a person?"

Summary

Empiricism is of significant importance to kinesiologists. In its many forms, most of which recognize "mind," empiricism has always been associated with psychology because of its concern with the origin of ideas. From this perspective ideas are seen as "citizens of the mind." What one experiences is stored in memory and subsequently analyzed.

Regardless of one's preferred definition of empiricism, then, understanding the various definitions and limitations of each can only help one understand how one acquires knowledge in kinesilogy, especially in the sciences, sport psychology, and pedagogy. Observations are also of import to sport historians, who through primary sources seek to establish generalizations that will explain how and why sport has changed over time. Finally, the discipline of motor behavior uses empiricism as a primary mechanism for creating knowledge. Closely related to and derived from sport psychology, motor behavior relies on observation and induction to facilitate the development of hypotheses that can be scientifically tested. The development of motor behavior as a discipline is its own study,[7] but one can argue that motor behavior is the unique discipline of kinesiology. Regardless of the status of motor behavior, empiricism is critical to this discipline as a mechanism for creating knowledge.

Discussion Questions

1. Construct the ideal program of study for a college physical education program using the epistemology of empiricism. Do this in groups of three or four. Everything you have learned in this chapter should be applied.
2. Compare your program of study from the perspective of empiricism to the program of study that you developed using the methods of authority and rationalism.
3. Use the collaborative learning session to answer the following questions:
   a. What are the metaphysical positions of the three empiricists discussed in this chapter? Describe each position separately.
   b. What is the epistemological position of the three empiricists? Describe each position separately.
   c. What would an empiricist's ideal curriculum (program of coursework) look like?
   d. What would be the most important course in the curriculum?
   e. What courses would be specific to the physical education part of the curriculum?
   f. How would an empiricist feel about athletics? about intramurals?
   g. How would an empiricist's program compare with the program that is currently in place at your school?

References

Cranston, M. (1972). Francis Bacon. *The encyclopedia of philosophy*. New York: Macmillan/Free Press.

Dewey, J. (1984). *Types of thinking*. New York: Philosophical Library.

Hobbes, T. (1995). Leviathan. *Classics of western philosophy* (pp. 475–532). Indianapolis, IN: Hackett Publishing.

Locke, J. (1995). An essay concerning human understanding. *Classics of western philosophy* (pp. 645–742). Indianapolis, IN: Hackett Publishing.

Melsen, A. (1967). Atomism. *The encyclopedia of philosophy* (p.193)*,* Paul Edwards (Ed.). New York: Macmillan/Free Press.

Runes, D. (1983). *Dictionary of philosophy*. New York: Philosophical Library.

Endnotes

1. One reason that the word "property" was not used in the Declaration of Independence is that not all of the farmers of the Constitution agreed with the idea that all individuals have the *right* to property. Instead, the framers argued that one has the right to *try to acquire* property and that this right is balanced with the possibility that one might not be able to acquire property. In addition, there was some discussion regarding slavery: Slaves were not allowed to own property in some states, and to include in the Declaration a statement that all individuals have the right to own property would have undermined the authority of the slave states.

2. For a more detailed explanation of induction, see Zeigler's comments on rationalism in the previous chapter. Of interest to us, and to anyone using empiricism, is that induction can be used in other philosophies than rationalism.

3. This idea explains why religious extremists drove Hobbes from England in the mid-1600s.

4. Remember that Descartes put himself in the good graces of the Catholic Church by arguing that free will does, in fact, exist. What would be the political consequences of Hobbes' philosophical position? Obviously, the truly religious would reject Hobbes' notions of God not being part of this reality and that there is no such thing as free will. These statements on Hobbes' part amounted to heresy!

5. This change in thinking shows how the times were changing in the Enlightenment. Philosophers began to take the corporeal world seriously, which is radically different than in the Middle Ages where the corporeal world was merely a bus stop on the way to heaven.

6. The *Dictionary of Philosophy* defines behaviorism as, "The contemporary American School of psychology—which abandons the concepts of mind and consciousness, and restricts both animal and human psychology to the study of behavior." (Runes, D., 1983, *Dictionary of Philosophy*. New York: Philosophical Library.)

7. Dewey, for instance, describing a weakness of empiricism in psychology, anticipated the discipline of motor behavior when he argued that, "The new psychology rejects this (strictly empirical) interpretation of experience, and defines sense perception as a stimulus which invites the creature to act. For this reason we speak of this new psychology as Motor Psychology." (Dewey, 1984, p. 116)

Knowing through Experimentation

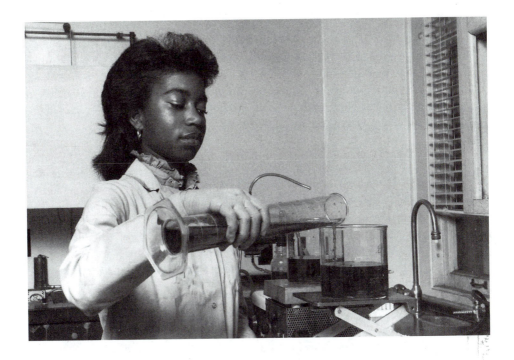

Chapter Objectives

Upon completing this chapter, the reader will be able to:

1. Define pragmatism as a way of knowing and relate it to the nature of being.
2. Understand that pragmatism is a combination of rationalism, empiricism, and test.
3. Understand the basis for the use of pragmatism in teaching, coaching, and other learning situations.
4. Understand how pragmatism is the basis for science.
5. Relate pragmatism to kinesiology, specifically areas of exercise physiology, biomechanics, motor behavior, and all areas where science is used.

You have probably noticed that the three philosophies covered so far—authority, rationalism, and empiricism—all have in common one characteristic: All of them seek "absolute" knowledge about reality—that is, they all argue that they and they alone provide a method for seeking the *truth*. Once a position on absolute knowledge about reality has been established, our "lived" experiences are *determined* by this knowledge. For better or worse, our lives, attitudes, and behaviors are explained totally by the philosophy. Many of you have noticed that these philosophies leave something to be desired. For instance, with Descartes we have an emphasis on mind and a deemphasis on the body, and all of our efforts toward generating knowledge aim at theory or the measurement of our bodies in motion. At the other extreme, with Hobbes' empiricism, we have a body without a mind and all knowledge is performance or behavior. With Plato we have knowledge that exists in the "reality of ideas," and we are limited to what we can infer of this reality, or to what we are told by some authority.

The philosophy of pragmatism was developed to overcome the limitations of the above types of thinking in that it argues that *there is no absolute truth*. We cannot emphasize this point enough: Truth is *relative* to the experiences of the person. There are versions of pragmatism that make this point in stronger or weaker terms, but the emphasis on experience, reason, and test are all the same.

The original pragmatists—Chauncey Wright, Charles Peirce (pronounced "purse"), William James, Oliver Wendell Holmes, and others—recognized that any philosophy that seeks to understand reality in terms that are absolute will often come up short in certain situations. At the very least, the epistemologies we have studied—authority, rationalism, and empiricism—come up with answers that make perfect sense in one context and are incomprehensible in another. How would one know when to accept one epistemology over another? Peirce, Wright, and James sought to answer this question by forming a group to discuss the limitations of traditional philosophy. This club, jokingly called the "Metaphysical Club" (none of these philosophers believed in metaphysics as we have discussed it so far), made significant contributions to a philosophy called *pragmatism* (Smith, 1980).

Pragmatism, also known as "experimentalism" and "instrumentalism," was developed with the idea in mind that all philosophies reflect the needs and concerns of the culture in which they are developed (Dewey, 1984). Philosophers are products of their times, sensitive to their culture's needs, who try to explain what they see in a logical manner. Seen in this way, pragmatism is an attempt to explain what was happening in nineteenth century America. In contrast, the philosophies we have studied so far attempted to explain what happens to humans at all times in all cultures—without exception. The members of the Metaphysical Club believed that the attempt to explain reality in terms that transcend time and culture cannot be done. For whatever reason, the context in which we exist cannot be dismissed in the attempt to find rules that explain reality. Since every context is different, there will be different rules that explain reality.

One of the best of the pragmatists is Richard Rorty, who argues that the best a culture can do is to understand the context in which it exists (Rorty, 1979). In so doing we must dismiss the attempt to find a set of rules that explains reality (metaphysics) and how we come to know (epistemology) it.

If we could bring ourselves to accept the fact that no theory about the nature of Man or Society or Rationality, or anything else, is going to synthesize (all philosophies), we could begin to think of . . . (metaphysics) . . . as little in need of synthesis as are paintbrushes and crowbars. . . . (All philosophies) are right, but there is no way to make (all) speak a single language." (Rorty, 1989, p. xiv.)

The language to which Rorty refers is the language of metaphysics, which can be understood as the seeking of the common set of rules that explains existence and knowledge the same for all people for all time. Rorty, then, is arguing that there is no such thing as a "metaphysics" that will help us understand our existence. What then is there? More importantly for this textbook, what are we going to study now?

The "Epistemology" of Pragmatism

While Rorty argues that there is no such thing as "metaphysics" in pragmatism, we will continue to use the term to refer to the rules of a philosophy that help define reality and knowledge. But with pragmatism we have a new kind of reality and a new kind of knowledge. The first thing one must do as a pragmatist is to accept the position that there is no such thing as *absolute truth* or *absolute knowledge*. According to pragmatists, there is no longer *one* answer to the question, "What is *the* truth?" There is no longer one truth. There can be many "truths." Put in a more humorous way, "do your own thing" is more easily understood with pragmatism than it is with the older philosophies. This statement is a radical contradiction from the previous philosophies we have studied. What are pragmatists to do? Basically, they ask a series of questions and make several assertions that will guide their thinking:

1. What is the *difference* as to whether we have absolute knowledge?
2. What is important is whether I have enough knowledge and the right kind of knowledge that will help me make an intelligent *decision*.
3. I want the best possible *outcome* concerning the problem I am addressing. (Dewey, 1984)

Pragmatism, looking at the above set of rules, is results-oriented rather than rule-oriented. This is the main difference between pragmatism and the philosophies studied so far. In more technical terms, the previous philosophies were based on an *a priori* system, while pragmatism is *a posteriori*. What do these terms mean?

A priori is a scholastic term, dating back to the Middle Ages. Its present use dates back to a famous German philosopher named Immanuel Kant and literally means "from what is prior." *A posteriori* literally means "from what is after." For a philosophy to be *a priori* it must set up the rules and then deduce how we are to live. *A posteriori* means that we will induce the rules after the fact, or after our experiences. Given these definitions, we can see that Plato, Descartes, Locke, Bacon, and Hobbes are so extreme because their philosophies are *a priori*. They establish the philosophy first and then deduce how we are to live. When a rule is carried to an extreme, extremely silly situations and consequences are the result.

Pragmatists, in contrast, believe that a philosophy developed without experience in the "real" world is totally arbitrary. As far as a pragmatist can tell, one philosophy is as good as another until one question is asked: "What is the difference between the two philosophies in the 'real' world?" Pragmatism was designed to settle the disputes between all previous philosophies by asking this question. One no longer seeks to establish a method first and then see what happens. Rather, one adds up all of the things that happen in the real world and then tries to see what all of these things have in common. If there is a commonality, then one can describe that as a rule. The rule is good as long as it works in practice.

With pragmatism, the *method* of gathering knowledge and making rules is far more important than asking questions about what is "real" or what is "knowledge." The *a priori* method of philosophy is dismissed. One no longer seeks to establish the set of rules that explain reality (metaphysics) or seek the nature of absolute knowledge (epistemology). Rather, one seeks to find out what works in the real world and *then* makes up the rules. One comes up with a very interesting (and practical) definition of knowledge and of reality from this position.

John Dewey's Epistemology

John Dewey may have been America's best philosopher. Dewey described best how pragmatism works; he began by listing the advantages and limitations of rationalism and empiricism in coming to know reality. In short, Dewey believed that the distinctions made by rationalists and empiricists are artificial and that in "reality" we combine these ways of knowing and put them to the test.

Dewey accepted the empiricists' position that one must begin with perception. He recognized that we live in the experienced world and that our senses are critical to understanding the lived world. However, he also argued that mere experience is limiting. Dewey was critical of philosophers like Hobbes who argued that we are bodies without minds. Here Dewey agreed with the rationalists, that we should *mediate* our experiences with our powers of mind or reason. The combination, then, of empiricism and rationalism overcomes some of the limitations of each epistemology. Furthermore, the processes of experience and of inference occur simultaneously. Remember, there is no distinction between mind and body in pragmatism; Dewey was a monist.

Pragmatism accepts the better parts of rationalism and empiricism, and consequently attempts to overcome the limitations of each. There are several ways to describe these limitations, but the easiest is to begin (as Dewey did) with the advantages and disadvantages of empiricism. Empiricism has several advantages: Knowledge is not in the exclusive domain of a minority (professors, priests, etc.), so empiricism overcomes the philosophy of authority (Plato). Next, everyone has experiences and knowledge from their experiences. Consequently, empiricism is very democratic. A limitation of empiricism is that not all of us can have the same experiences and occasionally our observations may be in error. Dewey argued, however, that just because they may be in error occasionally is no reason to dismiss them entirely. The idea that we all have experiences is good, not bad, and an occasional error is no reason to dismiss an entire method.

Rationalists, if you recall, are diametrically opposed to the positions of empiricists. Rationalists argue that since experience is unstable and changing, it is therefore not reliable. Furthermore, rationalists argue that the emphasis on the practical application of knowledge is a weakness. Since the scope of experience is limited, its practical application is limited to the mechanical and material aspects of life. Rationalists argue that humans should be concerned about the higher, spiritual, and ideal matters of Dewey, which is beyond the scope of experience and sense perception. To place experience and perception preeminent is to relegate the "higher" and spiritual aspects of life to second place. Finally, rationalists argue that when experience is preeminent, then we are limited by tradition. Since experience is limited to the past, it cannot provide perspective for planning the future or for deriving guidelines for the future.

Dewey, through the use of pragmatism, sought to take the best part of empiricism and combine it with the best parts of rationalism. In his words, "This new concept of experience preserves the strengths of empiricism, while avoiding the weaknesses which were the targets of the rationalists' criticism" (Dewey, 1984, pp. 113–124). Dewey argued that pragmatism provides a new means by which we can systematize and organize our thoughts. We can grasp the real meaning of knowledge only by organizing how well our ideas work in the "real" world. This point is carried out with the most rigor in the scientific method. But one does not have to be a scientist to be pragmatic. All one needs to do is to apply the pragmatic method to any aspect of our lives. Dewey says we must induce rules out of our experiences and test these rules in the "real" world. We can then move to the future, keeping the rules that work and discarding those that do not.

The Characteristics of the Pragmatic Method

According to Dewey there are three steps to the pragmatic method. Basically his argument is that the *mediation* of *experience* is the function of *reason*, and one's *actions* are the measure of this process. We have put these words in italics because these words emphasize the three aspects of the pragmatic method. *Mediation* and *reason* are components of rationalism and mind, while *experience* is a component of the body. *Action* is the test of this process in action. Specifically:

Step One: Begin with experience. The first act one performs is to observe, using the senses of the body. Dewey uses the example of crossing the street. The first thing one does is to look both ways and observe where the cars on the street are. The difference between Dewey's observation and that of empiricism is that, with pragmatism, observation is purposeful. "Mind" has been added to the observation. We are looking with a reason for looking, hearing with a reason for hearing, and so on. The purpose of looking is to get across the street; our eyes are not merely a camera receiving light that has bounced off automobiles. The *purpose* of looking is to *do* something.

Step Two: The next step after observing is *inference*. As Dewey says, this is the process that helps us move from the past into the future. Back to our example, the pedestrian decides, based on past experiences, if she can make it across the street.

She is comparing past experiences with what she is observing, and the comparison will dictate her actions. Inference, according to the pragmatists, is possible only when we have experiences comparable to the ones we experience in the present. If we have no experience that is similar, then we will be pretty lost. At any rate, we decide to cross (or not to cross). One *infers* a decision.

Step Three: The final step, and the one that separates pragmatism from other philosophies, is the step of *action*. The pedestrian walks across the street. *Action* is the proof of the decision made; it is the basis by which one determines the correctness of the first and second steps. Put differently, the pedestrian makes it across the street easily, or with difficulty, or she does not make it at all. Once completed, this *experience* is added to the database of all past decisions and will be used in the future to help the pedestrian cross the street.

Science in Physical Education

The *scientific method* is also the pragmatic method. The difference is one of degree, but not of kind. The scientific method follows the pragmatic method in a particularly rigorous manner. Experiences are recorded in a systematic, detailed manner. When one investigates in a certain area, the review of literature constitutes the sum total of *experiences*. These experiences are on record for all scientists to examine. The hypothesis is a clearly stated *inference* that will be tested. The *action* is the experiment itself; what happens is unknown before the experiment and known after its completion. The entire experiment is recorded, added to the database, and the scientist moves to the next experiment.

After a series of experiments is completed, one may *infer* a general principle based on the findings. For instance, after testing groups of joggers to determine the maximal use of oxygen (Max VO_2), one might infer that the more one runs, the higher one's Max VO_2. One would then test to make sure this is a true statement. Of course, one would find a certain truth to the statement, and the variations on this statement would warrant further investigation. One question emerges: Would one ever run out of variations to investigate? Put differently, Would one ever arrive at a final, ultimate truth? The answer, according to pragmatists, is no. There is no ultimate truth to arrive at. There is consensus, a sum total of experiences that can be communally shared, but there is no one "truth."

There are other assumptions that undergird the method of science as well. According to Rainer Martens, "Orthodox science holds that we can observe, know, and understand the universe in which we live; that by means of objective, inductive-empirical methods of science, we can fully comprehend the natural influences in our universe" (Martens, 1987, p. 32). Martens summarized the six general steps of the scientific method as follows:

1. Formulation of specific hypotheses
2. Design of the investigation
3. Accumulation of the data
4. Classification of the data
5. Development of generalizations
6. Verification of the results, both the data and generalizations

The scientific method needs very little support in the field of kinesiology. Indeed, it is accepted uncritically by many in the field, and it is the lack of criticism that has led to much of the debate regarding the hegemony of science in kinesiology. Often the debate centers on whether science is the desirable method of inquiry in certain disciplines such as sport psychology, or that the methods of science are so pervasive as to limit kinesiology to a narrow scientism and instrumental rationality. Other debates focus on whether other methods, such as qualitative research, are in fact a form of scientific inquiry at all, or if these alternate methods achieve knowledge of some higher quality than the method of modern science.

The criticisms of science itself we will leave to others (Kuhn, 1970; Polanyi, 1958; Popper, 1972). Our criticism is that too few of our students understand the assumptions that the critics attack, and consequently students accept the claims of science through an act of faith. Put humorously, kinesiology students often approach the "altar of science," light a candle, and pray for significance! On a more serious note, the benefits of the scientific method in kinesiology need to be made explicit to our students. When science is appropriate, and when it is not, is a topic worthy of study in a field that is composed of a dozen or so subdisciplines. Where science is particularly appropriate is in the subdisciplines of exercise physiology, biomechanics, and motor behavior. Its use is sometimes appropriate in the social sciences of sport psychology, pedagogy, and sport sociology, and science is of little or no use in the humanistic study of sport (philosophy, literature, history, cultural studies, etc.).

Pragmatism and Science Applied

Of interest to kinesiology students are those areas where pragmatism is especially appropriate. If one looks at the professions where knowledge is "applied," one will find pragmatism to be a very handy philosophy. In many instances professionals will be asked to make decisions that have significant practical impact. These decisions can often be framed in the practical language of pragmatism, where the consequences of one's decisions are played out in the real world. By examining the possibilities placed before the decision maker, one can select the best of all of the possibilities based on the predicted outcome of that decision. In theory, the decision will be better than one made solely on past performance because all past performances, are compared to one another, and the most desirable past performance is the one that will guide the decision-making process.

Situations where teachers might use the method of pragmatism range from the classroom to the playing field. Similarly, professionals in athletic training, sport law, exercise prescription, and many other kinesiology professions can use this process. Coaches are some of the best practitioners of pragmatism: Certainly coaches value results in the "real" world!

Courses in many university programs are designed to give students the opportunity to test for themselves the ideas that they have learned in their coursework. For instance, most programs that certify teachers require that students spend a semester in the schools as part of their academic coursework. These internships allow students to see for themselves specific pedagogical research in action. In such situations students can literally "test" this research. Assuming that the research is valid, students in internships will be able to continue the line of questioning on which pedagogy research is based. This research becomes the "observations" upon which new research will be done, and students can add to the body of knowledge and become professionals themselves.

Summary

Some final points should be made regarding pragmatism. In pragmatism there is no "cause and effect," but there are "means and ends." Means and ends imply a purpose, or a mind, behind the action. While a pragmatist will recognize "cause and effect" in the material world of objects, he will not limit human behavior to cause and effect. Pragmatists believe that humans have free will and that behavior is not determined exclusively by outside forces. Rather, "mind" makes behavior purposeful. The result of this union between mind and body is that a pragmatist is a monist: There is no distinction between a thought and an action. There is no such thing as a disembodied thought, or a mindless act. The two phrases are oxymorons.

Finally, pragmatism states that true knowledge occurs when observations and inferences have been tested in action. Action is the test of truth and validity. Some pragmatists have gone so far as to say that *knowledge is what works*. This epistemological statement is a little too harsh for some pragmatists, but it is a saying worth remembering. The purpose of pragmatism is to make knowledge and principles practical, of this world, and for our use. It is not to produce useless and ornamental knowledge. Pragmatism renders human behavior more intelligent and controlled by tested knowledge. The final part of this argument should go something like this:

> Rene Descartes: "Cogito, ergo sum." (I think, therefore I am.)
>   John Dewey: "Who cares? Does this information make any difference in my life? I don't think so. See ya, Rene."

Pragmatism is *the* American philosophy. It does not emphasize the philosophy itself, but instead focuses on the results of the method. A good pragmatist, however, never forgets that the ends and the means are so intimately connected that to consider one without the other is foolish. For instance, the muscle bulk added through using drugs is not a good choice to a pragmatist: The means (drugs) and the ends (muscle bulk) are connected. The ends are desirable, but the means are not, so using drugs is not the *best* course of action in the real world.

Discussion Questions

1. Construct the ideal program of study for a college physical education program using the epistemology of pragmatism. Do this in groups of three or four. Everything you have learned in this chapter should be applied.
2. Compare your program of study from the perspective of pragmatism to the program of study that you developed using the methods of authority, rationalism, and empiricism.
3. Use the collaborative learning session to answer the following questions:

a. What is the metaphysical position of a pragmatist? Do not limit yourself to the answer of the Metaphysical Club!
b. What is the epistemological position of a pragmatist? Tip: Use all of the steps.
c. What would an pragmatist's ideal curriculum (program of coursework) look like?
d. What would be the most important course in the curriculum?
e. What courses would be specific to the "professional" part of the curriculum? To the "scholarly" part of the curriculum?
f. How would a pragmatist feel about athletics? About intramurals?
g. How would a pragmatist's program compare with the program that is currently in place at your school?

References

Dewey, J. (1984). *Types of thinking*. New York: Philosophical Library.

Kuhn, T.S. (1970). *The structure of scientific revolutions* (2nd ed.). Chicago: University of Chicago Press.

Martens, R. (1987). Science, knowledge, and sport psychology. *The Sport Psychologist, 1*, 29–55.

Polanyi, M. (1958). *Personal knowledge: Towards a post-critical philosophy*. Chicago: University of Chicago Press.

Popper, K. (1972). *Objective knowledge*. Garden City, NY: Doubleday.

Rorty, R. (1979). *Philosophy and the mirror of nature*. Princeton, NJ: Princeton University Press.

Rorty, R. (1989). *Contingency, irony, and solidarity*. Cambridge, England: Cambridge University Press.

Smith, P. (1980). *Sources of progressive thought in American education*. Lanham, MD: University Press of America.

Chapter 12

Knowing through Awareness

Chapter Objectives

Upon completing this chapter, the reader will be able to:

1. Define somatics as a way of knowing and relate it to the nature of being.
2. Understand the basis for the use of somatic awareness in teaching, coaching, and other learning situations.
3. Understand the profound nature of somatic awareness on movement experiences.
4. Relate somatics to kinesiology, specifically sport psychology, pedagogy, and athletics.

Furthermore, because sport has the elements that produce, for many individuals, the stimulus necessary to extend themselves further than they do in any other facet of their lives, surely if we understood more about these great moments we would be able to help athletes experience more of them and get more out of them. After all, with pursuit of excellence and enjoyment on almost all competitive athletes' minds, the appreciation and facilitation of peak moments should be of interest to performers, coaches, and sport scientists alike. (McInman & Grove, 1991)

In Chapter 11, when discussing the virtues of pragmatism, we argued that the scientific method is one of the most frequently used epistemologies in kinesiology. However, one could make a strong argument that it is also the least used method of *students* of kinesiology, who know human movement (at least when they begin study in the field) by entirely different means (Randall, Buell, Swerkes, & Bailey, 1993). What we should emphasize now is that, while scientists, researchers, coaches, teachers, and other professionals in kinesiology use science to understand *about* human movement, science is woefully inadequate to understand the *subjective experience* of human movement.

This criticism of science, however, needs to be put in perspective. Science is not meant, and was never meant, to be a tool that helps one understand subjective experiences. Indeed, good scientists understand that science was not meant to help an athlete explain being in the "zone" when she hits her routine in gymnastics or when the baseball player hits everything coming over the plate. Science is meant to understand the *objective*, measurable world. Being in the zone, however, is not objective and measurable: It is *subjective* and immeasurable. Science, then, cannot explain the intensely personal, and often pleasurable, subjective experience of humans moving.

The subjective experience, or when one is aware of one's experiences, falls into the area of *somatics*. This term was developed from the word *soma*, which is defined as the unified nature of one's being. There is no separation in one's *soma* between mind and body. In this philosophy, the words do not make sense: There is no such thing as a disembodied mind, or an unconscious act. These concepts are literally *nonsense* in the philosophy of somatics.

There are several of philosophies that emphasize somatic knowing, or knowing through awareness of experience, particularly existentialism, phenomenology, Zen Buddhism, and other Eastern philosophies. These philosophies have an advantage over traditional Western ways of knowing in that they recognize, and help us organize and explain, our subjective experiences. Perhaps what will be helpful at this point is to explain what we mean by "subjective." "Subjective" literally means "of the subject." It has to do with an individual person and has nothing to do with anyone or anything else. "Subjective" means that an individual has an experience that often is observable *only* by that individual. A thought, an idea, an emotion, and a sensation are all "subjective" in the sense that an individual experiences it. However, when these types of experiences occur, the only person who knows that they occurred is the "subject" who experienced one of them.

Now one can contrast "subjective" with "objective." "Objective" is basically the opposite of "subjective": Those types of experiences that can be observed by all people can be "objectified." That is, anyone can measure or observe the "object." An individual moving can become an object, and from this perspective that person can be measured, the performance can be quantified, and the entire experience has a whole set of characteristics that can be understood through the methods of science. In Chapter 11 we discussed how science can be used to *objectively* understand human movement. In this chapter we will provide an introduction as to how we can *subjectively* understand human movement.

In short, somatic epistemologies are familiar to kinesiology students because they are based on experiences students have when they enter the classroom. And these experiences become much more legitimate and comprehensible when one examines and illustrates them with philosophies that assume the validity of subjectivity. There are many philosophies that emphasize the subjective experience, but the ones that we use in this chapter are existentialism, phenomenology, Zen Buddhism. These philosophies have in common one epistemological characteristic: To truly know something one must subjectively experience it.

Existentialism in Kinesiology

Jean Paul Sartre, the French existentialist, offered a classic example of this emphasis on subjectivity when he described the three dimensions of the human body (Kleinman, 1979). Sartre used as an example a climber making a difficult ascent. Before the ascent the climber is actively aware of his body. However, all of these thoughts vanish when he begins the ascent, and the climber becomes conscious only of the mountain. This is the first dimension of the body. "What remains, what *is*, is only the mountain. He is absorbed in it, his thoughts are completely given to it. And it is *because* he forgets his body that the body can realize itself as a living body" (Kleinman, 1979, p. 176). The climber is aware only of his climbing the mountain, he is enjoying climbing the mountain, he is, in a sense, the mountain.[1]

The second dimension of the body exists when the climber is watched by another, or when an observer sees the climber as an *object*. As Kleinman (1979) notes,

> That which holds least significance to the climber contains the most significance for the hidden viewer. It is this recognition of another as a functioning organism which makes anatomical and physiological analysis possible. (p. 176)

Kleinman has two points worth emphasizing. First, the second dimension of the body has nothing to do with the subjective experience of the climber. Instead, the second dimension is experienced by someone else. The "watcher" has turned the climber into an object, literally a moving piece of meat![2] Consequently, the second dimension of the body is the perspective another person has of the subject.

The second point Kleinman makes is that it is the second dimension of the body that is emphasized in Western science. Indeed, it is the perspective that is most used in the Western world. The emphasis on the subjective nature of moving in somatics provides a window into the Western perspective of objectifying our existence. If you recall the assumptions and axioms of science discussed in Chapter 3, all of these assumptions can be explained by

Sartre's second dimension of the body. We wish to emphasize here, though, that Sartre found this second dimension lacking: Sartre argued that this second dimension of the body was flawed because it lacked the subjective dimension that is essential to human existence.

Finally, the third dimension of the body occurs when the climber becomes aware that he is being watched. For Sartre, this perspective is destructive: The climber becomes annoyed, uncomfortable, and vulnerable under the gaze of another. Ultimately the look of the other results in alienation.[3]

In all three of Sartre's dimensions of the body, awareness and being are discussed in a manner so as to create an understanding of movement from the subjective perspective. In so doing Sartre provides perspective not only into the subjective nature of the movement experience and the body, but also provides perspective as to how and when we are *objective* about the body and human movement.

And it is no accident that Sartre used an activity such as climbing to illustrate his philosophy. To consciously move is to *be*. In Sartre's (1979) words, "Being-for-itself must be wholly body and it must be wholly consciousness; it cannot be *united* with a body. . . . There is nothing *behind* the body. . . . The body is wholly 'psychic.' (p. 164)

Phenomenology

Phenomenology offers insights into the subjective nature of human movement and of the body as does existentialism. As Kleinman (1979) argues,

> To the phenomenologist, to understand the body is to see the body not in terms of kinesiological analysis but in the awareness and meaning of movement. It's to be open to gestures and action; it's the grasping of being and acting and living in one's world. Thus movement becomes significant not by a knowledge about the body but through an awareness of the self—a much more accurate term. (pp. 176–177)

Kleinman argues, then, that the kind of knowledge created by phenomenology is *awareness*. Knowledge is not a thing, not an object, but an experience. It is not easily described, impossible to quantify, does not lend itself to grading, and is essential to our understanding of self and the experience of movement in the present moment. As Ravizza (1977) has argued, "Integrating mind and body so as to focus on what is happening in the present increases one's awareness; the experience is intensified as a result of full attention being given to the experience" (p. 104).

This type of knowing is not to be dismissed because it is so different from what we normally do in the West, such as using science to understand physical activity. Rather, it should be emphasized to students of kinesiology that this is the type of experience that led them to study movement, sport, or dance in the first place! Interestingly, because of the emphasis on objectivity, science, measurement, authority, and critical thinking, students of kinesiology are often led *away* from the aspect of *awareness* of their own movements. It is our argument that students will be much better off if they are taught to focus on their own awareness of the human movement experience.

Zen

Eastern philosophies such as Dhyana Buddhism, known in Japan as "Zen," offer similar approaches to the subjective nature of knowledge as do existentialism and phenomenology. In short, Zen focuses on experience and awareness. Perhaps the most well known exposition of Zen in the field of kinesiology is by Herrigel (1971), who defined Zen as

> not speculation at all but immediate experience of what, as the bottomless ground of Being, cannot be apprehended by intellectual means, and cannot be conceived or interpreted even after the most unequivocal and incontestable experiences: One knows it by not knowing it. (p. 7)

As with Sartre, who used a climber to describe the three dimensions of being, Herrigel used archery to try to describe a way of being. For Herrigel, though, archery is not the culmination of an epistemology well used. Rather, it is a window to the awareness of the "deepest ground of the soul . . . to one's becoming one with it." Exercises like archery become an art, and if all goes well an art "can in no circumstances mean accomplishing anything outwardly. . . but only inwardly, with oneself. Bow and arrow are only a pretext for something that could just as well happen without them" (p. 8).

The subjectivity of the experience, then, the *awareness* of the act of moving, is emphasized in Zen as it is in existentialism and phenomenology. Perhaps what distinguishes Zen from existentialism and phenomenology, and the point that Herrigel made in his argument, is that to focus on the awareness of the movement is to forget about the possible outcome(s) of the movement performance. Herrigel found that from a Zen perspective he erred when he was concerned with getting a bullseye when he shot. Instead, it was his awareness of the act of shooting that was important. Hitting the bullseye was only part of the act and not the most important part. The excellent shot is a measure of excellence, but being aware of the act of shooting and the quality of the shot are much more important than the location of an arrow in a target. When done well, archery as art does not distinguish between shooting the arrow and the bullseye. The outcome of the shot and the act of shooting are part of an integrated whole.

Peak Moments

What all of the above philosophies have in common is that they emphasize the subjective nature of experience. Applied to kinesiology, the three philosophies we described— existentialism, phenomenology, and Zen—can help students to explain, understand, and articulate the emotions and sensations that are part of the movement experience. Indeed, most students do just this when they talk about human movement. Statements such as, "That felt great!" or "I nailed it!" convey the pleasurable subjective feelings individuals experience when they move well.

One of the problems with somatic philosophies is that the aspects of existence for which they argue are not observable, nor are they measurable. In spite of this limitation, a vocabulary of particular types of somatic experiences has been developed to accurately describe the emotions or sensations that one can experience. These terms in philosophy and psychology help kinesiologists articulate and categorize their somatic experiences.

In kinesiology there is a growing body of scholarship that is concerned with the *peak moment* in human movement. In common terms that many students have used, a peak moment occurs when one is in the "zone," when one is performing at a personal best. Usually this performance is intensely pleasurable, and the individual is utterly absorbed by the experience. There are other characteristics as well, and understanding the terminology and the basic characteristics of the peak moment can provide kinesiologists with the language to articulate the quality and type of their experience. These experiences can range from one extreme to another. As McInman and Grove (1991) note,

> From utter contentment, with little desire to talk about the accomplishment, to elation and rapture, with a strong desire to articulate these feelings, athletes from a vast array of sports report an uncanny similarity of emotions and performance states when describing their greatest moments in sport. The fullness of such experiences is what makes sport not just recreational but also profound and life enhancing. (p. 333)

Working to eliminate some of the definitional problems that occur as a result of the highly personal nature of these experiences, McInman and Grove used the following definitions of particular types of peak moments to describe the pleasurable experience of moving well:

> Flow: "Enjoyment, an intrinsically rewarding, or autotelic, experience" (Privette, 1983, p. 1362)
>
> Peak experience: "A subjective experiencing of what is subjectively recognized to be one of the high points of life, one of the most exciting, rich and fulfilling experiences which the person has ever had" (Thorne, 1963, p. 248)
>
> Peak performance: "Behavior in any activity that transcends what normally could be expected in that situation" (Privette, 1981b, p. 51)

McInman and Grove developed these definitions out of a growing body of literature because so many different terms were being used to describe peak moments that it was difficult to compare one experience to another. Flow, peak experience, and peak performance have seven common characteristics, all of which can be understood by the philosophies described above. Yet they are all somewhat distinct as well. We will first describe the common characteristics of peak moments, and then we will describe how they are different. The end result is a description of what many students of kinesiology have already experienced through sport or physical education.

Peak moments in sport—flow, peak experience, and peak performance—have in common seven characteristics (Table 12-1). *Absorption* is the total immersion in the activity, and this condition is produced by intense concentration. *Detachment* is the feeling experienced by the athlete that she is performing without consciousness. A statement to the effect,

TABLE 12-1   **Common Characteristics of Peak Moments**

* Absorption: Total immersion in the activity or the experience.
* Detachment: Performance without consciousness; no fear of losing nor hope of winning.
* Emptiness: A sense of nothing; total loss of self.
* Ecstasy: The feelings of fun and joy.
* Larger energies: Unusually high levels of energy, strength, stamina, or fitness.
* Altered perceptions of time: Time "speeds up" or "slows down" depending on the nature of the activity.
* Sense of unity: Transcendence of dualities; no distinction between mind and body, or between self and team.

"You're thinking too much" would fall into this category. The athlete performs as if she can do no wrong, and there is no fear of losing nor hope of winning.

Emptiness is the feeling the athlete has when experiencing the peak moment. It is associated with a total loss of ego. *Ecstasy* is the feeling of "high" the athlete experiences. In short, a peak moment is fun! It is joyful, and it is this joy that attracts athletes to that experience over and over again. "In other words, their intrinsic motivation comes from the few rare moments when they lose themselves in something outside themselves, in the struggle, combat, or fight" (McInman & Grove, 1991, p. 344). *Larger energies* are the feelings of power and control athletes experience in peak moments. One experiences unusual levels of energy, strength, stamina, or fitness during such moments.

Altered perceptions of time occur, perhaps, because the athlete is so focused on the activity. It works both ways: Time either "speeds up" or "slows down" depending on the subjective nature of the experience. Baseball players see the baseball "float" toward the plate, while endurance runners have the finish line approach abnormally quickly. *Sense of unity* is the phrase used to describe how the athlete experiences a sense of "oneness" with the universe or with the environment. It seems as if all occurrences are related and almost expected. There are no distinctions between mind and body, or between individual and team (McInman & Grove, 1991).

If the above seven characteristics all characterize flow, peak experience, and peak performance, what makes these three types of peak moments distinct? The following definitions define the three types of moments. Following these definitions is a discussion of what makes these moments distinct.

Flow

Csikszentmihalyi (1975) argued that the essential characteristic of flow is the balance between what one can do and the demands of the task. When one is in this condition, the potential for the individual to experience flow is present. McInman and Grove elaborated on this principle:

> Only when there is a matching of ability and task demands will flow occur. In such circumstances, there is a unified flowing from one moment to the next. (McInman & Grove, 1991, p. 341)

TABLE 12-2 Characteristics of Flow

* Balance between what one can do and the demands of the task.
* Unified flowing from one moment to the next; there is no distinction between one moment and the next.
* Concentration comes easily and without coercion.
* Powerful feeling of control.
* Egoless with respect to the activity.
* Feelings of simple joy and happiness.
* Sought primarily because it is fun and pleasurable.

Flow occurs, then, when there is no distinction between one moment and the next. This is another critical component of flow: One is so immersed in the activity that one loses track of time.[4] Sartre's first dimension of the body (see page 172) emphasizes this aspect of flow.

Another major characteristic of flow is that one concentrates on a limited stimulus field and this concentration comes easily and without coercion (McInman & Grove, 1991). Individuals experience a feeling of control and appear to be "egoless" with respect to the activity. By "egoless" it is meant that the athlete does not attempt to associate status or power with the accomplishment of the flow state. Finally, "Of all of the aspects of flow, the most dominant characteristic must surely be the simple joy and happiness involved. People seek flow primarily because it is fun and pleasurable" (McInman & Grove, 1991, p. 341).

It is hard to say it better than did McInman and Grove: The flow state is one of the most pleasurable movement experiences one can have. It is our contention that the experience of flow is one of the prime motivating forces behind students entering the field of kinesiology. Swimmers approaching their peak prior to a final competition often experience euphoric feelings of competence, control, and speed. Runners experience "runner's high" unexpectedly, causing them to look forward to the next workout. Gymnasts hit their routine; dancers perfectly execute their choreography; basketball players make the blind pass and "can't miss." No matter what the movement activity, the possibility of flow is present, and in all cases the flow experience is described by the characteristics in Table 12-2.

Peak Experience

Perhaps the best scholar of the peak experience was Abraham Maslow, whose research into the hierarchy of needs culminated in the state of self-actualization. To reiterate what we stated above, the peak experience is a subjective experiencing of what is subjectively recognized to be one of the high points of life. It is one of the most exciting, rich, and fulfilling experiences that the person has ever had (McInman & Grove, 1991). This type of experience happens frequently in sports and is one of the reasons that many athletes seek to become coaches. In short, those who have had a peak experience find that this experience has in some way ordered their life, and these individuals hope either to pass along something of this experience to their students, or in some way to recapture the experience for themselves in some other aspect of their sporting life.

TABLE 12-3   Characteristics of Peak Experience

* Recognized to be one of the high points of life.
* The most exciting, rich, and fulfilling experiences one has ever had.
* Associated with fully functioning individuals in self-actualization.
* Characterized by feelings of bliss, great joy, and illumination.
* Strong sense of self and freedom from outer restrictions, very often unexpected, rare, and extraordinary.
* Associated with individuals who are more open minded.

McInman and Grove described Maslow's research below. Maslow saw peak experiences

> as an individual's most exciting, fulfilling, and meaningful moments in life. He also argued that they were associated with fully functioning individuals, in what he termed self-actualization. That is, self-actualizing people tend to report more peak experiences than less fully developed subjects. . . . Peak experiences are characterized by feelings of bliss, great joy, and illumination. There is a strong sense of self and freedom from outer restrictions. They are very often unexpected, rare, and extraordinary. (McInman & Groe, 1991, p. 340)

While many athletes, dancers, and others in a movement experience do have a peak experience, many do not. The reasons for this are unclear. However, there is some reason to believe that individuals who are more open minded are more likely to have a peak experience than those who are not (Table 12-3). This condition, however, warrants further study, and certainly is not a predictor of peak experience.

Peak Performance

In the words of McInman and Grove (1991), "Peak performance is superior behavior. It is behavior that exceeds what is normally expected of an individual in a specific situation" (p. 338). Usually peak performance is the best performance ever for a particular individual, but sometimes it is the best performance that *any* individual has ever had, such as a world record performance. The central characteristic of peak performance is that the level of the performance is of the very highest quality for that individual (Table 12-4).

The type of performance is irrelevant. Peak performances happen in all walks of life and in all different types of movement situations. "Thus, a peak performance can occur during physical activity, strength in a crisis, intellectual activity, creative expression, or human interaction. . . . It may also occur as a response to a placebo, via biofeedback, or to hypnosis" (McInman & Grove, 1991, p. 339). Peak performance, then, is not specifically associated with sport. Rather, peak performance is a highly subjective condition of human existence, and human movement is a particularly visible way of demonstrating peak performance.

TABLE 12-4 Characteristics of Peak Performance

* Superior behavior.
* Best performance ever for a particular individual; the level of the performance is of the very highest quality.
* Can occur during any experience or subjective condition.
* Can be characterized by (1) high level of performance; (2) clear focus, (3) spontaneity, (4) expression of self, and (5) initial fascination with the task.
* Athletes experience (1) fulfillment, (2) awareness of power, (3) lack of apt words, (4) temporality, (5) overwhelmed senses, and (6) feelings of being not companionable.
* Absence of an awareness of "the world" around the individual.

Peak performance can be characterized by five factors:

1. High level of performance
2. Clear focus (in terms of clarity and sharpness)
3. Spontaneity (although the action was planned, the performance is spontaneous)
4. Expression of self (strong sense of self)
5. Initial fascination with the task (the individual is interested in the type of activity to be performed and may spend a lot of time thinking about the activity prior to performing).

Athletes who experience a peak performance often try to describe it using the following terms:

1. Fulfillment
2. Awareness of power
3. Lack of apt words (indescribable)
4. Temporality
5. Overwhelmed senses
6. Not companionable

That athletes are not companionable, or that involvement by others is seen as an intrusion, is a bit surprising. There is some research to indicate that involvement by others may inhibit the ability of an athlete to experience a peak performance. Perhaps this is because involvement by another, such as a coach, may distract the athlete and disrupt his attention. Also important to peak performance is the absence of an awareness of "the world" around the individual. In other words, the athlete has narrowed her awareness to the activity itself and nothing else. The athlete's "global awareness" is at a minimum.

Distinctions between Peak Moments

McInman and Grove summarize the differences between peak moments as follows:

Very simply, peak experience is intense joy, flow is an intrinsically rewarding experience, and peak performance is superior functioning. . . . A more in-depth statement suggests peak experience is characterized by (a) fulfillment, significance, and/or spirituality . . .,(b) highest happiness . . ., or (c) cosmic, pure psyche and absolute ecstasy. . . . Flow, on the other hand, is fun, enjoyable, and/or the matching of one's abilities with the challenge...Finally, peak performance is superior behavior, a high level of performance, and a clear focus of attention. . . . A joyful event is exclusively peak experience when it does not specifically involve (superior) behavior. An event is exclusively peak performance when superior performance is not accompanied by joy, or enjoyment. An activity is exclusively flow only at the lower levels of joy and performance. (McInman & Grove, 1991, pp. 345–346)

Table 12-5 summarizes McInman and Grove's major characteristics of peak moments in sport.

One final note regarding the peak moments in Table 12-5. It is not necessary that all of the characteristics of any type of peak moment be present at one time. Also, one can move between these different types of experiences.

Obviously, peak moments are desirable types of experiences. How can one facilitate having one of these peak moments? Unfortunately, there is no guarantee that one can do so. There are some conditions, however, that seem to coincide with peak moments. Basically, the more experienced the athlete, the greater the possibility of the peak moment. And with more experience athletes experience peak moments more frequently. This stands to reason: The best athletes perform at peak more frequently by definition. Put differently, what makes a "better" athlete is, in part, the fact that he or she performs at "peak" more frequently than does his or her peers. Also, as athletes mature, better athletes have stayed with their sport *because* they have had more peak moments. Indeed, it is the desire to have a peak moment that keeps the athlete in the sport at all.

There is much research to be done on how to "cause" a peak moment. What little we do know can be summarized as follows: Athletes must focus attention so as to concentrate only on the important elements of the task. Extraneous information must be filtered out. The ability to focus takes practice, and athletes who experience peak moments practice having them. At the same time, the athlete cannot try to "have" a peak moment. As soon as one focuses on trying to have a peak moment, one is for the most part precluded from hav-

TABLE 12-5   Major Characteristics of Peak Moments in Sports

Peak experience	Flow	Peak Performance
High level of joy (ecstasy)	Fun	Superior behavior
Transpersonal and mystical	Enjoyable	High level of performance
Passive	Loss of ego	Clear focus (absorption)
Feeling of unity and fusion	Playful	Strong sense of self
Loss of self	Feeling of control	Fulfillment
Spontaneous	Lost time and space	Not playful
Feeling of peak power	Intrinsic motivation	Intended action but spontaneous performance

ing one. Catfish Hunter, the famous baseball pitcher, described this "having and not having" consciousness:

> Catfish Hunter, in describing the perfect game he pitched against the Minnesota Twins in 1968, says, "I wasn't worried about a perfect game going into the ninth. It was like a dream. I was going on like I was in a daze. I never thought about it the whole time. If I'd thought about it, I wouldn't have thrown a perfect game—I know I wouldn't." (McInman & Grove, 1991, p. 347)

Hunter, then, says that "thinking too much" is a cause of failing to achieve a peak moment. McInman and Grove summarize other means of facilitating the peak moment:

> Such comments provide justification for practicing imagery from an internal perspective and not an external perspective: If you perceive yourself and your actions from the outside, you are thinking about yourself, and thus flow halts. . . .This noneffort is very similar to the necessary condition of not aiming for a peak performance, or flow. If you set out with that in mind, it almost certainly won't occur. These moments are usually spontaneous, and thinking about them can only be a hindrance. . . . Similar to the need for an absence of conscious thought is the use of rituals in order to facilitate a peak moment. If athletes have a set routine, both prior to and during the game, then they can expend less conscious effort on unnecessary thoughts and stimuli. (McInman & Grove, 1991, pp. 347–348)

Somatics in Kinesiology

Perhaps the use of somatics is most frequently found in the subdiscipline and profession of sport psychology, where an awareness of performance in the activity itself leads to increased levels of performance. Ravizza (1977), for instance, has argued that awareness, or "focus," is a clear advantage to the enhancement of performance:

> The technique of focusing attention on the present and bringing mind and body together will enable the athlete to concentrate on an awareness of his body. This concentration is common in athletics as evidenced by the psyching-up process. The athlete often prepares for a game by narrowing his thought process on the immediate contest. He dismisses all thoughts that are irrelevant to the actual playing of the game. His concentration is intense and centered only on the game. The player is not consciously thinking about what he is doing, he is just doing it. (p. 106)

Summary

One use of somatic experiences in sport psychology, using any or all of the ways of knowing described above, occurs when one examines optimal performance in athletics. Sport psychology is the discipline most closely allied with the understanding of the qualities of

peak performance and is where most of the research has been performed in order to significantly improve performance.

Other disciplines such as pedagogy, motor behavior, sport philosophy, and sport literature utilize the methods and assumptions of subjective epistemologies to generate knowledge. Using subjective ways of knowing in these disciplines makes understanding subject
matter easier for the student because these methods utilize knowledge the students already
have: their own experiences. Students merely need to made aware—in a much more rigorous and introspective way—of their own experiences. Indeed, the subdisciplines of kinesiology that emphasize the actual movement experience of the student will find subjective
ways of knowing informing and informative.

Discussion Questions

1. Construct the ideal program of study for a college physical education program using
   the epistemology of somatics. Do this in groups of three or four. Everything you have
   learned in this chapter should be applied.
2. Compare your program of study from the perspective of somatics to the program of
   study that you developed using the methods of authority, rationalism, empiricism, and
   pragmatism.
3. Use the collaborative learning session to answer the following questions:
   a. What is the metaphysical position of one with somatic awareness?
   b. What is the epistemological position of one with somatic awareness?
   c. What would the ideal curriculum (program of coursework) look like if one were
      somatically aware?
   d. What would be the most important course in the curriculum?
   e. What courses would be specific to the "professional" part of the curriculum? To the
      "scholarly" part of the curriculum?
   f. How would one who is somatically aware feel about athletics? About intramurals?
   g. How would a somatics program of kinesiology compare with the program that is
      currently in place at your school?

References

Csikszentmihalyi, M. (1975). Play and intrinsic rewards. *Journal of Humanistic Psychology, 15,* 41–63.

Herrigel, K. (1971). *Zen and the art of archery.* New York: Pantheon Books.

Huizinga, J. (1953). *Homo ludens: A study of the play-element in culture.* Boston: Beacon Press.

Kleinman, S. (1979). Jean Paule Sartre. In E. Gerber & W. Morgan (Eds.), *Sport: A philosophic inquiry.* Philadelphia: Lea & Febiger.

McInman, A., & Grove, J.R. (1991). Peak moments in sport: A literature review. *Quest, 43*(3), 333–351.

Privette, G. (1983). Peak experience, peak performance, and flow: A comparative analysis of positive human experiences. *Journal of Personality and Social Psychology, 45,* 1361–1368.

Randall, L., Buell, C., Swerkes, B., & Bailey, I. (1993). Learning style preferences of physical education majors. *Discipline exchanges: Physical education.*

The California State University System Institute for Teaching and Learning.

Ravizza, K. (1977). The body unaware. In *Being human in sport* (pp. 99–109). Philadelphia: Allen & Fahey/Lea & Febiger.

Sartre, J. (1979). The body. In *Sport: A philosophic inquiry* (pp. 163–165). Philadelphia: Lea & Febiger.

Thorne, F.C. (1963). The clinical use of nadir experience reports. *Journal of Clinical Psychology, 19,* 248–250.

Endnotes

1. Coaches and athletes will sometimes joke about this experience. In such situations one might say, "Be the ball!" In other words, don't let anything separate the athlete from the experience he or she desires. Get into it!

2. An example of this condition exists when construction workers watch a woman walk past their worksite. Often the workers have no interest in the *subjective* experience of the woman walking past their location. Rather, the workers have turned the woman into an "object" of desire. This situation was reversed recently, and rather famously, when Coca Cola advertised Diet Coke by having a group of women in an office viewed with much appreciation a handsome construction worker as he took his Diet Coke break. Our point is that one's sex does not limit the ability to turn another into an object. Rather, the experience is one of perspective.

3. Using again the example of the woman or the man being watched by others, the person being watched often becomes very uncomfortable when he or she becomes aware that he or she is being watched. Have you ever been in the situation when you are being watched and evaluated solely because of your physical appearance? While some do, in fact, enjoy this situation, most do not. This discomfort is what Sartre called *alienation*.

4. It should be noted that this is also a characteristic of play. See Johann Huizinga's *Homo Ludens* (1953) for a more specific definition.

Chapter 13

Knowing through Story Telling

Chapter Objectives

Upon completing this chapter, the reader will be able to:

1. Define narrativism as a way of knowing and relate it to the nature of being.
2. Understand the basis for the use of narrative knowing in teaching, coaching, and other learning situations.
3. Understand the profound nature of narratives on how we understand and experience movement.
4. Relate narrativism to kinesiology, specifically sport history, sport philosophy, and sport literature, as well as to all areas of kinesiology.

The next epistemology discussed is that of narrative knowing. Recent scholarship in kinesiology argues that narrative ways of knowing are used both in the real world to understand the meaning behind movement (Estes, 1990; Newburg, 1992) and in kinesiology to illustrate or explain "reality" in the field (Kretchmar, 1990). Briefly, a narrative is a kind of organizational scheme expressed in story form that fosters the creation of meaning. Polkinghorne (1988) defines a narrative as "the fundamental scheme for linking individual human actions and events into interrelated aspects of an understandable composite" (p. 13).

Thus, a "narrative" can be understood as both the story and the interpretation of the events that make up the story. What we are interested in is the interpretation: What does a story mean? Why is it believable? Why do we act on stories more easily than we do on "rational" ways of knowing like science, empiricism, or rationalism?

Narratives have not been studied by philosophers to the extent that other rational methods of knowing have. Yet at the same time it is one of the more enjoyable ways of knowing that humans have devised. We will not explain the philosophy behind this way of knowing as much as we will argue that students should appreciate this way of knowing kinesiology because reading stories, telling stories, and watching films comprise one of the most potent, yet misunderstood, epistemologies.

While we are not going to spend much time explaining this philosophy, several descriptions of narratives reveal the following. The metaphysical position of the "narrativists" is that of monism. There is no distinction between the story that is told and the teller. Put differently, the story and the story teller are, philosophically speaking, indistinguishable.

Have you noticed that your feelings toward a person go hand-in-hand with the stories that person tells? If a person tells you stories about his life, his experiences, his successes and failures, and if you eventually come to "like" this person, what is "it" that you like? Is it not the "stories" that this person tells you? Certainly there may be something about the person's appearance, his physical stature that you find attractive. But just as likely it is the "person" who embodies these stories with whom you are friendly. In sum, there is no distinction between the stories, or narratives, one tells and embodies, and the person. Consequently, reality is both the story and the person woven into one complete package.

The epistemological position of a narrativist is a bit more complex. How do we come to know through hearing a narrative? An empiricist would argue that the "hearing" part is the most important, but a narrativist would argue that the story has meaning to us as we are told the story. The meaning that is conveyed in the story explains and interprets reality to us. It stands to reason, then, that the study of narratives, how they are told, and how they convey meaning is also the study of reality. Scholars have found that narratives are an ideal vehicle for studying reality because narratives exist in all aspects of our lives. A scholar by the name of Roland Barthes argued just this point:

The word narrative covers an enormous variety of genres . . . : the narrative may incorporate articulate language, spoken or written; pictures, still or moving; gestures and the ordered arrangement of all the ingredients. It is present in myth, legend, fable, short story, epic, history, tragedy, comedy, pantomime, painting, . . . stained glass windows, cinema, comic strips, journalism, conversation. In addition, under this almost infinite number of forms, the narrative is present at all times, in all places, in all societies; the history of narrative begins with the history of mankind. (Barthes, 1988, p. 14)

Narratives are so much around us that they are hard to see—much like the saying "you can't see the forest but for the trees": We are so surrounded by narratives that we take their existence for granted. Narratives are like water to a fish, or the air we breathe—they are so common we take them for granted. Consequently, narratives are an ideal method by which we can understand meaningful experiences in any walk of life. And since sport and playful experiences are an essential part of human existence, the stories that we tell in the world of sport can reveal much about how and why sport is meaningful to us.

Narratives are passed on from one individual to another, or from one group to another. Consequently, narratives often describe "shared meanings," or those meanings that define a specific social group such as a team, a school, or a nation (Estes, 1990). One needs only to say the words "Notre Dame football" and the images of autumn Sundays, gold helmets, and pleasant (or not so pleasant, if you are not a fan of Notre Dame) memories of college football. The shared meanings of all of us who are fans of the Notre Dame football team are passed along from one to another, until there is a distinct group of people who have very similar attitudes and beliefs about that football program, what it stands for, and how fans relate to the program.

Philosopher Richard Rorty (1989) argues that narratives are a powerful vehicle for the expression of personal meaning as well, and that narratives are an aspect of culture that is becoming the mechanism by which we redescribe ourselves. The novel, the movie, and the television program have, gradually but steadily, replaced the sermon and the treatise as the principle vehicles of moral change and progress. Put differently, philosophers now recognize that the stories we tell each other are a more powerful mechanism for exchanging shared meanings than more traditional philosophical methods such as science or rationalism. Studies of kinesiology majors support this idea: Students who enter our field as freshmen are much more familiar with the talk that goes on in the locker room than the rational methods of philosophers and scientists. The stories told in the locker room are much more powerful, and convey to us our understanding of the experiences we have had. It is not just the athletes, either. Who could have predicted the wave at a football game? The end zone dance? "Trash" talk?

While one might be convinced that personal and public meaning can be conveyed through narratives, what are some of these shared meanings? One answer is that these shared meanings are the myths used in contemporary culture that make our sporting existence meaningful are passed along in narratives. Myths are part of an ideology and are often the models people refer to when they try to understand their world and their behavior in it (Robertson, 1980). Ernst Cassirer (1979) argued that humans use the "language of myth" in all of their experiences, "For this language is not restricted to a special field; it pervades the whole of man's life and existence" (p. 245). Sport owns its share of myths. Sport myths are perpetuated and dynamic and are a source of many beliefs about sport. They can be understood as purveyors of meaning in popular culture,

> both teaching and interpreting social reality to those who partake and (they) can come in many packages, ranging from the newspaper to the novel, the TV or the

film, the radio or the conversation or even within the sacred temples of action. . . . Sport as social myth is often found embodied in the Heroes of Sport, who are really the purveyors of myth rather than heroes of Sport. (Crepeau, 1981, p. 24)

One can even claim that sport itself is myth in the sense that one's sporting reality is defined as the sum total of experiences and narratives one has created and lived through in sport (Estes, 1990). And if one accepts the idea that myth is a powerful explanation of one's attitudes and behaviors, the influence of sport myths on behavior should not be under-estimated. As Oriard (1982) has argued, "Sport, in fact, as Malamud has taught us so well that we now take his insights for granted, is the most important and quite possibly the sole repository for myth in American society today" (pp. 211–212).

Various myths are evident in specific narratives. For instance, Bernard Malamud (1952), Jack London (1985), and Irwin Shaw (1985) have described powerful images of how athletes age, and how the aging athlete is an expression of our mortality. More recently, this theme was examined in the films "Bull Durham" and "The Natural." Mala-mud (1952) and Kinsella (1982) have also examined the pastoral and mythic images asso-ciated with baseball. The concept of the hero has been expressed often in sport films and sport fiction (Oriard, 1982). One can argue that "Rocky" is an American legend, exhibiting the characteristics of the American athlete hero, muscular Christianity, rugged individual-ism, the Great White Hope, and a Horatio Alger figure (Estes & Gibson, 1987). The devel-opment of certain themes, at the expense of others, speaks volumes about sport in American culture. For instance, one does not have to look far to notice that American sport heroes are almost always white, male, and middle class. The absence of women in mainstream sport narratives reveals much about American sporting attitudes.

It is the study of heroes that is perhaps most revealing to students in kinesiology. Many students enter the field because they admire the athletic role models they see on television or have competed with and against. What, then, is a "hero"? Michael Oriard (1982) has summarized the characteristics of the hero in what he calls a "morphology" of the Ameri-can athlete hero. Oriard's morphology, or the study of the body of a story, is in turn based on the timeless myths of western civilization:

The mythological hero, setting forth from his commonday hut or castle, is lured, carried away, or else voluntarily proceeds to the threshold of adventure. There he encounters a shadow presence that guards the passage. The hero may defeat or conciliate his power and go alive into the kingdom of the dark (brother-battle, dragon-battle; offering, charm), or be slain by the opponent and descend in death (dismemberment, crucifixion). Beyond the threshold, then, the hero journeys through a world of unfamiliar yet strangely intimate forces, some of which severely threaten him (tests), some of which give magical aid (helpers). When he arrives at the nadir of the mythological round, he undergoes a supreme ordeal and gains his reward. The triumph may be represented as the hero's sexual union with the goddess-mother of the world (sacred marriage), his own divination (apotheosis), or again—if the powers have remained unfriendly to him—his theft of the boon he came to gain (bride-theft, fire-theft); intrinsically it is an expansion of con-sciousness and therewith of being (illumination, transfiguration, freedom). The final work is that of return. If the powers have blessed the hero, he now sets forth under their protection (emissary); if not, he flees and is pursued (transformation flight, obstacle flight). At the return threshold the transcendental powers must remain behind; the hero reemerges from the kingdom of dread (return, resurrection). The boon that he brings restores the world (elixir). (Oriard, 1982, p. 37)

The typical plot of the stories told in the world of sport, both our own experiences and the stories we read and the movies we watch, follows a similar pattern. As Oriard (1982) describes it,

> The hero leaves him home and parents to go off to a challenging prestigious school. He encounters a rival and overcomes him, gaining admittance not only to the school itself but to the elite circles within the school. The hero then undergoes a series of adventures and adversities, with the aid of loyal friends and the hindrance of rivals, until he achieves his final triumph, creating joy for all the deserving and particularly elevating himself to great fame. The story ends. (Oriard, 1982, pp. 37–38)

Some stories come to mind quickly: "Rocky," the Academy Award winning film about a down-on-his-luck boxer in Philadelphia in the 1970s, is an excellent example of this formula. Rocky comes from the slums of Philadelphia, overcomes adversaries (his own self doubt, his background, the doubts of his coach and peers) to defeat Apollo Creed in a climatic ending. He is united with Adrian and elevated to the position of hero through his boxing skills. The story ends.

Similarly, the film "Field of Dreams" describes the story of a man going on a quest, entering a "world" of unreality, and returning to grant a boon of happiness of the world. As the character of Terrance Mann, played by James Earl Jones, notes, "It's money they've got, and it's peace they lack." In the end the hero in field of dreams grants "peace" to all of those people coming to see the baseball field.

Summary

Students entering kinesiology find that their understanding of sport, dance, and human movement has been confined to their subjective experiences and their narrative interpretations. An examination of their narrative beliefs, and how narratives impart meaning, can help students understand the origins of their own attitudes and behaviors. Specific to kinesiology, narratives are used in the disciplines of sport literature, sport philosophy, sport history, sport sociology, and sport psychology. An understanding of what a narrative is and how it shapes meaning in the sport context is helpful in understanding all or parts of these disciplines. Perhaps most importantly, an understanding of narratives can provide a bridge between the meaningful experiences the student brings into the classroom and the rigorous, analytical type of knowing routinely used in contemporary kinesiology.

Discussion Questions

1. Construct the ideal program of study for a college physical education program using the epistemology of narrativism. Do this in groups of three or four. Everything you have learned in this chapter should be applied.

2. Compare your program of study from the perspective of narrativism to the program of study that you developed using the methods of authority, rationalism, empiricism, pragmatism, and somatics.

3. Use the collaborative learning session to answer the following questions:
   a. What is the metaphysical position of a narrativist?
   b. What is the epistemological position of a narrativist?
   c. What would the ideal curriculum (program of coursework) look like if one were to emphasize narratives?
   d. What would be the most important course in the curriculum?
   e. What courses would be specific to the "professional" part of the curriculum? To the "scholarly" part of the curriculum?
   f. How would a narrativist feel about athletics? About intramurals?
   g. How would a program of kinesiology that used narratives compare with the program that is currently in place at your school?

References

Barthes, R. (1988). Introduction to the structural analysis of the narrative. In D. Polkinghorne, *Narrative Knowing and the human sciences* (p. 14). Albany, NY: SUNY Press.

Cassirer, E. (1979). The technique of our modern political myths. In D. Verene (ed.), *Symbol, myth, and culture* (pp. 37–48). New Haven: Yale University Press.

Crepeau, R. (1981). Sport, heroes, and myth. *Journal of Sport and Social Issues, 5*(1), 23–31.

Estes, S. (1990). *Sport myth as lived experience.* Unpublished doctoral dissertation, The Ohio State University.

Estes, S., & Gibson, J. (1986). *Rocky: An odyssey of muscular thespianism.* Annual Conference for the North American Society for Sport History, Columbus, Ohio, May 5.

Kinsella, W. (1982). *Shoeless Joe.* New York: Ballantine.

Kretchmar, S. (1990). Values, passion, and the expected lifespan of physical education. *Quest, 42*(2), 95–112.

London, J. (1985). A piece of steak. In P. Schwed & H.W. Wind (Eds.), *Great stories from the world of sport* (vol. 2, p. 134). New York: Simon & Schuster.

Malamud, B. (1952). *The natural.* New York: Avon Books.

Newburg, D. (1992). Images and insights: Joseph Campbell and heroism in performance. *Contemporary Thought on Performance Enhancement, 1*(1), 141–146.

Oriard, M. (1982). *Dreaming of heroes: American sports fiction 1868–1980.* Chicago: Nelson-Hall.

Polkinghorne, D. (1988). *Narrative knowing and the human sciences.* Albany, NY: SUNY Press.

Robertson, J., (1980). *American myth, American reality.* New York: Hill and Wang.

Rorty, R. (1989). *Contingency, irony, and solidarity.* Cambridge, England: Cambridge University Press.

Shaw, I. (1985). The eighty yard run. In D. Vanderwerken & S. Wertz (Eds.), *Sport inside out* (pp. 9–19). Fort Worth, TX: Texas Christian University Press.

Chapter *14*

The Nature of Human Movement

Chapter Objectives

Upon completing this chapter, the reader will be able to:

1. Compare and contrast the salient concepts of human movement with those of "traditional" physical education.
2. Understand the significance of the contributions made by Per Henrik Ling to the development of human movement theory.
3. Discuss the basis of the body of knowledge reflected in Human Movement Studies and why advocates of Human Movement Studies claim it is superior to physical education's theory base.
4. Understand the concepts and ideas that reflect the nature of human movement outcomes as espoused by Rudolph Laban.
5. Identify various outcomes of human movement theory that lend themselves to inclusion in contemporary American educational philosophy.
6. Discuss the positions relative to the value of human movement as espoused by Brown, Cassidy, and Renshaw.

In general, this chapter will focus on the rational for understanding the nature of human movement, the content of human movement, and how it is supposed to articulate with kinesiology. Salient information derived from classic scholarship in this area will be presented that establishes human movement as more accurately representing the nature and scope of the field than physical education. While some of the activities and methods used in traditional physical education are sound, most professionals and academics in the field believe that human movement is more advantageous than physical education because of its theoretical base and educational outcomes; a shift to human movement does not necessarily preclude the elimination of physical education. This chapter will differentiate human movement from physical education and will provide a compelling rationale so that the reader can understand why human movement, not physical education, is the "soul" of kinesiology and the essence of our field.

The initial impression that most people have regarding contemporary human movement as a curricular offering is identified with those types of activities commonly found in the elementary schools, from kindergarten through the sixth grade. In many schools, the activities and methods that reflect the concepts of modern human movement continue to operate under the traditional label of "physical education." However, a more contemporary label for the K–6 curriculum teaching human movement fundamentals is "Movement Education." It is important to note that, traditionally, physical education has been, and continues to be, identified with physical activity instruction that is taught in grades K–12. In addition, there are a number of colleges and universities faculties, that to this day, retain their identity as the Physical Education Department as opposed to identifying with kinesiology, human movement, human performance, exercise science, or other more contemporary and timely academic designations. Advocates of human movement argue that the term physical education is to limiting and the term human movement represents the future. After reading this chapter, you will understand why.

Human Movement: The "Soul" of Kinesiology

Movement education, as you may have experienced it, is an essential developmental course in grades K–6 that ideally articulates with the overall physical education curriculum that is traditionally identified with grades K–12. Movement education is a critical curricular component in colleges and universities preparing students in kinesiology, especially in the area of pedagogy. It is important to understand that *Movement Education* in grades K–6 *is but one component of Human Movement Studies.*

Human movement is the essence of our field, and for this reason, human movement has been identified as the "soul" of kinesiology, as well as physical education. All of the other elements that comprise our field are drawn from other academic disciplines; teacher preparation originates from research in the discipline of education, biomechanics originates from the disciplines of engineering and physics, kinesiology originates from anatomy, physiology, and physics, psychology of sport originates from psychology, and so on. Human movement is the one entity that distinguishes our field from others; it is the singlemost important element that makes our field unique.

The Influence of Per Henrik Ling

The concept of human movement, in the form of movement education, as the focus of contemporary physical education has its origins in England. Before World War II both the English system of physical education and much of the American system of physical education was grounded in the Swedish gymnastics system developed by Per Henrik Ling (Mechikoff & Estes, 1998, p. 187). A strong case could be made that Ling's system of gymnastics, which was established in the early 1800s, provided the conceptual framework for the development of human movement theory.

The Swedish system of gymnastics, developed at the Royal Gymnastics Central Institute in Stockholm, Sweden, was implemented to support the military goals of that country. Europe in the early 1800s was in a constant state of political turmoil and war, and after suffering military defeats at the hands of the French and the Russians, the King of Sweden became very receptive to Ling's proposal of creating and administering a physical training program that would help his armies do better in war.

Ling's Swedish gymnastics system was based on the medical and scientific knowledge of the early 1800s. The basis of his Ling's system was as follows:

> Physical exercise must be based on the laws of the human system, and influence not only the body but also the mind. The fundamental principles can be briefly comprised in the following four clauses:
>
> 1. The aim is all-around harmonious development of the body.
> 2. The attainment of this is sought by means of biologically and physiologically grounded physical exercises in definite forms and, as far as possible, of known effect.
> 3. The exercises must have developmental and corrective values, be easily understood, and satisfy our demand for beauty.
> 4. The exercises must be carried out with a gradually increasing degree of difficulty and exertion. (Thulin, 1938, pp. 625–631)

What Ling did was to ground his system in the science of the day, thereby incorporating (1) aesthetic, (2) military, (3) pedagogical, and (4) medical aspects of movement. His system was quite formal, and to the eye it appeared very "rigid." It seems clear to the modern student of kinesiology that the goals of Ling's Swedish system of gymnastics, even though they were developed over a century ago, are not necessarily incompatible with the concepts and goals used today. Human movement education places great value on aesthetics, on the teaching of movement skills, as well as understanding and applying the scientific and medical aspects of human movement. As the new millennium approaches, we have expanded the goals and methodology of our field to a degree that Ling never would have dreamed. However, we remain committed to the value and benefits of human movement to enhance life in much the same manner as did Ling and his contemporaries.

British physical education, in contrast to Ling's gymnastics, enjoyed a strong emphasis on athletic competition that had reached a high degree of organization and widespread participation by the nineteenth century. To complement the sports and games made popular in the "public" schools (British "public" schools are much more like our private schools), the British incorporated Swedish gymnastics. The appeal of Swedish gymnastics may have been as much educational as it was utilitarian. England had been hurt by World War I, and by the time the physical education teachers in Britain changed their association's name to the Ling Association of Teachers of Swedish Gymnastics, Adolph Hitler had begun to attract a considerable following. Like the King of Sweden who was attracted to Ling's claims that physical education would build a stronger army, England bought into gymnastics as physical education.

The Contribution of Rudolf Laban

The need to support England's military by teaching physical fitness was the job of physical educators. Swedish gymnastics was combined with the rough and tumble games that were a tradition in England. Compared to gymnastics, sport was believed to mold the character and physical fitness of British soldiers. It was during this era that Rudolf Laban, an extraordinary dancer living and working in Germany, designed a system to observe and analyze the efficiency of movement of factory workers. In order to accomplish this, Laban focused on four components:

1. Body
2. Space
3. Effort
4. Relationships (DeLaban, 1964; Laban, 1920, 1960; Laban & Lawrence, 1947)

In doing this, he established the concept of "Human Movement." Laban was forced to leave Nazi Germany in 1937 and relocated to England. He arrived in England where a number of his disciples, primarily dancers, took him in and helped him to advance his ideas about human movement. During World War II, Laban provided exercise instruction to factory workers.

Laban's concept of human movement initially had limited appeal. With the exception of the dancers who were familiar with his revolutionary concepts, there was little interest in his work. Still, the ideas put forth by Laban in his classic work, *Die Welt des Tanzers* (in English, *The World of Dancers)* were nothing less then revolutionary. Juana DeLaban, Rudolph Laban's daughter, stated that her father believed that movement as the basis of our existence is not well understood (DeLaban, 1964, p. 15). Rudolf Laban argued that the obligation of the dancer is to assist humans in knowing themselves through their movements. Furthermore, the discovery of the "self" and the ability of human movement to provide meaning cannot be overestimated. DeLaban wrote, "There is no emotion (affective process) or intellectual action without bodily movement manifestations or vice versa" (DeLaban, 1964, p. 15). His belief that no emotional or intellectual action can occur without prior bodily movement strongly suggests that the beginning point for everything human is movement. In conclusion, DeLaban argued that her father, "not only valued dance for contributing both to artistic growth and to the search for individual worth, for its scientific benefits and educational implications, but also to effect the discovery of self—a synthesis of existence achieved through movement" (DeLaban, 1964, p. 15).

Laban recognized that dancers are some of the most gifted athletes and tried to understand why dancers were able to perform so well the difficult movements of the dance. Foster speculates that Laban's quest to understand the dance led him to study the classic philosophies of the Enlightenment such as Froebel (1782–1852), Rousseau (1712–1778), Guts Muths (1759–1839), and Pestalozzi (1746–1827), all of whom strongly believed in the value of human movement as an important curricular component of education. According to Foster (1977):

> It is possible to show a sympathy between Laban and Rousseau. The latter thought it was through movement that the child learned the difference between the self and the not self, and through this movement he discovered the concept of space. This idea is very much akin to Laban's thinking. . . . Guts Muths "the grandfather of German gymnastics," stressed the importance of linking physical activity with "the education of the head and the heart"; an idea found throughout Laban's thinking, i.e., that movement stimulates intellectual activity and problem solving. . . . In the same way [speculation] Pestalozzi's "natural" as distinct from his "art" gymnastics (where the emphasis was on the development of the innate capacities of the child), can be linked with Laban's ideas. . . . The basic tenets of Laban's philosophy can be linked to Froebel's concept of *Darstellung*—"creative self-expression" (the satisfaction of an innate urge to push out to a greater life and to adjust to a greater unity). (pp. 39–40)

It is important to understand "that [Laban's] thinking was predominantly dance oriented, and only part of his work has ideas with educational significance. The inference that movement education is a basic training for all activities of life is a central theme of educationists who use Laban's work" (Foster, 1977, p. 40). The language of dance—more precisely, human movement as described by Laban—manifests itself in many forms. One form is "Laban notation," a system of signs and symbols that express dance movements much as Egyptian hieroglyphics express language. Some of Laban's notations describe tone as gesture, thought as gesture, an analysis of gestures in spatial relationships, feelings and moods (in terms of nonverbal communication), the logic of movement actions, harmony of gesture, physiology and psychology of dance, the dancing "being," dance as art, the significance of dance notation, as well as dance as an experience of living (DeLaban, 1964, Kleinman, 1975).

According to those who argue that human movement is central to kinesiology, dance provides a window into the body of knowledge that has as its basis both science and art. Human movement is valued for its ability to effect the discovery of the "self," provide meaning to life, to facilitate expression and communication, and to provide the means to achieve individual identity. Human movement represents a methodology and theoretical foundation that many advocates believe could have a tremendous impact on the nature and scope of contemporary physical education (grades K–12) as well as the study of kinesiology.

Laban's Impact on British Physical Education

Laban's human movement theory appealed to a small group of British physical educators who were not satisfied with the physical education curriculum in England. While the combination of Swedish gymnastics and rough and tumble sports appealed to men, it was not nearly as attractive to women. The rigid and formal structure of the Swedish system of gymnastics was seen as limited and did not suit physical educators who considered themselves to be progressive. Human movement, in contrast, held out the promise of a "new physical education." One of the strong attractions of Laban's approach was the use of the "discovery method," which was actually developed by Heinrich Medau and utilized extensively by Laban (Foster, 1977, p. 42). Laban and Medau never met, but the work of Medau, especially the "discovery method," had a significant impact on Laban and his methodology of human movement.

The teachings of Laban found a receptive audience in British physical educators, especially women, who were determined to carry the banner of human movement education as the "new physical education." As Foster noted, "These women physical educators were closely connected with emancipation. Mary Hankinson, a founder of the Ling Association, was a suffragette. The women's colleges often saw new ideas and approaches as an opportunity to assert the independence of women. Any activities which helped this ideal were studied" (Foster, 1977, p. 76). In retrospect, it is clear that Laban's emphasis on the development of the "self" was an attractive argument for women who were working to promote the status of women.

In addition to the support of Laban's human movement ideas from women physical educators, England was going through social change following World War II that helped Laban spread his ideas. During these post-war years educators began to stress theories that emphasized individual differences among students, an idea that fit nicely with the ideas of Laban. Laban's approach was expressive, and the English encouraged self-expression.

Perhaps the most influential and dedicated follower of Laban, whose ideas had to be spread through a devoted following of physical educators, was Lisa Ullman, Principal of the Laban Art Studio. Ullman was charged with creating a school curriculum, but even Ullman had enormous difficulty writing the human movement curriculum articulated by Laban. According to Foster, "She knew Movement but could not help teachers to use the knowledge she gave them to enrich their work" (Foster, 1977, p. 81). Ulmann had no training in education, and, as a consequence, she was the subject of a great deal of criticism. Furthermore, Ullman utilized clichéd terms to promote "Movement" as the basis of living. The ready use of popularized phrases angered the women physical educators who were so necessary to promoting Laban's ideas. Most women physical educators were trained in curriculum development and knew that their devotion to human movement as the basis for the new physical education would fall on deaf ears without a sound curriculum. Although the relationship between Lisa Ullman and the physical educators who embraced Laban's work was sometimes strained, there is little doubt that without Lisa Ullmann, Laban's work would not have been accepted as much as it was in England.

Since women physical educators were the primary advocates of human movement, spread primarily though educational dance, the popularity of human movement was highest among girls. Consequently, the influence of Laban upon boys' physical education programs, as well as men's physical education programs in the colleges, was not nearly as significant. Foster (1977) observed that:

> The work of Laban has influenced the education of girls far more than boys partly because of the historical accident that during the early days of the growth of

Laban's influence, men were fresh from HM [His Majesty's] forces [World War II] and still focused on military movements. Attempts have been made to rectify this but there is a persuasive school which does not accept Laban's ideas uncritically as a vehicle for boys' work. In fact, Laban's devotees have spent more time in regularizing their position with girls and younger children than persuading others of the relevance of their work to older boys. (p. 103)

R.E. Morgan, Director of Physical Education at Leeds University, witnessed firsthand the hostile reception Laban received when he traveled to Leeds University to speak with male students. Laban's reception was proof that his ideas were far more popular with women physical educators than with men. Lisa Ullman believed that the refusal of men to accept his ideas always worried Laban.

The debate between those who favor human movement as the focus of physical education and the anti-Labanites continues to cloud the identity of our field. It is safe to say contemporary women physical educators at the elementary school level are closely identified with human movement in the form of movement education. To this day, male physical educators remain resistant to human movement, in part because of the identification or labeling of human movement with dance and elementary school physical education. Opponents have criticized human movement supporters for claiming that "skill and creativeness in dance provides an appropriate base for creativeness and skill in other fields" (Foster, 1977, p. 102). For instance, human movement argues that there is a training effect developed from what one learns by engaging in dance and other specified human movement activities, and that this training effect will carry over to games and sports. However, there is no scientific evidence that this training effect exists in practice. Another problem with human movement is how movement is defined. The Labanites' definition does not appeal to other constituents in our field. Laban implored us to establish our individual identity. One of the reigning issues of physical education has been one of establishing a proper identity. Laban's identity for our field is human movement and all that it encompasses.

The Content of Human Movement

What is the position of contemporary kinesiology relative to the study of human movement? This philosophical question has yet to be resolved to everyone's satisfaction. Brown and Cassidy (1963) described human movement in the following way:

Human movement is the expression or activity of the human organism. Human movement is the change in position of the individual in time-space resulting from force developed from the individual's expenditure of energy interacting with the environment.

The human, interacting with his [her] environment, moves. In moving, the individual may be expressing, communicating or coping with the environment. Movement is developmental and changes both the individual and environment. Human movement may be considered from the standpoint of each or all together: (1) movement is expressive, (2) movement is communicative, (3) movement is developmental or changes the individual, and (4) movement is environmental or changes the environment as man copes with the environment. (p. 10)

Laban, Brown, and Cassidy believe that the focus of human movement is upon development of the individual, the "self." Those movements that do not promote development of the "self" are not appropriate activities for the school program (K–12) of human movement, or what many in kinesiology still refer to as physical education. Brown and Cassidy were early American proponents of the change from physical education, which they considered limiting, to human movement. Human movement could still retain the concept of physical education as part of a school program, although it would be subject to modification.

An important point to consider is the fact that a number of physical educators, especially in the middle school and high school, are resistant to the "new physical education" in the form of human movement. These opponents are primarily found in the boys' physical education departments and believe in the value of sport and games to build character, discipline, teamwork, cooperation, achievement of personal goals relative to fitness, and other similar outcomes that traditionally have been associated with participation in games and sports. Physical education means different things to different people involved in the field.

Brown and Cassidy described human movement in their seminal work, *Theory in Physical Education: A Guide to Program Change* (1963). Brown and Cassidy, along with Eleanor Metheney and Lois Ellfeldt, helped to establish the theoretical basis for human movement as a curriculum that would supersede traditional (and some would say—outdated) physical education programs in the United States. Brown and Cassidy (1963) argued that,

> Physical education is the school program of study of the art and science of human movement needed in today's world designed for development through movement, and human performance restricted to expressive form and/or restricted through the use of representations of environmental reality. (p. 36)

Renshaw (1973) attempted to distinguish between physical education and human movement in his excellent article, "The Nature of Human Movement Studies and Its Relationship with Physical Education" (Renshaw, 1973; see also Corbin, 1989). Renshaw taught courses on the philosophy of education at the University of Leeds Institute of Education. His perspective on the "great debate" relative to physical education versus human movement is unique because he is a detached observer and does not teach either physical education or human movement. He observed that "But, whilst many of the conflicting arguments form part of a territorial dispute, some of the underlying problems raise questions which are essentially philosophical" (Renshaw, 1973, p. 79). Renshaw hit the nail squarely on the head! What is important to understand is that if the philosophical justification of our field is "weak" or lacks academic integrity, there is no credible argument to support the position that what we do has any value. In this same article, Curl (1973) notes that

> Human Movement has been developed largely under the aegis of Physical Education, where the theory underlying Physical Education is similar to educational theory in so far as both draw on a range of disciplines in order to formulate principles for practice. If one takes this position, then physical education can be seen as a

practical theory which serves extrinsic ends, where "Human Movement" can be seen as a field of knowledge with its own intrinsic standards of relevance. (p. 81)

Not all human movement qualifies for inclusion in Human Movement Studies. For example, mowing the lawn, painting the house, working at the computer, or digging a ditch does not lend itself to individual development, especially with respect to Laban's criteria of the "development of the self." However, many of the traditional subjects in physical education—such as the study of sport, play, and games—take on a new educative function, the development of the "self." What is critical to understand is that the definition of physical education by Brown and Cassidy ensures that play, games, and sports remain an important part of human movement theory because of their capacity to develop the individual and impart cultural values. As they argued, "Within games and sports are found the built-in values of a culture and the movement skills needed to cope with the physical world" (Brown & Cassidy, 1963, p. 36).

While games and sport are the premier focus in traditional physical education programs, they do not occupy the same position in Human Movement Studies. Games and sport are just ONE TOOL in the repertoire of human movement theory that physical educators can use to develop the individual. Adapted physical education programs are particularly well suited to human movement because of their ability to build self-esteem, a positive identity, and enhance the life of the individual through movement. Dance and physical fitness activities represent human movement activities that are designed to help develop the individual and enhance not only the quality of life but the identity of each of us. Advocates strongly believe that human movement is highly educative and directed toward the development of the individual, both cognitively and physically. Physical education has traditionally held the goal of individual development as important. However, the approach of the traditional physical education program, according to human movement advocates, has not succeeded in this regard.

Physical Education versus Human Movement: A Comparison

In all cases, the essential feature of human movement theory is to "live the movement, experience the corporeal [the physical]." Human movement is to be experienced, and knowledge of the "self" is generated as a result of movement experience. The personal meaning derived from engaging in human movement manifests itself as an expression of the self. In this way, human movement becomes a means of both communication and self-discovery. Discovery then leads to identity. Laban, if you remember, valued human movement activities, especially dance, for their scientific and educational implications as well as discovery of the self.

Human movement is ignored by many physical educators in favor of physical education activities that revolve around play, games, and sport. However, many of these traditional activities have come under frequent attack by educational critics because of their "questionable" educational value. For example, the strong emphasis on sport skills leaves out many students who simply have little or no interest in competitive activities. Consequently, the general public's perception of physical education, and quite possibly their experience with physical education while in school, has not been very positive, often because of the emphasis on games and sports. A basic question is raised by Renshaw (1973) when comparing the difference between human movement and traditional physical education:

> How valid is the assertion that physical education as part of education . . . shares the criteria [credibility] of [mainstream] education . . .? Certainly the term "Physical Education" can function in a purely descriptive way to embrace all the physical activities that go on in schools and colleges. But this is not to equate these [physical] activities with education in [the] . . . evaluative sense of the word . . . for many of the activities are more concerned with therapy, training, or socialization. Further, the educational value of [physical] activities has to be demonstrated, not just assumed." (p. 81)

Renshaw poses some profound questions about whether physical education can be a component of mainstream educational theory and practice. He is not the first to question the legitimacy of physical education's claim to a sound theoretical basis on order to justify its existence. Renshaw continues his scrutiny of physical education by stating:

> Finally, is it possible to identify any systematic body of knowledge which can legitimately be termed "physical education theory"? Can a set of distinctive principles be located which support the professional authority and autonomy of the teacher of physical education? I would suggest that the body of theory underlying Physical Education is a myth. It would seem more logical to view this in terms of building up an understanding of concepts, skills, procedures and principles culled from the study of Human Movement, and then relating this knowledge to the study of children and to the educational process. It is not meaningful to talk about historical education theory, so why should Physical Education set itself up as a possible candidate for having its own body of theory? (1973, p. 81)

Renshaw's skeptical view of physical education (as opposed to human movement, which he supports) seems to be supported by Abernathy and Waltz (1964) when they state that "the justification [of Physical Education] in the long run, will rest upon the utilization of principles drawn from scholarly inquiry into the phenomenon of human movement" (p. 6). Abernathy and Waltz see physical education as knowledge of human movement that is applied in education, specifically school physical education programs. Abernathy and Waltz made this statement over thirty years ago. However, their concern about the educational validity of physical education and the apparent questionable theoretical basis from which it proceeds remains one of the most important issues of the field as it enters the twenty-first century.

Renshaw justifies his ideas about the study of human movement. He believes that

> Human movement can be studied for both intrinsic and extrinsic reasons. In colleges and universities such study can take three forms:

> **1.** The academic study of different kinds of theoretical and practical knowledge underlying Human Movement.

2. Actual engagement in the language of symbolic movement.
3. The applied study of Human Movement. (1873, p. 82)

There is no doubt that Renshaw favors "Human Movement Studies" as the label and focus of our field. He presents his ideas of the study of human movement from an academic, cognitive, experiential, and applied format that is consistent with the content of the subject matter. He looks upon physical education, as do most human movement proponents (and much of the general public), as suspect with regard to its educational value:

> Games . . . can be viewed as part of the educational process if a student is encouraged to structure his movements and consciousness according to the public standards [educational criteria] internal to the activity. The emphasis must be on knowledge with understanding, thus allowing for critical objective appraisal, rather than on mindless physical drill and conditioning. But how far are physical activities pursued in schools and colleges for such educational reasons? (Renshaw, 1973, p. 85)

Renshaw argues that the traditional outcomes of physical education such as (1) promotion of physical fitness and health, (2) the acquisition of neuromuscular skills, (3) the development of social adjustment, and (4) development of emotional stability and formation of a positive attitude towards physical activity can hardly be considered as educational. These outcomes should be viewed logically as the ends of some therapeutic or socialization process but not "masquerade as valid aims of physical education, if the term education is functioning in an evaluative rather than a descriptive sense" (Renshaw, 1973, p. 85).

Renshaw views traditional outcomes of physical education as socialization and therapeutic processes, but certainly not as an educational process in an evaluative sense. He seems to imply that instead of delivering "Physical Education," it appears that what has been delivered is "Physical Mis-Education." Consider the following questions:

1. Do you take exception to his position or do you agree with him?
2. How would you define the nature and purpose of education?
3. Which one, traditional physical education or human movement, is easier to philosophically justify as an essential educational component that utilizes both mind and body?

Let's examine these issues further. Do you believe that sports and games as a part of the curriculum of school physical education lend themselves to the achievement aspects of education? The human movement advocates claim that a cognitive frame of reference can be established through the systematic study of human movement that has its foundation a solid "body of knowledge." The movement people ask whether games and sports offer the educational breadth and cognitive development that human movement does. According to advocates of human movement, when a game is played merely as a game, there can be no educational value because the game fails to satisfy the wider cognitive conditions of education. To illustrate this point, have you ever seen a "physical educator" simply provide equipment and a place to play the game and then stand back and watch? When it rains or the weather is bad, how many "physical educators" send their students to the gym to sit around?

This is not to say that games lack any cognitive content. Many games and sports are very complex. This is the case with games such as basketball, which is an open skill activity requiring a high degree of perceptual judgment as opposed to the closed end skills such as throwing a javelin. The drawback to physical education programs that rely on games and sports as their core focus share a common problem: All skills, whether they be open or closed contain their own internal cognitive content; however, their scope is *limited*. To illustrate this point, understand that the human movement supporters will argue that the simple acquisition of physical skills cannot generate new personal and educational discovery the way that human movement activities can. This is because skill development, as it occurs in traditional physical education programs for approximately the past fifty years, revolves around training, not education, say the proponents of human movement. How much credibility do you find in the rationale used by the movement advocates relative to their position that physical education is essentially built upon training, socializing, and therapeutic outcomes, not educational processes?

It is important to know that as far back as 1964, advocates of a scholarly physical education "reinvented" physical education as an academic discipline (Henry, 1964, 1978; Nixon, 1967; Rarick, 1967). The development of physical education as an academic discipline was an important milestone and is discussed elsewhere in this book.

Although we have presented the merits of using human movement as the theoretical foundation of our field, it is important to note that The Battle of the Systems—Human Movement versus Physical Education—has not abated. Make no mistake, there are many current physical educators who adhere to the traditional program in physical education and are skeptical about the utility and approach utilized by those who support human movement.

Camille Brown was a Professor of Physical Education at UCLA and a leader in the effort to make human movement the theoretical basis of the field. She presented a compelling argument in her article titled "The Structure of Knowledge of Physical Education" (1967). Professor Brown identified:

1. Areas of Study within the body of Knowledge of Human Movement.
2. The Structure of Subjects [instruction].

Study her analysis that follows carefully and be prepared to respond to several questions. She identifies the Body of Knowledge of Human Movement as shown in Table 14-1.

The structure of knowledge in the form of the Body of Knowledge in Human Movement may in fact lend itself to represent the Body of Knowledge in Physical Education as well. This position would mean that physical education and human movement are one in the same; there is only the question of semantics to wrestle with. Physical education has been historically presented as a form of instruction, a method of training the body (Brown, 1967, p. 56). As you can see, the Body of Knowledge of Human Movement offered by Brown goes far beyond the basic instruction in training the body that historically has been identified with our field. Are human movement and physical education the same thing? If not, is physical education as a process of instruction in the schools part of the Body of Knowledge in Human Movement? With regard to the Body of Knowledge of Human Movement, to what extent did you experience the type of curricular opportunities presented by Professor Brown when you took physical education?

TABLE 14-1   Areas of Study Within the Body of Knowledge of Human Movement

1. The areas of study that are derived from human movement explanation.
   A. The study of the substantive structure of human movement; its explanation and classification.
   B. The study of the syntactical structure of human movement.

2. The nature of and the development of man [woman] affect his [her] movement.
   A. The study of the nature of the development of man [woman], including the materials and conditions necessary for healthy growth and development and the effect and effects on man's [woman's] environment.
   B. The study of individual differences in the development of man [woman] and their effects on his [her] movement, including such variable factors as skeletal and muscular structure, purpose or motivation of the individual, concept of self, maturation, strength, training, endurance, flexibility, state of tension-relaxation, materials and conditions necessary for health and full functioning, perception, movement skill, kinesthesis, rhythm, height, weight, body proportion, general health status.
   C. The study of man's [woman's] development, his [her] unique expressive behavior and the meaning he [she] gives his [her] movement.

3. The nature of the environment affects man's [woman's] movement.
   A. The study of the nature of the physical and geographical locale, both in motion and not, and their specific variables and the sanction of each for human movement, including: sense objects; objects of simple location, animate and inanimate, having characteristics of weight (ounce, pound, etc.), shape (circle, square, etc.), dimensions (thickness, breadth, length); media (land, water, air); time (minute, hour, etc.); time and space (speed, acceleration); space, illusory, or actual direction (rotation, horizontal, etc.), distance (foot, yard, etc.); others.
      1. The study of the movement patterns and designs possible within a particular physical environment.
   B. The study of the nature of the culture at any moment in time and place and its specific variations and the effect of each on human movement, including societal problems, events (work, play, subsistence unity), materials and conditions needed for man's [woman's] healthy growth and development, philosophy, and attitudes of valuing others.
      1. The study of the particular and possible patterns and designs within a culture.

4. Development of man [woman] through movement.
   A. The study of the nature of man [woman] and the effect of man's [woman's] movement on the development of man [woman] generally.
   B. The study of each modification of development through movement, including muscular-skeletal, purpose, flexibility, tension-relaxation, perception, movement skill, kinesthesis, rhythm, concept of self, strength, endurance, height, weight, body proportion.

5. Changes in the environment through movement.
   A. The study of the nature of the physical environment, identifying the variations and describing the effect of movement on these environmental variations.
      1. The study of the nature of movement patterns and designs possible within these environmental variations and the effect of these on the environment.
   B. The study of the effects of human movement on its culture.
      1. The study of the nature of the culture and the movement patterns and designs which appear in the culture at any moment in time or place.
   C. The study of the movement needed to cope with the environment in time and place.

6. The study of the development of movement in man [woman] and movement learning.

7. Human movement as nonverbal expression and communication.
   A. The study of man's [woman's] movement expression.
   B. The study of man's [woman's] communication through movement.

From Brown (1967), pp. 55–56.

The Body of Knowledge has been identified by Brown. It now remains for the student to decide about the appropriateness of the structure of subjects, as Brown refers to them, that she sees as the academic, theoretical, and educational content of human movement. She identifies the structure of subjects as consisting of four subject areas. "Each subject area is uniquely different from each other subject area, yet each is related to the others" (Brown, 1967, p. 58)

Examine the content and theoretical basis of the four subject areas. According to Brown, these four subject areas are supposed to produce the following outcomes:

1. Each subject area should emphasize different human and environmental variable factors and different movement within its learning opportunities.
2. Each subject area should make a unique contribution to the biological (socio-psycho-somatic [physical]) development of man [and woman].
3. Each subject area should make a unique contribution to the development of man's [and woman's] movement.
4. Each subject area should develop unique cognitive concepts.

We have "distilled" Professor Brown's Outcomes and have come up with the following goals:

A. Develop mind and body utilizing movement.
B. Provide social, psychological, and physical development by utilizing movement.
C. Provides a method of personal discovery through the "joy of movement."
D. Utilizing movement, the individual should be able to understand and apply unique cognitive concepts. For example, understand and apply Newton's Laws of physics to human movement.

Carefully read and think about the information that is depicted in Table 14-2. While studying Table 14-2, can you locate the concepts and experiences that seem to correspond with the "goals" identified above?

The subjects ordinarily a part of traditional physical education (track and field, gymnastics, correctives, etc.) can be placed within the preceding structure. What Brown sees is that learning to use the raw materials of movement in problem solution and learning an activity in its final form represent two different sides of an issue. They may both be used as a means of self-discovery; however, it is important to recognize the difference between them (Brown, 1967, p. 67).

In summary, Brown concludes that it seems to be possible to identify a Structure of Knowledge of Human Movement that could encompass a Body of Knowledge of Human Movement. It also seems to be possible to identify a structure of instruction for human movement. From such material it should be possible to think about the following questions:

1. Are human movement and physical education the same?
2. Is physical education an identifiable part of human movement as a body of knowledge?
3. Does physical education represent the structure of instruction of human movement? (Brown, 1967, p. 67)

TABLE 14-2   Human Movement Curriculum

The structure of subjects is outlined as follows:

I. CONDITIONING AND TRAINING (exercising)
  Conditioning I, II, etc.
  Training I
  Relaxation I

  Subjects: Conditioning
             Training
             Relaxation

  A. Body of Knowledge of Human Movement
    1. Substantive organizing elements
      a. Human variable factors emphasized: meaning given to strength, endurance, flexibility, tension-relaxation, body proportion
      b. Environmental variable factors: factors utilized but not emphasized
      c. Principles relating to the development of these particular factors: principles of overload using own body, weights; principles relating to timing and spacing practice and progressive resistance
      d. Facts relating to muscle attachments, movable body members, and direction of movement
      e. Principles of circulation-respiration and exercise
      f. Principles of flexibility or normal range of movement
      g. Principles of relaxation
      h. Principles of weight and figure control; balance of rest, food, and activity
      i. Others
    2. Behavioral organizing elements: movement classification—exercises, or basic movement, performed for a specific developmental purpose

  B. Learning Opportunities
    1. Determining one's status in relation to the human factors and composing an exercise program to meet one's needs: e.g., a weight-training program or a circuit training program
    2. Setting up a conditioning program for a specific performance or seasonal sport
    3. Setting up procedures for becoming trained and/or staying trained
    4. Maintaining proper weight through planning food and activity relationships
    5. Participating in games and sports having identified particular developmental objectives
    6. Others

  C. Developmental Results
    1. Cognitive concepts: facts and principles relating to the meaning of strength, endurance, flexibility, tension-relaxation, and body proportion and to their development through movement and through other health factors
    2. Biological development: strength, endurance, flexibility, relaxation, change in body proportion
    3. Movement skill development: exercises

  D. Behavior
    1. Making one's own conditioning and/or training program according to one's own needs
    2. Acting on the program

  E. Sequence: Achievement is related to the growth and developmental stage of the person, the performance or life for which he [she] is conditioning, the training he [she] needs in time and place.

TABLE 14-2 *Continued*

II. MOVEMENT MECHANICS (managing oneself in movement in various environments)
Body Mechanics
Basic Movement Mechanics
Movement Mechanics in Varied Environments I, II, etc.

    Subjects: Body Mechanics
                Basic Movement Mechanics
                Movement Mechanics in Varied Environments

A. Body of Knowledge of Human Movement
    1. Substantive organizing elements
        a. Human variable factors emphasized: body structure for human movement; posture, postures
        b. Environmental variable factors emphasized: matter as animate and inanimate objects having various weights, shapes, and dimensions; media of land, water, air; earth and outer space forces; resistance; degrees of weightlessness; variations in time and space
        c. Principles of mechanics of movement: Newton's laws, principles of equilibrium, laws of levers and simple machines; emphasis on both human and environment as matter and the human having his own energy system, centers of gravity, body levers, and balance mechanism; study of equilibrium, force, motion.
        d. Principles of movement learning: readiness to act, including purpose or motivation, will to act, attending on sensory cues, thinking and relating to past experience. Positioning to act; translating to action, including coordinating muscular movement with sensory data and disequilibrium; terminating action utilizing controls of both self and environment

B. Learning Opportunities
    1. Managing one's own alignment and postures in simple environments found in everyday living
    2. Managing oneself in water, air, land when time or space is changed to make for differences in speed and acceleration; when space is changed in distance and direction
    3. Managing oneself when objects are changed in weight, shape, and dimensions
    4. Managing oneself in moving an object; moving an object with an object; moving oneself and an object together; moving oneself within a moving object to cause the object to move
    5. Propelling oneself through the use of objects both in motion and not in motion
    6. Moving oneself and an animate object; moving oneself competing against an animate object
    7. Moving oneself to move an object in a competitive goal structure.
    8. Moving oneself in strange and stressful environments; moving oneself on strange objects in strange environments
    9. Others

C. Developmental Results
    1. Cognitive concepts: facts and principles relating to learning new movements and facts and principles relating to managing oneself as the environment is changed
    2. Biological development: general conditioning and specific conditioning dependent upon the environmental change; ability to manage oneself in varied environments; openness to experience
    3. Movement skill development: posture, postures; jumping, landing, throwing, catching, balancing, gymnastics, aquatics from swimming through sailing to scuba diving

Continued

TABLE 14-2 *Continued*

D. Behavior
   1. Using mechanical principles and movement learning principles in coping with environments whether the tasks be for subsistence, work, or play
   2. Being able to manage oneself in movement in varied environments
   3. Being open to the experience of new and strange environments

E. Sequence: Complexity is described by changing the environmental variables of matter, energy, time, space.

III. MOVEMENT COMPOSITION (composing movement)

Basic Ground-Covering Movement
Movement Self-Expression
Expressive Forms I, II, III
Cultural Movement Forms

Subject: Basic Ground-Covering Movement*

A. Body of Knowledge of Human Movement
   1. Substantive organizing elements
      a. Human variable factors emphasized: skeletal-muscular structure including movable body members; purpose, internal controls, and force
      b. Environmental variable factors emphasized
         (1) Matter, having characteristics of amount (mass), weight (pound, ounce), shape (circle, rectangle, sphere, etc.), dimensions (thickness, breadth, length)
         (2) Energy, gravitational force; resistance: air, liquid, material—animate or inanimate
         (3) Time: minute, second; before, after, during
         (4) Space: place in space; distances between places; direction in space.
         (5) Time and space: speed, acceleration
   2. Behavioral organizing elements
      a. Movement classification: basic movement (flexion, extension, abduction, adduction, rotation, circumduction, pronation, supination, glide, depression, elevation); basic movement pattern (giving and receiving impetus of self on flat unencumbered surface as in running, walking, leaping, turning, landing, etc.); structured form as in stunts and tumbling

B. Learning Opportunities
   1. Identifying movable body members by using them in movement possibilities; varying human shape
   2. Using body and body members to propel oneself over space; taking off and landing using various possibilities
   3. Dissipating momentum using internal controls
   4. Maintaining equilibrium bearing weight on different parts of the body
   5. Moving, changing space variables; time and space variables; effort or energy variables
   6. Using these variables in composing movement sequences, in ground-covering movement; thinking, remembering, acting, feeling
   7. Others

*There are three additional entries to Subject Area III, MOVEMENT COMPOSITION. The remaining entries are labeled (1) Movement Self-Expression, (2) Expressive Form, the Art of Movement, and (3) Cultural Movement Form. The authors have selected "Basic Ground-Covering Movement" to provide the reader with a basic understanding of the subject areas.

TABLE 14-2   *Continued*

   C. Developmental Results
      1. Cognitive concepts: the meaning of man [and woman] as matter having weight, shape, dimensions; the meaning of gravity and human movement; time and space meanings in speed, acceleration; space meanings in terms of place in space, distance, and direction
      2. Biological development: openness to experience, time and space awareness
      3. Movement skill development: basic movement and basic movement patterns

   D. Behavior
      1. Being open to other movement experiences
      2. Using basic movement variables of human instrument and movable body members, energy, time and space in composing movement

   E. Sequence: This area is basic to the study of movement and is emphasized at each growth stage.

IV. STRUCTURED MOVEMENT FORMS (participating in nonverbal group movement forms)
   Games
   Sports (Basketball, etc.)
   Folk and Social Dance

   Subjects: Games
             Basketball, Football, Hockey, Baseball, etc.
             Tennis, Badminton, etc.
             Folk Dance, Social Dance, Other Social Forms

   A. Body of Knowledge of Human Movement
      1. Substantive organizing elements
         a. Human variable factors emphasized; those utilized but not emphasized
         b. Environmental variable factors emphasized; those utilized but not emphasized
         c. Movement knowledges; knowledges needed to play or to participate in game, sport, or dance (these include all rules particular to the form; strategies where appropriate; descriptions and explanations of movement skills needed and human relationships specific to the game, sport, or dance.)
      2. Behavioral organizing elements
         a. Movement classification: structured nonverbal movement forms having established frameworks and participated in by two or more people; structured frameworks having unstructured, problem-solving, internal frameworks

   B. Learning Opportunities
      1. Participating in game, sport, or dance, studying the knowledges needed to participate; practicing the movement skills needed; continuing in the act.
      2. Studying movement strategies in team play for a specific game or sport; putting these into operation
      3. Others

   C. Developmental Results
      1. Cognitive concepts: knowledges needed to participate in game, sport, or dance
      2. Biological development: human relationships; general development; specific development depending upon the form; problem solving related to solving complex interactions within structure.

   D. Behavior
      1. Conducting one's own games, sports, and dances
      2. Participating in school and community games, sports, and dances

Continued

TABLE 14-2 *Continued*

E. Sequence: It may be based on student interest or need. If based on interest, the student may take a beginning, intermediate, or advanced course. If based on need for belonging or development, he [she] may become as well skilled as he [she] needs to be to belong to the group or until he [she] has achieved the needed development.

From "The Structure of Knowledge of Physical Education" by C. Brown, *QUEST* (Monograph IX/December 1967), pp. 55–56, 58–67. Copyright 1967 by the Quest Board of 1967. Reprinted by permission of Human Kinetics Publishers.

You have read and may have discussed the ideas of Brown and others relative to human movement. Would you agree or disagree with the content, educational objectives, and methodology of (1) the Body of Knowledge of Human Movement and (2) the Structure of Knowledge of Human Movement presented by Brown? To be sure, there is disagreement about the nature of our field although everyone from physical education (athletic?) supporters to human movement advocates agree that human movement/physical activity is foundation of the field and the one element that makes us unique from all the other areas of study.

Some physical educators frequently avoid using human movement terms when presenting instruction in sports skills, with the possible exception of gymnastics. Is it because these terms are equated with "dance terminology"? Broer (1964) states, "It is unfortunate that movement education has become, to many physical educators, synonymous with expressing and communicating dance objectives. For this reason they have restricted the term to 'dance movement education.' Have they overlooked the fact that movement is also the individual's only means of 'coping with the environment?' " (pp. 20–21).

"The expressive and communicative outcomes of movement are linked primarily to movement as an art; the developmental effects on the moving individual involve movement as an art and a science, while the effects of movement in developing and changing the environment may be considered to involvement the science of movement" (Broer, 1964, pp. 20–21). Broer has beautifully articulated what Brown, Cassidy, Laban, and other movement scholars have long advocated: the field embodies both a Body of Knowledge and Method of Instruction that reflect "the art and science of Human Movement."

One of the goals of obtaining a college education is developing the ability to engage in critical thinking through reasoned inquiry and analysis. You have been asked to engage in critical thinking throughout this book primarily through discussion questions. As in any field, there will always be individuals and groups who are critical of the status quo and seek change. This is both healthy and necessary if the field is to advance the frontiers of knowledge and refine its own particular art of discovery. By this point you know that Physical Education is no exception to this internal and external critical review.

Summary

The human movement "movement" believes that for physical education to remain a viable part of the school program, the concepts underlying physical education as well as its justification will be based upon the principles drawn from research and scholarship originating in human movement as opposed to traditional Physical Education "beliefs." Abernathy and Waltz (1964) observe that:

> Attention to the structure of physical education as an application of disciplined knowledge in an educational situation does not negate the functional role of traditional activities in the conduct of the program. Organized experience in sports, dance, gymnastics . . . is not incompatible with a program based upon movement inquiry. However, in such a program, [these] activities cannot be perceived as ends in themselves since they [sports, dance, gymnastics] do not define the nature or purpose of the experience. (p. 7)

In conclusion, do you think physical education is a means to an end, as do the human movement advocates, or an end in itself that does not need to rely upon the theoretical foundation of Human Movement but can stand alone on its own merits?

Our field continues to search for an appropriate identity and suitable body of knowledge. Human movement as an academic discipline continues to be debated, as does the scope and educational rational of physical education. If you were to construct a body of knowledge that framed your version of our field, what would you side with human movement or the traditional approach of physical education?

Discussion Questions

1. What are the concepts and ideas of "human movement theory" that were espoused by Rudolph Laban?
2. How did the ideas of Laban differ from those of Brown, Cassidy, and Renshaw? How were they similar?
3. How do the concepts of human movement compare to those in "traditional" physical education?

References

Abernathy, R., & Waltz, M. (1964). Toward a discipline: First steps first. *Quest, 2*, 1–7.

Broer, M.R. (1964, April). Movement education: Wherein the disagreement? *Quest*, Monograph II, 20–21.

Brown, C. (1967, December). The structure and knowledge of physical education. *Quest*, Monograph IX, 55–67.

Brown, C., & Cassidy, R. (1963). *Theory in physical education: A guide to program change*. Philadelphia: Lea & Febiger.

Corbin, C. (1989). The evolving undergraduate major. *The American Academy of Physical Education Papers, 23*, 1–4.

Curl, G.F. (1973). An attempt to justify human movement as a field of study. In J.D. Brooke & H.T.A. Whiting (Eds.), *Human movement—A field of study*. London: H. Kimpton. Cited in Renshaw, P., The nature of human movement studies and its relationship with physical education. *Quest*, Monograph XX, Summer Issue, June 1973, 79–81.

DeLaban, J. (1964). Modus operandi *Quest, II*, 15–18.

Foster, J. (1977). *The influences of Rudolph Laban*. London: Lepus Books.

Henry, F. (1964). Physical education: An academic discipline. *Journal of Health, Physical Education and Recreation, 25*, 32–33.

Henry, F. (1978). The academic discipline of physical education. *Quest*, Monograph XXIX, 13–29.

Laban, R. (1920). *Die welt des tanzers*. Stuttgart, Germany: Verlag Walter Seiffert.

Laban, R. (1960). *The mastery of movement*. London: MacDonald and Evans.

Laban, R., & Lawrence, F. (1947). *Effort*. London: MacDonald and Evans.

Kleinman, S. (1975). Movement notation systems: An introduction. *Quest, 18*, 44–50.

Mechikoff, R., & Estes, S. (1998). *A history and philosophy of sport and physical education: From ancient civilizations to the modern world* (2nd ed.). Madison, WI: WCB/McGraw-Hill.

Nixon, J.E. (1967, December). The criteria of a discipline. *Quest*, Monograph IX, 42–48.

Rarick, G.L. (1967, December). The domain of physical education as a discipline. *Quest*, Monograph IX, 49–52.

Renshaw, P. (1973). The nature of human movement studies and its relationship to physical education. *Quest, 20*, 79–86.

Thulin, J. (1938). The application of P.H. Ling's system to modern Swedish Ling gymnastics." *Mind and Body* (November), 625–631.

Chapter *15*

An Overview of the Development and Reform of Modern Physical Education and Sport

Chapter Objectives

Upon completing this chapter, the reader will be able to:

1. Identify the individuals, social themes, and outcomes that influenced the development and reform of modern physical education and sport.
2. Identify and discuss the contributions of immigrant groups in developing physical education.
3. Understand and discuss the emergence of physical education as a profession.
4. Understand and discuss salient social and educational issues that impact the reform of education in general and physical education in specific.
5. Discuss the rationale for developing the academic discipline of physical education.
6. Understand the social issues and attendant rationale that suppressed the development of women's athletics.
7. Understand the impact of Title IX on the reform of sport.
8. Identify and discuss the events and societal concerns that brought about attempts to reform sport in the colleges and universities.

From our earlier discussion, we know that both religious beliefs and climate impacted on the development of physical education. Pre-modern colonial America did not provide much in the way of organized physical education. Benjamin Franklin, Noah Webster, and Thomas Jefferson all advocated keeping the body healthy, primarily because of the belief that a sound body enhanced the mind. America was an agrarian land, and working the land in order to raise food and cash crops resulted in plenty of exercise. Schooling was rare during this time and the Latin Grammar School model that was in existence did not see much need for a formal program in physical education. Children who were fortunate enough to attend school played before school and during recess if the teacher so allowed.

The first formal program of physical education was formulated by two men, George Bancroft and Joseph Cogswell, who started the Round Hill School for Boys in 1823. Located in Northampton, Massachusetts, the school required mandatory physical education. The idea of including physical education as a "core course" was the result of the desire of Cogswell and Bancroft to continue their education in Germany. While studying in Germany, the two Americans became involved with the Turners, who were a group of people who were devoted followers of Friedrich Jahn, head of the Turners. Jahn developed a series of gymnastics and exercise programs and urged in his followers a strong patriotic duty. Upon returning to the United States, they opened the Round Hill School and hired Dr. Charles Beck, a political refugee who had emigrated to America from Germany. Beck was a Turner, and along with help from Cogswell and Bancroft, built a Turnplatz, which was an area that was used for exercise and housed the gymnastic apparatus of the Turner system. Beck taught Latin and physical education and is credited as being the first physical education teacher in the country. The Round Hill School is historically significant for two reasons. First, it was the first educational institution that had a formal, organized system of sports and physical education for students: Round Hill employed Charles Beck who was trained to teach physical education in Germany. The second significant aspect that occurred was that the formal training of Beck and the inclusion of a conventional curriculum in physical education reflected the societal need to make the transformation from pre-modern to modern culture. Specialization is one of the benchmarks of modernism. The physical education program at the Round Hill School reflected the trends towards specialization and educational expertise.

The Round Hill School fell on hard financial times and closed in 1834. A few public schools were being operated by some of the larger cities in the country, but these schools were primarily located on the East coast. Boston was the first city to require that students have the opportunity for exercise on a daily basis. By 1860 students in Toledo, Brooklyn, Hartford, and Cincinnati had come to enjoy the gymnasiums that were built as part of the high schools. These gymnasiums provided students the opportunity to play games, sports, and engage in physical fitness activities in the form of exercise. In general, boys frequented the gymnasiums more than the girls, but this is not to say that women were denied access to physical education. Nineteenth-century America was an era when men were the predominant social and political spokesmen for cultural and societal behavior; many would say that this remains the case today in many parts of the country. Women were taught to be very feminine and the thought of women exercising and playing sports troubled men. Men were generally opposed to having women exercise and sweat; it was not feminine. However, two people appeared who vigorously promoted exercise and health for women.

Women and Physical Education

Catherine Beecher (1800–1878) along with Dioclesian Lewis (1823–1886) were the pioneer physical educators who promoted physical education for women. Their approach can be considered to be another example of modern thinking. Beecher taught at a girls' seminary in Hartford and later opened the Western Female Institute in Cincinnati. She wrote several books on physical education; the most influential was *A Manual of Physiology and Calisthenics for Schools and Families*, published in 1856. Her system of calisthenics was based on twenty-six lessons in physiology and two courses in calisthenics. She had two programs, one for the schools and one for exercise halls and gymnasiums. Beecher and Lewis developed a gymnastics system exclusively for women and spent their lives promoting health and exercise for women. Both Beecher and Lewis were opposed to the two most popular systems of exercise that were based on gymnastics and calisthenics from Germany and Sweden.

The Influence of Germans and Swedes on the Development of American Physical Education

Initially, the development of American physical education was based on two systems of physical education that were promoted by immigrants from Germany and Sweden. Tens of thousands of Germans emigrated to the United States before the Civil War. They came here, like all immigrants, seeking a better life in a land noted for opportunity and freedom. They came to America with their Old World customs. Thousands of Turners came to America with their formal and systematic gymnastic system. They settled primarily in the Midwest: Kansas City, Cincinnati, and Milwaukee were home to large populations of Turners. The Turners built Turnvereins, the building complexes where they would meet to socialize and participate in gymnastics out on the Turnplatz. The Turners were highly patriotic and did their best to assimilate into their new country and at the same time preserve the culture of the Old World. The Turnvereins provided the opportunity to continue the customs of their former land. Many Turners joined the Union Army and fought in the Civil War, in the same manner as their founder, Friedrich Jahn, rallied the Turners to join the army and drive the French out of Germany. The Turners went into the schools and community and volunteered to teach physical education, in the form of German gymnastics, to the students. They held gymnastics competitions, known as Turnfests. The gymnastics program favored by the Turners was based on gymnastic apparatus such as vaulting horses, climbing ropes, ladders, beams, rings, and bars. The Turners wore uniforms and practiced a rigid form of calisthenics that was military in form and function. Discipline was the operative word during calisthenics. The Turner system was rivaled by the Swedish system developed by Per Henrik Ling (1776–1839).

Ling developed the Swedish system in approximately 1814 while teaching at the Royal Gymnastics Central Institute in Stockholm. His system was based on the medical and scientific knowledge of the day and, in this respect, claimed to have an advantage over the German system. Ling's attempt to incorporate science into his physical education program reflected the trend toward modern culture. Ling incorporated (1) aesthetic, (2) military,

(3) pedagogical, and (4) medical aspects of exercise. These four components were supposed to enable students to achieve health, which was described as harmony among the nervous, circulatory, and respiratory systems. He believed in a unified relationship between mind and body and claimed his system could achieve this. He preferred "free exercises" without the use of dumbbells or other hand held items. Stall bars, Swedish broom, and the window ladder were some of his inventions. He focused on posture and correct body positions and movements. Students were required, as a class, to "hold" a particular position while the teacher observed and corrected the faults of each student. Ling believed that the German system was too complicated; his system was criticized because it was said to be inconsistent.

Hartvig Nissen and Baron Nils Posse traveled to Boston to promote Ling's Swedish system. There they made the acquaintance of Mary Hemingway, a wealthy Boston philanthropist. She financed the building of the Boston Normal School of Gymnastics, which trained individuals to teach Swedish gymnastics. The Boston schools made Swedish gymnastics the official program of physical education in 1890. The argument among physical educators during this era over which system was better was known as the "Battle of the Systems." Swedish gymnastics were practiced in the Northeast United States but never did gain the respect and popularity that German gymnastics did.

By the turn of the century, most states were in the process of passing laws requiring that physical education be taught in the schools. Ohio is credited with being the first state to pass such a law in 1892. California had passed a law in 1866 requiring instruction in health and exercise, but this policy was terminated in 1879 when a new state constitution took effect. Legislation requiring that physical education be mandatory in the public schools was strongly promoted by the Turners and other groups, especially the Women's Christian Temperance Union (WCTU).

Early College Physical Education Programs

For the most part, colleges did not spend much time insuring that the physical health of their students was cared for. In 1789 Georgetown University was established in Virginia and was an exception. Their 1814 Prospectus stated that "the garden and court where the students recreate, are very airy and spacious . . . cleanliness, exercise and whatever contributes to health are attended to with particular care." Georgetown employed a fencing master and set aside daily periods for recreation. A backboard for handball was available and ball games were played, even on Sunday!

Harvard, Yale, Brown, and a few other colleges set aside space for gymnasiums between 1825 and 1830. There was little faculty supervision and students were left on their own most of the time. The students at the University of Virginia hired a Frenchman to operate the outdoor gymnasium, which opened in 1852 and closed during the Civil War. It is safe to say that prior to the beginning of the Civil War, few college administrators had interest in providing physical education experiences for their students. Students played games and exercised but not with formal structure or professional supervision.

The Contributions of Dr. Edward Hitchcock

It was not until Dr. Edward Hitchcock was hired by Amherst College as a Professor of Hygiene and Physical Education in 1861 that college physical education programs took root. Hitchcock, like almost all of America's early physical educators, was trained as a physician, having received his degree from Harvard Medical School. Amherst required that students attend physical education classes taught by Dr. Hitchcock four times per week for thirty minutes each. He kept vital statistics on each Amherst student and prescribed appropriate exercises for each student depending on physical and medical status. Other colleges followed Amherst and built gymnasiums and hired physical education professors.

The Contributions of Dr. Dudley Sargent

One of the most prominent physical educators of all time was Dr. Dudley Sargent, who was appointed to the faculty at Harvard as an Assistant Professor of Physical Training and Director of the Hemenway Gymnasium. Sargent was a dynamic force in the promotion of physical education, and, along with other devoted leaders, was a significant force in shaping the discipline. He demanded that physical education teachers receive appropriate training and, in this respect, was one of the first to promote the professional preparation of physical education teachers. He opened a private school in Cambridge called the Sanatory Gymnasium where he trained physical education teachers. The course was one year in duration and he taught it for free. His first attempt attracted six women with one actually completing the course. His original intent was to offer the course to both men and women, however, women comprised the great majority of his pupils and he made the decision to admit only women. Among his graduates were some of the most influential and prominent women in the history of physical education. Dr. Delphine Hanna of Oberlin College, Helen Blackwell of Boston University, and Dr. Helen Putnam of Vassar were but a few of his many students who made lasting contributions to the profession.

Developing the Profession of Physical Education

Dr. Sargent was one of several physical educators who opened private teacher training schools. Other prominent physicians who operated similar proprietary schools were Dr. Watson Savage, who ran the Savage School of Physical Education in New York, and Dr. William G. Anderson, who founded the Brooklyn Normal School for Physical Education in 1886. The YMCA Training Schools also produced physical educators who made solid contributions to the field. Dr. Luther Gulick and Dr. James McCurdy are credited for developing the excellent course of instruction at the Springfield YMCA. However, it was Dr. William G. Anderson who called the most important meeting in the early professional history of physical education.

On November 27, 1885, Dr. William G. Anderson convened a meeting of physical educators in order to discuss their common interests. Forty-nine people attended and discussed the merits and drawbacks of the German and Swedish systems, professional preparation of physical education teachers, Beecher's calisthenics for women, physical education in the YMCAs (which was outside the schools and may have caused some anxiety among some of the attendees), and developing a body of knowledge in physical education that was based on a sound theoretical basis. The large representation of physicians who attended the meeting (there were twenty-five) were concerned that the body of knowledge reflect science and have a strong medical focus. The meeting resulted in the formation of the American Association for the Advancement of Physical Education (AAAPE), which was renamed in 1903 as the American Physical Education Association (APEA).

The professionalization of physical education was underway due in a large part to the efforts of Dr. William G. Anderson and the group of physical educators who turned out for the historic meeting on that winter day in 1885. Today the APEA has evolved into one of the largest professional organizations in the nation, the American Alliance for Health, Physical Education, Recreation, and Dance (AAHPERD). Early American physical education was grounded in medicine and, over the course of time, deviated away from medicine into the teaching of play, games, and sports, among other things. Recently there has been a strong shift back towards the medical aspects of exercise and health, and in many colleges and universities, sports medicine is among the most popular areas of study.

The New Physical Education: Reforming the Nature of Physical Education

Physical education, like other professions, has undergone significant reform. One of the most dramatic reforms occurred between 1915 and 1930 when three physical educators unveiled the "New Physical Education." The three architects of the New Physical Education were Clark Hetherington, Rosalind Cassidy, and Thomas D. Wood. The New Physical Education was based on the book written by Hetherington titled *School Program in Physical Education*. The New Physical Education was strongly influenced by the work of three of America's most revered educators, John Dewey, G. Stanley Hall, and Herbert Spencer, who all believed in the value of play, games, and sports.

The New Physical Education incorporated the psychological and sociological practices that were an important component of mainstream educational practice. In addition, the New Physical Education divided physical education into four separate but cooperative areas, (1) organic, (2) psychomotor, (3) character development, and (4) intellectual development. Physical education as redefined by the New Physical Education was in a position to reflect mainstream thinking that embraced the educational and social objectives of mainstream educational philosophy. The New Physical Education curriculum was influenced by the strong biological, evolutionary, and psychological orientation of a nation that was coming into its own. Modern thought and the scientific movement shaped American society and educational goals, and the New Physical Education mirrored mainstream educational thinking, which was critical if physical education was to remain a valued curricular component in the schools.

Change did not come easy for many of the senior physical educators who remained firm in their conviction that gymnastics was the core of physical education. The play, games, and sports that the New Physical Education utilized to achieve its goals was not seen as being as useful as gymnastics by the older physical education teachers who had been educated via German gymnastics. It was not long before the rigid gymnastics—and the accompanying boredom that was a frequent complaint by students—was replaced by the New Physical Education, which held the promise of fun, health promotion, personal development, and instilling those ideals and behaviors that would make for productive citizens.

Physical education became a national security issue during World Wars I and II. Over 25 percent of the men who were drafted failed their draft physicals. These men were overweight and in very poor condition. This state of affairs was alarming, and physical educators in many schools responded by replacing physical education with military drill and calisthenics. The rationale in this was that these types of activities (military drill) prepared youth for the military and in this way contributed to the national defense. After the war, most schools returned to traditional physical education programs.

Professional preparation of physical education teachers gradually shifted from the private teacher training schools to the colleges. Because of the mandatory physical education requirement that the vast majority of states passed into law, physical education teachers were in demand. As a result, colleges and universities began to offer degrees in physical education to meet the requirements of the profession and to add teachers to the schools. Between 1914 and 1921 the number of state normal schools preparing teachers of physical education jumped from three to twenty-eight, the number of state universities preparing physical education teachers rose from four to twenty, and the number of endowed colleges offering a bachelor's degree in physical education climbed to twenty-two. The first graduate program in physical education was started at Columbia University by Dr. Thomas D. Wood. Columbia awarded the first master's degree in physical education in 1910. The first Ph.D. degree program in physical education was started by New York University and Teachers College, Columbia University, in 1924.

The growth of physical education and sports after World War II was rapid. High schools and colleges fielded more and more teams and the seasons became longer. The level of competition and the sophistication that coaches were able to employ moved sports to a level that increased the expectations and pressure to excel to new heights. Millions of students became involved in competition that ranged from youth sports, to high school sports, to college sports, to professional-level sports. The recreational adult athlete emerged in great numbers in the mid-1960s. Physical education underwent change and began to promote lifetime sports that allowed for the enhancement of health and an active lifestyle. No longer did physical education cease after formal schooling. This New Physical Education was designed to educate and promote a healthy lifestyle, catching the attention of millions of Americans. Jogging, cycling, power walking, aerobics, and other fitness activities are lifetime activities that are enjoyed by millions. Physical education entered a new era where health promotion and physical fitness spawned a new culture of symbolized by health clubs, nutrition and dietary expertise, and a highly scientific and medical approach to insuring quality of life.

Since the 1885 meeting called by Dr. Anderson, the profession of physical education has enjoyed impressive expansion to the point where it is among the most popular of all undergraduate and graduate majors. The emphasis on health and fitness in conjunction with America's insatiable appetite for play, games, and sports strongly suggests that interest in the field will remain high for years to come. We will watch carefully how mainstream American education reacts to a changing multicultural society. Instead of remaining "reactive" to the direction of mainstream educational thought, it is time for physical educators, human movement specialists, and kinesiologists to become strongly proactive and help lead the way to educational reform and health reform. As the next section in this chapter will detail, history has shown what is likely to befall our profession when we remain complacent and reactive (instead of proactive) to changes looming on the horizon.

Reforming American Education

Since the last half of the nineteenth century the educational system in the United States has placed strong emphasis on certain subjects and less emphasis in others. The discoveries of Charles Darwin (1809–1882), the Cold War, and the launching of the Soviet Union's first orbital satellite, Sputnik, have led to science and mathematics sitting atop the educational hierarchy. When Americans perceive that science and math are not well taught, there is much talk of educational reform. For instance, there is a fair amount of concern over the declining scores over the past several decades on standardized tests that measure educational achievement; even though there has been an emphasis on teaching analytical and verbal skills, test scores in these two areas continue to slide. Numerous leaders in American education have called for educational reform to "fix" the problem.

One of the more well-known documents to address educational reform was titled "A Nation at Risk" (1983). The authors of this study indicted American education, stating that if there were no serious reforms, then an entire generation would lack the basic skills traditionally provided by public education. In 1993, the authors of this study held a meeting to discuss the changes that (hopefully) had occurred as a result of their work. Unfortunately, the writers felt they had little to cheer about. Their report was the latest effort at educational reform, a hot topic among politicians, parents, and educators everywhere.

The Coleman Report

Educational reform is not a recent development. In 1966 James Coleman was the chief author of a government report on education titled "Equality of Educational Opportunity." The *Coleman Report,* as it was called, addressed the long-held belief that public education acted to insure equal opportunity among the cultural and economically diverse segments of American society. The *Coleman Report*, surprisingly, condemned the failure of public education to prevent and eliminate alienation against minority students. It turned out that "equal opportunity" was a myth. Even after tremendous amounts of money had been expended in an effort to "fix" the system, very little progress seemed to have been made. The impact of foreign immigration, combined with the disadvantages that a significant population of minority children bring with them when they enter school, caused the students to perform poorly on standardized tests. The *Coleman Report* concluded that education as an institution had failed to overcome the disadvantages of poverty and race.

Thirty years later the same problems are still being discussed, and not only among educators. In 1993, Lynn Franey a reporter for the Copley News Service, wrote a story quite similar to the findings of the *Coleman Report*. Franey reported that on average only *27 per-*

cent of the students who attended Manual Arts High School in Los Angeles would graduate. The dropout rate was a staggering *73 percent*, the highest in the Los Angeles Unified School District. Approximately 40 percent of all students fail to graduate from high school in Los Angeles. As Franey (1993) noted:

> Latino students drop out here at a rate of 40 percent. In Latino enclaves like South Central and East Los Angeles, drop-out rates routinely exceed 60 percent. Latinos account for about two-thirds of the district's 630,000 students. African Americans quit school in higher proportions than do Latinos—44 percent—but blacks make up just 15 percent of the district enrollment. The drop-out rate for white students, who are 13 percent of the student population, is 26 percent. (p. A33)

The problem is serious. The concerns that were presented in the *Coleman Report* over thirty years ago and are still reported by the media unfortunately continue to remain as we enter the next century. Teachers and school administrators continue to search for solutions in the name of reform. To be sure, there have been some successes; however, most of these efforts have fallen short of their goal. To be sure, there has been significant social change in the cultural fabric of America since the *Coleman Report* was issued. However, both the *Coleman Report* and "A Nation at Risk" accurately predicted the pressures with which public education would have to contend, and yet the state of affairs in public education has not significantly improved. The process of education, as witnessed by the *Coleman Report* and "A Nation at Risk," clearly needs modification. All of us will have to contribute to the solutions. Unfortunately, the problem is so large that it is hard to frame the questions. For example, What is it you would like to see eliminated or changed regarding how education is "delivered" to students from kindergarten to the twelfth grade? Would you change the curricular content? Do you think the curriculum you were exposed to was too difficult, about right, or not difficult enough? Are these even the right questions to be asking?

Educational reform has and will continue to be an important issue that has a strong impact on all of us. You no doubt have some thoughts about educational reform. As a student who was a product of our educational system prior to your matriculation into college, you know that there are many dedicated teachers who are sincerely interested in the academic progress of their students in addition to their personal development. Looking back, what is it that you believe these teachers needed in order to support their instructional efforts but never received? Is the decline of our educational system the result of the inability of (1) the student to learn, (2) the teacher to teach, (3) attitude of the student (some students do not want to be in school), (4) the failure of students and parents to value education, or (5) some other reason?

Education or Mis-Education?

There have been numerous voices calling attention to the failure of our schools and the consequent alienation of students. Jonathan Kozol's *Free Schools*, Paul Goodman's *Compulsory Mis-Education and the Community of Scholars,* Neil Postman's and Charles Weingartner's *Teaching as a Subversive Activity*, and Allen Graubard's *Free the Children: Radical Reform and the Free School Movement* are some of the classic books that are highly critical of the educational system, substance of education (curriculum), and educational process. All of these educational critics have demanded the reform of education for quite some time and have offered controversial and radical innovations in the name of reform.

The issue of reform and "what it means to reform" is of critical importance to the social, moral, and intellectual fabric of our society. There will be numerous views regarding the content and scope of educational reform. Some of the models will be liberal, such as Graubard's, and some will be considered conservative. Suffice it to say, educational reform is an ongoing process and is a major component of the political agenda of the nation. The history of educational reform seems to be the attempts by many dedicated educators, over time, to enact significant change against forces resistant to change.

The Reform Movement in Sport and Physical Education

Reform of physical education and athletics is no different from "mainstream" educational reform. Historically, our field attracts a great deal of attention in the name of reform. There have been, and no doubt will continue to be, panels of distinguished scholars, citizens, coaches, and "experts" convened to study and document the abuses in interscholastic and intercollegiate sports. There will continue to be educators and other public-minded people who will call into question the legitimacy of physical education as a necessary part of education. While not necessarily comforting, the close scrutiny that our field receives ensures we cannot become complacent. Instead, we must remain vigilant and receptive to reform if the reform is beneficial to our field, our students, and our nation. We have and will oppose reform merely for the sake of change, or if the reform is without educational and academic merit. It will now be our purpose to present a brief historical overview of selected events in sport and physical education that were the catalyst for reform. When you read the following accounts, it is important to ask yourself if all that much has changed today and if not, why?

Sport

Football remains one of the most popular sports in America. Unfortunately, statistics in football show that there are numerous injuries among players, and the litigious nature of contemporary American society has caused many coaches to leave the coaching profession. What may be surprising is that in the past football was even more violent than it is today. Over a century ago, football was characterized by mass formation plays that were deadly. In 1891 Amos Alonzo Stagg designed the "Turtleback" formation: A mass of players situated themselves into an oval resembling a turtle's shell, bearing down in mass on the opposing ball carrier. A year later, Harvard University's football team employed the "Flying Wedge," a formation that enabled the receiving team on a kickoff to form a wedge as each player held on to the jersey or locked arms with his teammate. The ball carrier was tucked safely within the confines of the wedge, and woe be the man that was designated the "Wedge Breaker"! Representatives from Yale, Harvard, Princeton, the U.S. Naval Academy, and the University of Pennsylvania convened in 1894 and accomplished two significant rule changes: (1) to reduce the length of the game from 90 minutes to 60 minutes and

(2) to abolish the deadly "Flying Wedge." While these attempts at reform were only partially successful, the reform movement in intercollegiate athletics had begun in earnest.

In spite at this attempt at reform, the number of serious injuries continued to increase as more and more Americans played the game. In 1905 eighteen football players were killed because of mass formation plays. The "Flying Wedge," surviving the attempted ban in 1894, was one of the main reasons for all of the mayhem on the field. As a result, Northwestern University and Columbia University dropped football and Stanford and the University of California at Berkeley substituted rugby in place of football.

In 1905 President Theodore Roosevelt, an avid football fan, convened a meeting with representatives from Yale, Harvard, and Princeton to both regulate the game and to teach players sportsmanship. In addition to the problems of players being killed on the field, there were eligibility problems. Football players would simply enroll at another college when their eligibility expired at their first school. Heated discussions and stories appeared in the nations' newspapers over questions of eligibility and the carnage and violence that was associated with the game. Shortly after President Roosevelt's meeting in October, the Chancellor of New York University, Henry McCraken, convened a meeting in December of the same year to discuss the fate of college football. Thirteen college representatives attended the meeting. The result was the decision to form an association that was to regulate collegiate sports.

A few weeks later sixty-two colleges sent representatives to a meeting that established the Intercollegiate Athletic Association of the United States that changed its name in 1910 to the National Collegiate Athletic Association; the NCAA, as it is commonly referred to today. The NCAA was devoted exclusively devoted to men's sports when it was first organized. Title IX of the Educational Amendments of 1972 reformed both women's sports and men's sports and eventually saw the NCAA change from an exclusive male membership to an organization that represents both men and women, but the "reform" of the NCAA was anything but easy.

During the decade of the 1960s, there was a great deal of social and civil unrest in the country. Change and reform were the operative buzz words of that era. Among the more vocal and action-oriented organizations that demanded reform were the National Organization of Women (NOW) founded in 1966. Women's rights, along with the civil rights movement, became very political and as a result, an agent for social change. Prior to the passage of Title IX, it was rare to find coeducational physical education classes at the high school or college level. After passage and full implementation of Title IX, coed physical education classes were the norm, not the exception. However, the greatest impact of Title IX was in the area of women's athletics. Prior to Title IX, sports for women in high schools and colleges was one step up from an intramural sports program at best. There was little if any funding for women's athletics from the athletic departments. Virtually all the money allocated by the schools and generated by the men's teams went directly back to fund the men's programs. The women's sports programs were funded to pay for a coach and some meal money in the event the team had to travel. The reasoning went that women don't eat as much as men and therefore don't need all that much money. The same belief was held for overnight lodging. It was perfectly fine to cram four to six women in a hotel room, two and sometimes three to a bed. Prior to the passage of Title IX, women's sports were not taken very seriously, even by some women.

The Department of Girls' and Women's Sports was adamant that athletic programs be conducted under the aegis of the women's physical education department and under no circumstance were women to participate as members of male teams. They also were opposed to awarding athletic scholarships to women. Since money was not readily available for this purpose, it could be considered a moot point. Radical changes occurred during the 1960s and 1970s and women's sports were not immune, much to the consternation of a number of women physical educators who opposed intense competition.

In 1967 the DGWS, which functioned as an arm of the American Association for Health, Physical Education, and Recreation (AAHPER), conducted national collegiate championships for women. In 1971 the Association for Intercollegiate Athletics for Women (AIAW) was formed to bring women's sports into the "big time." National championships were sponsored by the AIAW for the next ten years, their last one held in 1981. However, the AIAW folded in 1981. What caused the demise of the AIAW?

Title IX was an amendment to the Civil Rights Act of 1964 and in part said that no institution receiving federal funding could exclude on the basis of sex anyone from participating in any program, sports and physical education included. There are specific references to sports and physical education that opened the doors for women and enabled them to participate and receive the same type of facilities, financial resources, coaching, and accommodations that the men have enjoyed for close to a century.

Section 86.41 Athletics, part C of Title IX states:

> Equal opportunity. A recipient which operates or sponsors interscholastic, intercollegiate, club or intramural athletics shall provide equal athletic opportunity for members of both sexes. In determining whether equal opportunities are available the Director will consider, among other factors:
>
> (i)   Whether the selection of sports and levels of competition effectively accommodate the interests and abilities of members of both sexes;
> (ii)   The provision of equipment and supplies;
> (iii) Scheduling of games and practice time;
> (iv)   Travel and per diem allowance;
> (v)   Opportunity to receive coaching and academic tutoring;
> (vi)   Assignment and compensation of coaches and tutors;
> (vii) Provision of locker rooms, practice and competitive facilities;
> (viii) Provision of medical and training facilities and services;
> (ix)   Provision of housing and dining facilities and services;
> (x)   Publicity. (*Federal Register*, June 4, 1975)

While women were elated over Title IX, the National Collegiate Athletic Association (NCAA) was anything but happy, and the athletic directors in colleges and universities all over the country, along with the men's coaches, were furious. In order to continue receiving federal funds, the colleges and universities had to implement Title IX. That meant taking money from men's sports and funding the women's sports programs that would mirror what the men had. This was very expensive and, so the men believed, would cut their programs drastically. While the AIAW and NOW were celebrating, the NCAA went to court in order to stop the implementation of Title IX.

The NCAA eventually lost and then realized that it was better to bring the women into the fold. The NCAA would then regain control of intercollegiate sports and at the same time eventually realize television revenues from conducting women's championships. The NCAA offered a much better financial package for women's championships then the AIAW could. Since the vast majority of college athletic departments were hurting financially, the NCAA's promise to pay all expenses of women's teams that qualified for NCAA Championships was eagerly embraced by most of the nation's athletic directors. The AIAW could not begin to match the offer of the NCAA, and this was a major cause of its demise.

You don't have to read very far into the sports pages or wait very long while listening to the evening news to find about yet another alleged scandal in college sports. The pressure to win and the attendant demands and expectations of fans across the nation have and will continue to be a plague that is largely responsible for the moral and ethical decay of college as well as some high school sports programs. In order for colleges to field teams in "big-time" sports, a considerable amount of money must be secured in order to fund these programs at the Division I-A and I-AA level. Funding teams at the Division II level is likely to run in the neighborhood of a million dollars, and Division I-A and I-AA programs need millions of dollars each year in order to operate.

The Cartel

In general, big-time college athletic programs operate as a cartel. Cartels are formed by a group of independent business organizations that work together to regulate pricing and marketing strategies. For example, colleges may join forces so they can regulate various sports as well as market these sports and make money. The Big 10 Conference could be considered a cartel, as could the Bowl Alliance, which is supposed to regulate major college football bowl games that will send the two top-rated teams to play for the national championship.

Athletic departments frequently operate as corporations or foundations that must raise money in order to run the programs and collectively promote the interests and advancement of the cartel. Most big-time athletic departments are, in fact, separate from the college or university they represent. In a number of cases and while they may receive money from student fees, they rely heavily upon corporate sponsorships and donations from boosters. Most of the major college bowl games are funded by corporations and many college athletic departments will actually "sell" a football or basketball game to a corporate sponsor in exchange for large sums of money. Corporate sponsorships of intercollegiate athletics are the future, so we are told. Before too long, corporate sponsorships will provide the majority of revenue for many college athletic departments.

We all know that coaches have been hired and fired because of the wishes of wealthy alumni and boosters who contribute to the college. What kind of clout do you imagine Corporate America will be able to use regarding its sponsorship of numerous college athletic departments? If institutional control over athletics is an issue now (it has always been a concern of faculty), what sort of demands and influence could be placed on athletic directors and coaches by corporate sponsors who fund a large part of the budget?

Reform of college athletics must be an ongoing process. It can be argued that financial reform of college athletics is taking place. All we have to do is look at the number of corporations that are involved with intercollegiate athletics. Reform is taking place; however, the cost of the "financial reform" that stems from corporate involvement with intercollegiate athletics (and in some regions of the country, high school athletics) may put sport in a debt situation that is expressed in morale and ethical terms as opposed to revenues lost. After all, Corporate America has a less then sterling track record as an ethical and moral entity. Intercollegiate athletics have a history of scandal. Merging the two could produce a volatile situation, all in the name of economic reform.

After World War II the NCAA had to assume the role of policeman because too many college coaches engaged in recruiting violations, under-the-table payments to athletes, using academically ineligible players, and conducting out-of-season practices. The situation has not improved. In 1951 more than thirty college basketball players engaged in fixing games. Gamblers would play the players to throw the games, which they did. The colleges involved were the University of Kentucky, Bradley University, City College of New York, Long Island University, Manhattan College, New York University, and Toledo.

Alteration of transcripts to change grades on behalf of athletes caused the basketball coach at the University of New Mexico his job. In the late 1970s, the football and basketball programs at California State University, Long Beach were so scandal ridden that the NCAA put the university on probation for several years. The athletic director got a new job at Arizona State University and the basketball coach took a job at the University of Nevada, Las Vegas, where he built a basketball powerhouse and won a national championship with questionable practices and athletes who invited intense scrutiny from the NCAA.

The NCAA includes a staff of investigators who are charged with investigating fraudulent practices by member institutions. The "win at all cost" mentality that some coaches seem to favor has resulted in the NCAA passing the "Death Penalty" rule. This rule was imposed on Southern Methodist University in 1987 after SMU was found guilty of continuing to pay money to its athletes even though the university had previously been on probation for paying athletes several years earlier. SMU was ordered to drop football for the 1987 season, and the University decided to cancel the 1988 football season as well. In 1993, Auburn University's football team completed an undefeated season but could not appear on television or play in a bowl game because of violating NCAA rules.

The bowl games would probably suffer, but it seems that there is a great deal of interest in a national championship to determine, conclusively, the "king" of college football. There is opposition to this proposal. A number of football coaches and college presidents oppose the concept; however, there is a great deal of money to be made for all of the NCAA Division I-A schools that play football. We already have national championships for every sport in Division I except for football. The opponents often claim that the season is already to long for the student-athletes, and a championship game would extend the season. Besides, the bowl system would suffer. Why is the argument about the long season only applicable to Division I-A football programs? The NCAA sponsors national football championships in Divisions I-AA, II, and III.

The curious student may want to add up all the games that are necessary in order for a national championship game to be played at the "lesser levels" of college football. The student-athletes who participate in national football championship games sponsored by the NCAA or the National Association of Intercollegiate Athletics (NAIA) are involved in football from August through December. The major bowl games all occur on or about New Year's Day. Consider the following questions:

1. Do you see any benefit to the student-athletes who participate in a season that lasts five months?
2. Is there any "down side" to the length of football season and the demands that are placed on players and coaches involved with high-profile programs?
3. Would you reform college athletics or high school athletics in some way, shape, or form?
4. Would you keep the current governing structure in college sports or replace it with something "better"?
5. Do you believe that the "win-at-all-cost" attitude still exists in sports? If yes, to what extent does it exist—where can you find this attitude easily?
6. Can cheating ever be eliminated, for the most part, from serious athletic competition, no matter what the level?

Sports have certainly captivated the attention of the American public. Reform has taken place; however, the entry of Corporate America into college athletics as a major source of revenue could threaten the institutional integrity of the college that is not vigilant, thus necessitating still further action in the name of reform.

Physical Education

Physical education has generated a great deal of interest with regard to reform. Some educators would like to "reform" us out of education entirely. There are numerous calls to reform physical education, which are presented in Chapter 14.

Early in our historical development, the content of physical education until the turn of the century was based primarily on German and Swedish gymnastics that came to this country by way of immigration. Initial reform in physical education centered on which of the two systems was better suited for delivering the benefits of physical education to a young nation. The Battle of the Systems, as it came to be called, was a step to reform the content of physical education as well as the goals of our field. Each system was very formal and reflected the formal environment of the educational process over a century ago.

The Young Men's Christian Association (YMCA) offered an alternative that included games that were not part of the curriculum of the Swedish system or the German system. To a large extent, it was the inclusion of games as a means to develop students that reformed the German and Swedish system out of physical education all together.

Educational Developmentalism

Educational developmentalism and the scientific movement were the catalyst for reform in physical education between 1900 and 1930. Politically, physical education as well as most subject fields taught in the schools, reflected mainstream conventional thinking. Historically, it is this "middle-class" concept of conventional mainstream beliefs that shapes the curriculum in our schools. Physical education conformed itself to reflect this approach. Educational developmentalism and the scientific movement influenced America's middle class and physical education responded.

The development of athletic achievement tests, anthropometric measurement, use of statistics, and research in physiology was physical education's move toward reform that would complement the scientific movement that was defining and reforming science. Two pioneers in the field of physical education, Dr. Thomas D. Wood and Clark Hetherington, were the architects of the "New Physical Education" that reflected the ideas of educational developmentalism. The proponents of educational developmentalism came from the fields of education and psychology and believed that play was an important part of growth. The popularity of educational developmentalism resulted in the recognition that physical education was an essential part of education and therefore, must be a compulsory subject. Social education was a component of educational developmentalism and seemed to lend itself well to the goals of physical education during this era.

The reform of physical education during this era resulted in shifting away from the German and Swedish gymnastics. Physical education sought to reflect the mainstream conventional values and beliefs embraced by middle class America. Play, games, and sports based on the outcomes of educational developmentalism and the scientific movement became effective tools to develop students physically, morally, and socially.

The most prominent names in American education during the early part of the twentieth century were John Dewey, G. Stanley Hall, and Edward Thorndike. These three men, while not physical educators, believed in the value and contributions that our field would make to society. This was probably the last time that physical education was to enjoy such support. A new group of educators would emerge to question—and rightfully so—the value of physical education to the educational and developmental mission entrusted to our nation's schools. Our academic content would be seriously questioned, especially in the colleges.

The end of World War II brought with it enormous political and social changes throughout the world. The world that had emerged from the war was divided into three "camps": democratic nations of the West, communist nations of the East, and nonaligned Third World Nations scattered all over the planet. This was a serious world, a world that was under the threat of nuclear war. America was the leader of the "Free World" and needed an effective and efficient "modern" infrastructure that would not only perpetuate our global role but would be the catalyst for economic, social, and educational reform. As a nation we were working quite diligently towards these goals, or so we thought.

In 1956 the Soviet Union launched the first satellite into space, which escalated both the space race and the arms race, lest we let the Soviets "nuke" us from space. It became apparent that our schools were not doing the job (America was behind in the "race for space") and once again the demand for educational reform echoed from main street to Washington, DC. The professional preparation of teachers was called into question as well as the academic programs that "educated" teachers. Physical education was no exception.

James B. Conant

In 1961 the Carnegie Corporation of New York provided the funding that allowed James B. Conant, former President of Harvard University, to undertake a study of the education of America's teachers. The results of his study were published in his classic text titled *The Education of American Teachers* (1963). Conant visited 77 colleges and universities in 22 states and spoke to countless professors and students. In addition, Conant scrutinized state regulations and certification requirements of teachers, and related college curriculum to the elementary and secondary school level. His evaluation and analysis of physical education was interesting and revealing. Eventually, Conant's arguments concerning curricular content and graduate work in physical education became one of the major catalysts for reform in our field.

Conant argued that foreign languages, art, music, and physical education were "of a kind" because they have more in common then most people assume. According to Conant:

> The American public and the professional educators, then, are still a bit uncertain as to why instruction should be provided in art, music, foreign language, and physical education. This uncertainty is reflected in the amount of time allotted to these subjects in the schools and in the varying practices as to the optional nature of the work. In a sense all four fields are in competition. In only a few of the schools I have visited are the teachers of all four satisfied with their positions accorded to their specialties. . . . Physical education as a required subject one period a day five days a week obviously takes time away from music and art, as do the academic subjects. Therefore, a certain tension exists, to put it mildly, among the proponents of all these fields. (Conant, 1963, p. 181)

Conant argued that physical educators seem to suffer from an academic inferiority complex, and in their attempt to gain academic respectability, physical educators adopted the phraseology and symbols of more intellectual academic areas of the arts and sciences. With regard to the attempt by physical educators to gain academic respectability by identifying with the arts and sciences, Conant (1963) says, "The consequences are most ridiculous in the [their] graduate programs" (p. 181).

Conant did argue, however, that physical education teachers must be competent performers, and that such competency should be a prerequisite for admission into a teacher training program. Prospective music and art teachers were to be held to the same standard. In Conant's words,

> In the areas of music, sport, and art, since skills are to a considerable extent developed on an extracurricular basis by high school students, *the total youthful experience* must be considered in establishing the level of attainment demanded for admission to the teacher training program. Admission should depend on the demonstration of a high level of performance. (p. 183)

According to Conant, the experience and teaching that the prospective physical education teacher receives in high school is of critical importance. He makes the point that "Thus, it is during the pre-college years that the future leaders of . . . physical education must receive the basic training on which their competence as teachers eventually depends" (Conant, 1963, p. 184). Conant, then, was strongly opposed to physical educators teaching anything but the activity courses that are offered in elementary and secondary schools:

> Teachers of physical education are today suspect because superintendents and principal of high schools have far too often required them to teach academic subjects that they have hardly studied in college; moreover, they are subject to so much

public pressure in their role as coaches that they are often forced to neglect their classroom work." (p. 185)

Conant believed that the demands of coaching and teaching physical education are too great to expect that physical educators should take on an additional academic burden. He recognized that the emphasis the public places on athletic success is extraordinary and very stressful.

Today every state regulates teacher preparation programs. These programs have a number of different educational certifications depending upon the subject, type of student, and grade level taught. Conant had called for reform of this type. In early 1962, the state legislature in California passed the Fisher Bill, which created a single-subject teaching credential limiting the teacher to a specific subject field, such as physical education. As a result of the Fisher Bill, it takes an additional year of college study, a fifth year, before a California teaching credential can be granted. In addition to the additional year of college, the Fisher Bill identified areas of study that are academic and nonacademic. Potential school administrators must major in an academic area. As you may have guessed, physical education was identified as a nonacademic area but could be classified as an academic area if certain conditions were met. As a result of the *Conant Report* and the Fisher Bill, physical education departments in colleges and universities across the nation underwent reform. In California, the reform of physical education was the transformation from an educational department to an academic department in order to qualify as an academic subject.

Gone are the days when a teacher who received a college degree in music could be assigned to teach physical education. Interestingly enough, Conant was an opponent of California's answer to reform, the Fisher Bill. He believed that four years of college is enough, provided that an adequate high school preparation is assured. Conant saw the fifth year as an attempt to provide the teaching profession with more status in the eyes of the public. The other reason for the additional year, so Conant was told, was that a teacher should be first of all a liberally educated person, the implication being that four years of college should be devoted to a liberal education, with the fifth year for teacher education. Conant's response to this rationale, espoused by proponents of a fifth year prior to becoming a teacher, was as follows. " And if all graduates of a liberal arts faculty are to be considered 'liberally educated persons,' it is important to remember that they include graduates with a major in physical education" (Conant, 1963, p. 202).

While Conant did not believe that an undergraduate degree in physical education should be equated with a traditional college education in the liberal arts and sciences, he did believe that there was room for physical education in the schools. However, the content and goals that Conant identified with physical education were not at all complementary with the arts and sciences, which form the traditional core of a liberal arts education.

Conant noted in his research that because of the high degree of visibility that coaches receive, they are frequently candidates for administrative positions. As a result, Conant argued that,

unless there is a change in the direction of this trend, I conclude that the physical education teacher should have an even wider general academic education than any other teacher. . . . More likely than not, the man preparing to be a physical education teacher is, perhaps unconsciously, preparing to be an educational admin-istrator. He needs to start early on a course of wide reading in the humanities and social sciences. (1963, pp. 185–186)

In California, the Fisher Bill seemed to be a response to Conant's belief that an acad-emic background in the social sciences and humanities was mandatory preparation for prospective school administrators who majored in physical education. Under the Fisher Bill, physical education departments that underwent reform to become academic depart-ments include coursework in the humanities and social sciences.

It is important to remember that Conant argued against assigning physical educators to subjects other than physical education because of their academic background. The fact that Conant was adamant about this is proof enough that he found the practice of assigning physical education teachers to subjects in which they had little or no academic preparation to be widespread. He believed that physical educators and coaches were likely candidates to become administrators and suggested reform, "that physical educators should have an even wider general academic education than any other teacher" (Conant, 1963, p. 201). He certainly did not dismiss or ignore the impact of physical education and athletics at the secondary school level. He did notice an inferiority complex by physical educators (dare we suggest defensive posture?) because of the educational establishments' labeling of phys-ical education as "nonacademic." He suggested areas where physical education could ben-efit from reform, but when he came to post-baccalaureate, graduate course work in physical education, he condemned the curriculum in a manner that alarmed physical educators throughout the country and was a catalyst for further reform in physical education.

The Response

In 1963 the American Alliance for Health, Physical Education, and Recreation (AAHPER) called for the formation of a panel that would address the professional preparation of phys-ical education teachers. The panel was designated as the AAHPER Professional Panel and was headed by Arthur Esslinger. The Panel accomplished the following:

1. Publicized the work of the Professional Preparation Conference of 1962. Two impor-tant recommendations emerged out of the conference: (1) Develop a five-year under-graduate program and (2) specify that half of the current four-year program be devoted to general education courses.
2. Developed a self-evaluation form that was sent to every college that offered a degree in physical education. The college president was asked to complete the form.
3. Was able to establish a positive working relationship with the National Council for the Accreditation of Teachers (NCATE).
4. Established a nationwide program that provided resources and leadership that helped college physical education departments improve their instructional effectiveness.
5. Called for a Conference on Graduate Education in Physical Education. (Snyder, 1968, p. 73)

The AAHPER Professional Panel went public in order to refute the views of James B. Conant. The Fisher Bill attracted national attention for a number of reasons. However, the most important feature of the Fisher Bill to our field was the classification of physical education as a "nonacademic" degree. Several hundred state legislators in California voted in favor of the Fisher Bill, believing that there was very little, if any, academic content in physical education degree programs. Always the setter of national trends, the status of physical education in California sent a wake-up call to physical educators across the nation. Reform of physical education came to be of critical concern to not only our field but to countless educators who questioned the value of physical education.

Franklin Henry: The Academic Discipline of Physical Education

Physical education responded to the above challenges of Conant's arguments and the Fisher Bill by convening a number of meetings and conferences all for the express purpose of establishing physical education as an academic discipline. Perhaps the best case for establishing both the curriculum and methodology of physical education as an academic discipline was presented by Franklin M. Henry. Trained as an experimental psychologist, he was a Professor of Physical Education at the University of California at Berkeley. In 1964, Henry delivered an address before the annual meeting of the National College Physical Education Association for Men titled "Physical Education—An Academic Discipline." He later published "The Discipline of Physical Education" in the *Journal of Health, Physical Education, and Recreation* (September, 1964) and fifteen years later published "The Academic Discipline of Physical Education" in *Quest* (Winter 1978). Henry insisted that physical education must become a bona fide academic discipline and must reign supreme over the profession of physical education, which he identified as an applied field.

Prior to becoming an academic discipline, physical education was considered a profession. To review, the profession is based on practical application and trains physical education teachers. The discipline of physical education is grounded in theoretical constructs and a body of knowledge that exists for the purpose of generating basic research that expands the body of knowledge. Basic research is "pure research" in that it need not have any practical application but does add to the body of knowledge. The profession of physical education devotes itself to teacher training and offers sports skills classes—activity classes to the general student body. Historically, physical educators identifying with the profession do not engage in basic research and have expressed little interest in doing so. The exception is the area of pedagogy, which is devoted to the training of teachers in physical education in addition to improving instructional effectiveness. Within physical education, pedagogy is usually based on behavior modification techniques, as opposed to the traditional professional preparation of teachers, which has not consciously or by design employed the behavior modification techniques made popular in some circles by B.F. Skinner.

Henry stated that before physical education can achieve academic status, it must have a body of knowledge that is grounded in scholarship and has a specific focus unique and distinct from other academic areas. The discussion relative to the body of knowledge in our field is also discussed in Chapter 14. The concern with the body of knowledge continues to receive considerable attention from scholars in human movement, kinesiology, physical education, sport science, and so on. It will be helpful to once again review Henry's concept of an academic discipline in his own words. We will spend some time discussing his impact on the reform of physical education into an academic discipline:

> An academic discipline is an organized body of knowledge collectively embraced in a formal course of learning; the acquisition of such knowledge is assumed to be an adequate and worthy objective as such, without any demonstration or requirement of practical application; the content is theoretical and scholarly as distinguished from technical and professional. (Henry, 1978, p. 13)

Henry was careful to point out that he does not discount the contribution of the profession when defining the academic discipline,

> Keep in mind that we are talking about a discipline that is erudite and based on confirmed theories (i.e., on established knowledge)—there is no intent to belittle the importance of the professional discipline which centers on pedagogy and the technology of motor skills, and is conceptually different in purpose. (Henry, 1978, p. 13)

The body of knowledge espoused by Henry reflects the academic emphasis that Conant and many others found lacking. Henry asked:

> What is the scholarly field of knowledge that constitutes the academic discipline of physical education? It was stated (Henry, 1964) to be constituted of certain portions of such diverse fields as anatomy, physics and physiology, cultural anthropology, history and sociology, as well as psychology. The focus of attention is on the study of the human as an individual, engaging in the motor performances required in daily life and in other motor performances yielding aesthetic values or serving as expressions of a persons physical and competitive nature, accepting challenges of one's capability to cope with a hostile environment, and participating in leisure time activities that have become of increasing importance to our culture. (Henry, 1978, p. 14)

Henry stated that the academic study of physical education must be cross-disciplinary as opposed to interdisciplinary. Traditional fields such as history or psychology are organized as "disciplines," which are the body of knowledge of those fields and are taught to students as such. "Interdisciplinary" means that one's curriculum is composed of a variety of disciplinary courses. The limitation of this approach is the assumption that a history or psychology instructor will provide physical education students with the necessary content that is specific to our field.

In contrast, cross-disciplinary programs of study are developed for in depth study of psychology of sport or sport history. Henry used the following example to argue the merits of a cross-disciplinary curriculum,

> For instance, a motor learning course must incorporate neurophysiology and related anatomy as well as specific aspects of experimental psychology. Should such a course be taught in the psychology department, it would be expected to devote

more attention to learning small movement tasks than to gross motor or large muscle phenomena and kinesthetic perception, and thus be inadequate for physical education. (Henry, 1978, p. 14)

Franklin Henry's impact on the reform of the curriculum of physical education is apparent in contemporary programs of study in kinesiology. Upper division course work in many colleges revolves around knowledge that is specific to kinesiology and developed using a cross-disciplinary approach. At the graduate level, kinesiology seems to utilize both the cross-disciplinary and interdisciplinary approach, which is primarily due to the specialized nature of graduate work. The combination of the interdisciplinary and cross-disciplinary approaches at the undergraduate level exists as well. It is not unusual to find physical education majors completing prerequisites in biology and chemistry before enrolling in upper division physical education courses. However, the overwhelming majority of physical education courses reflect Henry's belief in a cross-disciplinary approach.

When Henry joined the physical education department in 1936, the bachelor's degree was offered in the form of a Group Major in Physical Education and Hygiene. This degree, a minor, and an additional year of graduate study were required for a teaching credential. The Group Major was under the auspices of the College of Letters and Science, the liberal arts college at the University of California. In the early 1940s, the physical education department came under attack from the College of Letters and Science. After completing a review of the physical education department, the College Executive Committee determined that the curriculum in physical education lacked sufficient academic content. As a result, students in the department had to meet additional criteria that would insure the academic integrity of the degree. The College Executive Committee informed the physical education department that any degree granted by the physical education department would be under the jurisdiction of the College of Letters and Science. The handwriting was on the wall—reform or eventually disappear.

In 1945 the department of physical education proposed a new Group Major in Physical Education and the academic major in physical education was born. The proposal was accepted and the additional criteria that had been imposed on the physical education department to ensure academic integrity were removed. The physical education faculty at Berkeley had "dodged a bullet" and in turn developed and implemented the concept of the academic discipline of physical education. The physical education faculty at Berkeley communicated with their colleagues across the country and retold the story of why and how physical education must reform as an academic discipline. To ignore the situation that had occurred at Berkeley was to invite trouble, but ignore it we did. The "red flags" waving in California during post–World War II relative to the status and future of our field were passed off as an isolated incident by the majority of college physical education departments. As a result, the reform of physical education was a subject that Franklin Henry would speak often about. He and his colleagues had seen the future, and without reform the future was dark.

Two decades after the academic reform of the physical education department at the University of California at Berkeley, Conant brought to light what the College Executive Committee of the College of Letters and Science at Berkeley had unearthed in the early 1940s—physical education lacks adequate academic content and without reform, must be abolished, especially at the graduate level. Fortunately, Franklin Henry and other scholars in our field had prepared for the inevitable and were able to offer models for reform that would propel physical education as an academic discipline.

Reform: A Continual Process in the 1990s and Beyond

The reform of our field into an academic discipline is easy to find at some colleges, harder to find at others. The transition from physical education to kinesiology is an example of reform. Change does not come easily to the human race; institutional and organizational change often moves at a snail's pace. The position that "we have always done it this way" is not a defense when administrators and review panels issue their findings that are detrimental to programs. Our field is not immune from attacks, this much should be apparent. As a profession, departments and individuals should conduct self-study reports, establish and analyze departmental and individual goals, and never lose sight of our mission or fail to publicize our mission. We must remain a field known for its academic and professional expertise and contribution to society. Reform is an ongoing process and should be welcomed as an opportunity to retool if necessary and reflect mainstream current thinking. If we ignore calls from our constituents for reform, or bury our heads in the sand when reform is suggested because we are threatened with "change," we are quite likely to insure our own demise.

Summary

Our field has enormous potential for betterment of the "common good." The health benefits and psychological and physical well-being that we are capable of bringing to society at times seem without equal. Health and wellness are concepts that reflect the belief that achieving a quality lifestyle for all Americans is essential as we approach the new millennium. What better medium exists to achieve optimum health and wellness than that of engaging in human movement? Who is best educated to deliver quality instruction and information in the areas of play, games, sport, exercise, and all the other salient practices that help insure optimum health and wellness? Make no mistake about it! Students engaged in the study of human movement are the professionals who will continue to serve as catalysts for educational reform and who excel in the delivery of information and instruction that will promote the established connection between exercise and health.

As professionals, we must continue to refine our skills and seek new ways to deliver our message, our product. Reform is an ongoing process that reflects our commitment to not only remaining current but also to chart new directions for the field. It has been shown that if we become complacent as educators, researchers, or coaches, we will be replaced or eliminated because our contributions no longer have utility or the support of the community.

The cultural influence of sport continues to have great potential in bringing people together. However, the reform of sport, as is the case with kinesiology, must be a constant process if we are to continue to improve and refine our field and gain increased academic and public respectability. Medicine and other fields are constantly seeking to improve their ability to study and research their chosen field in a superior fashion. We must do no less.

Discussion Questions

1. What were the causes behind the development and reform of modern physical education and sport?

2. How did the contributions of immigrant groups facilitate the development of physical education in the United States?

3. What was the process of the emergence of physical education as a profession?

4. How did the educational reforms that occurred in the United States have an impact on physical education?

5. What was the rationale behind the development of women's athletics?

6. What have been the reasons behind the attempted reform of athletics in colleges and universities?

References

Carter, M., Grebner, F., & Seamen, J., (1991). AAH-PERD—Professions in transition. *JOPERD, 62,* 20–23.

Conant, J. (1963). *The education of American teachers.* New York: McGraw-Hill.

Federal Register, 40, no. 108 (June 4, 1975): p. 24141

Franey, F. (1993). Failure stalks the hall in L.A. *The San Diego Union-Tribune,* 12 December, A33, A42.

Goodman, P. (1966). *Compulsory mis-education and the community of scholars.* New York: Vintage Books.

Graubard, A. (1972). *Free the children: Radical reform and the Free School Movement.* New York: Pantheon Books.

Henry, F. (1964). Physical education: An academic discipline. *Proceedings of the 67th Annual Conference of NCPEAM* (pp. 6–9), January 8–11, 1964.

Reprinted in *Journal of Health, Physical Education and Recreation, 35,* 32–33; 69, 1964.

Henry, F. (1978). The academic discipline of physical education. *Quest, 29* (Winter), 13–29.

Kozol, J. (1972). *Free schools.* New York: Bantam Books.

Postman, N., & Weingartner, C. (1969). *Teaching as a subversive activity.* New York: Delacorte Press.

Sperber, M. (1990). *College Sports Inc., the athletic department versus the university.* New York: Henry Holt.

Snyder, R. (1968). Work of the Professional Preparation Panel. *Journal of Health, Physical Education, and Recreation, 39.*

Suggested Readings

Carter, M.J., Grebner, F., & Seamen, J.A. (1991, April). AAHPERD—Professions in Transition. *JOPERD, 62,* 20–23.

Sperber, M. (1990). *College Sports Inc., the athletic department versus the university.* New York: Henry Holt.

Index